English
Romantic
Poetry

English Romantic Poetry

ETHOS, STRUCTURE, AND SYMBOL IN
COLERIDGE, WORDSWORTH, SHELLEY, AND KEATS

by
Albert S. Gérard

UNIVERSITY OF CALIFORNIA PRESS
BERKELEY & LOS ANGELES 1968

University of California Press
Berkeley and Los Angeles, California

Cambridge University Press
London, England

Copyright © 1968, by
The Regents of the University of California

Library of Congress Catalog Card Number: 68-12348

Preface

COLERIDGE and Wordsworth, Shelley and Keats were all prodigal of abstract generalizations about nature, knowledge, and art. Some twelve years ago, in *L'Idée romantique de la poésie en Angleterre*, I attempted to define the theories of the English romantics by resorting primarily to their letters, notebooks, treatises, and the explicit statements made in their poems. Yet it is the poetry itself which best expresses the romantics' desire to interpret and convey a unified intuition, reflecting their vital experience of the world and of the puzzling processes of creation.

Every successful poem is an organic whole. When we consider in isolation the eloquent passages where the romantics strove to express their grandest intuitions, we singularly oversimplify the processes of imaginative creation in their minds, and we do far less than justice to their intellectual ability. By lifting extracts out of their contexts, we are dangerously apt to miss not only the searching seriousness but also the aching perplexities which accompanied their efforts to reappraise the nature of the universe and the secret springs of its living oneness. And we overlook an ambiguity and an anguish which account in considerable measure for their modern appeal. The well-tried method of close analysis of individual poems seems to be the procedure most likely to provide a firm interpretative basis for any comparative generalizations about the major romantic poets of England.

In order to lay the necessary conceptual foundation for the ensuing analyses, the first chapter will provide a brief summary of those poets' theoretical thought on nature, knowledge, and art: their ontology, their epistemology, their aesthetics. But the main purpose of this book is to dissect the romantics' poetry, in full awareness that great poetry is not abstract statement although it may contain abstract statements, that it is never the description of a world view but its embodiment, never the application of an aesthetic code but its fountainhead, and it is to this purpose that chapters 1–9 are devoted.

A good poem conveys a unique insight through a unique form, and the shape is the key to the sense. I shall be very much concerned with such questions as: What light does the structure of a poem, that is, the arrangement of its parts, throw upon the relative function and significance of each of its elements? What light does it throw, therefore, on the poet's outlook at the time of writing? How does any particular cluster of sense perceptions grow into a symbol? Why was it a matter of necessity for the romantics, and especially for Coleridge, to devise an original definition of the symbol? How far does poetic practice agree with theoretical definition? What sort of correlation is there between structure and symbol on the one hand, and the seminal insight which the poem is intended to communicate on the other? Only through close analysis of individual poems is it possible to provide cogent replies to such questions, that is, to disentangle the above-mentioned elements and at the same time to bring out their reciprocal relation, which constitutes the unity of each poem.

Although, ideally, the whole corpus of romantic poetry ought to be studied in this minute way before a word of generalization can be spoken, some selection is inevitable. The choice I have made is based not on form but on meaning. For although form is undoubtedly essential to poetry inasmuch as no work using language for its material can be a poem if it is shapeless, it is not the least paradox of poetry that the meaning is even more essential: no great poem ever resulted from the sole pleasure of playing around meaninglessly with words and sounds and images; a true poet writes because he wants to convey something—a unique message which could not be communicated in any other form than this or that particular poem. The present selection, then, is based on the similarities and the variations in the romantics' ethos, a conveniently vague word which does not connote any rigid set of theoretical principles, but suggests the loose configuration of general attitudes, of hardly realized assumptions—about the nature and function of the universe, about man and his proper place in the scheme of things, what he is and what he ought to be—which, more than any consciously elaborated system, control man's behavior, including the poet's behavior in the writing of poetry.

The works that I have chosen to discuss in this book fall into two groups. Those in the first group may be termed "poems of perplexity," for they exemplify in one way or another the poet's puzzlement and/or anguish as he becomes aware of the contradiction between his youthful idealism and the hard realities of life. Jacques Barzun once observed that the primary common source of inspiration for most romantic poets was the Pascalian apprehension of "the contrast between man's greatness and man's wretchedness; man's power and man's misery," and the ensuing "search for a philosophy, a religion, a faith, which transcend and unify the felt disharmony." The romantic awareness of disharmony is nowhere more perceptible than in the poems written at an age when the lamp of youthful idealism is shattered, or at any rate threatened, by the fearsome blows of reality.

Coleridge was twenty-five when he wrote his *Reflections on Having Left a Place of Retirement;* Wordsworth, whose inner growth seems to have proceeded at a slower pace, was twenty-eight when he composed *The Thorn;* Shelley wrote *Alastor* at twenty-four; Keats was twenty-one when he wrote the *Epistle to John Hamilton Reynolds,* and he put the finishing touch to *Endymion* a year later. All those poems, and, we may add, *The Eolian Harp* and *Tintern Abbey,* spring from souls in ferment. In the Preface to *Endymion,* Keats wrote that "the imagination of a boy is healthy, and the mature imagination of man is healthy; but there is a space of life between, in which the soul is in ferment, the character undecided, the way of life uncertain, the ambition thicksighted." It is part of the purpose of this book to explore that "space between."

The second group of poems may be called "poems of reconciliation." In *This Lime-tree Bower my Prison,* in *Resolution and Independence,* in the *Ode to the West Wind,* and in *Ode on a Grecian Urn,* we can observe how enlarged experience and deepened meditation enabled the romantic poets of England to emerge from puzzlement, to overcome the temptation of despair, and to reconcile the antinomies of expectation and experience into a positive synthesis.

Unless I am mistaken, scholars dealing with romanticism as a cultural phenomenon are in the habit of defining it by contrast with other large cultural movements such as classicism. This is as it should be, and I too have made use of such comparisons, which are so convenient for bringing out the peculiar identity of the romantic mind. But what struck me as even more significant, and this is what I attempt to show in the concluding chapter, is that English romantic poetry, in spite of its intentional rebellion against the classical literary tradition, has its place in the mainstream of the deeper tradition of Western wisdom, which ever strives for balanced clear-sightedness, positive acceptance, and creative reconciliation.

Every author likes to fancy, in the secrecy of his undivulged expectations, that his book will revolutionize the scholarly world. I can entertain no such fond hope, for my debts are heavy. In a number of specific cases, I have been able to acknowledge my indebtedness to, and my departure from, the interpretations of previous students of romanticism. On larger and more general issues, after reading and imbibing hundreds of essays and dozens of books on romanticism in the course of the last twenty-five years, I must leave it to the reader to decide what the original contribution of the book, if any, may be.

Acknowledgments

I AM VERY grateful for editorial permission to make use, often in considerably altered form, of the following articles: "Coleridge, Keats and the Modern Mind," *Essays in Criticism*, I (1951), 249–261; "*Alastor*, or the Spirit of Solipsism," *Philological Quarterly*, XXXIII (1954), 164–177; "On the Logic of Romanticism," *Essays in Criticism*, VII (1957), 262–273; "Keats and the Romantic *Sehnsucht*," *University of Toronto Quarterly*, XXVIII (1959), 160–175; "*Resolution and Independence*: Wordsworth's Coming of Age," *English Studies in Africa*, III (1960), 8–20; "Clevedon Revisited: Further Reflections on Coleridge's 'Reflections on Having Left a Place of Retirement,'" *Notes & Queries*, New Series, VII (1960), 101–102 (published by the Oxford University Press); "The Systolic Rhythm: The Structure of Coleridge's Conversation Poems," *Essays in Criticism*, X (1960), 307–319; "Counterfeiting Infinity: *The Eolian Harp* and the Growth of Coleridge's Mind," *Journal of English and Germanic Philology*, LX (1961), 411–422; "Romance and Reality: Continuity and Growth in Keats's View of Art," *Keats-Shelley Journal*, XI (1962), 17–29; "Symbolic Landscape in Wordsworth's *Tintern Abbey*," *Publications de l'Université de l'Etat à Elisabethville*, IV (December, 1962), 21–30; "Dark Passages: Exploring *Tintern Abbey*," *Studies in Romanticism*, III (1963), 10–23; "Of Trees and Men: The Unity of 'The Thorn,'" *Essays in Criticism*, XIV (1964), 237–255.

Contents

1. Souls in Ferment: Reality, Knowledge, and Romantic Art — 3
2. The Discordant Harp: The Structure of Coleridge's Conversation Poems — 20
3. Counterfeit Infinity: Coleridge and the Symbol — 40
4. Emblems of Misery: Wordsworth's *The Thorn* — 64
5. Dark Passages: Wordsworth's *Tintern Abbey* — 89
6. A Leading from Above: Wordsworth's *Resolution and Independence* — 118
7. The Hopeless Quest: Shelley's *Alastor* — 136
8. The Unextinguished Hearth: Shelley's *Ode to the West Wind* — 163
9. Greeting Uneasiness: Keats's *Endymion*, Book IV — 194
10. Truth is Beauty: Keats's *Epistle to John Hamilton Reynolds* and *Ode on a Grecian Urn* — 215
11. Conclusion: The Proper Bound — 237
    Bibliography — 265
    Index — 281

We hate poetry that has a palpable design upon us.
                    John Keats

1 Souls in Ferment: REALITY, KNOWLEDGE, AND ROMANTIC ART

Romantic poetry derived much of its revolutionary character from an intense and outspoken dissatisfaction with the dualistic world view which had prevailed during the eighteenth century. The young Coleridge and the young Wordsworth were persuaded that the established dichotomies—between spirit and matter in ontological thought, between subject and object in the theory of knowledge, between content and form in the sphere of art—were as unjustifiable and harmful as was the petrified division of society into an aristocratic ruling class and an oppressed majority; and once they had both settled into a more sedate—or, perhaps, more resigned—recognition of the limitations of the human mind and of the inherent imperfections of human society, they were stridently disavowed by Shelley, who, together with Keats, resumed the fight and the quest which the Lake poets had apparently relinquished. If one impulse can be singled out as central to the romantic inspiration, it is the *Sehnsucht*, the yearning toward the absolute, the aspiration to oneness and wholeness and organic unity, the dream of perfection. To many, both before and since the romantic period, this impulse has appeared juvenile. Nevertheless, it was the fountainhead of the intellectual and poetic activity of the romantics, in England as elsewhere. And it was taken seriously because its validity seemed to be guaranteed by visionary experiences which all young romantic poets found crucial, since they provided what appeared to them convincing evidence that such yearning was by no means illusory or utopian.

In these germinal experiences—such as those described in *The Eolian Harp* and *Tintern Abbey*, not to mention *The Prelude*, or those that are allegorically conveyed in *Alastor* or *Endymion*—there were many individual variations. Each of England's four major romantic poets was a man of strong personal temperament. And of course, they belonged to two generations, one of which reached manhood while the French Revolution was in progress, and the other at the time of Waterloo. The younger writers were bound to be influenced by their elders and in some measure to react against them. Nor is it immaterial that Shelley and Keats died at an early age, which prevented them from developing as their predecessors did. While Wordsworth and Coleridge reinstalled themselves—somewhat smugly, as many think—in the main current of Christian tradition, Shelley and Keats did not live to reach the stage when a man begins to feel humble enough to seek the help and comfort of guidance from above. But in spite of this diversity, they all participated in a similar *Sehnsucht*, and the quasi-mystical experiences that stirred their imaginations had much in common.

It used to be said disparagingly that romantic poetry is poetry of feeling. It is indeed suffused in emotion. But the strong feelings which overwhelm the poet's soul, the joy, the sense of glory, should rather be considered a psychological consequence of the poetic experience, and the subjective proof of its vital importance. The experience itself is not only emotional; it is also, and indeed primarily, cognitive. It includes sensory and intellectual elements; it brings the whole soul into activity; as a result, it is rich in moral and metaphysical implications.

Basically the poetic experience is a form of knowledge. It is not a strictly sensory form of knowledge, like that which often inspires the Imagists, since through the particular and the sensuous it aspires to reach to the universal. But it does not reach the universal by way of abstractions, like the philosophical poetry of eighteenth-century neoclassicism. In fact, it is felt as an intuition of cosmic unity: the sudden realization that the universe is neither an unintelligible chaos, nor a well-regulated mechanism, but a living organism, imbued throughout with an idea which endows it with its unity, its life, its harmony, its ultimate significance.

This was a staggering experience indeed, to which, until then, only the religious mystics claimed to have been privileged. Because of its intensity and scope, it demanded to be expressed and to be interpreted, and it is to this twofold need that the best romantic poetry owes much of its urgency and depth. But because the insight it procured was so obviously subjective, once the experience had receded the poet was left alone to grapple with the crucial question: Was it a vision, or a waking dream?—a query which, as I hope to show, is as central to Wordsworth's *Tintern Abbey* as it is to Shelley's *Alastor*.

Although many of the romantics' finest works are poems of vatic assertion, underneath their overt design there runs a more or less conscious, more or less perceptible trend of uncertainty and anguish. It is true that when they tried to work out the abstract, metaphysical implications of their visionary insight, the young romantics resorted to a variety of philosophical attitudes ranging from Coleridge's devout Unitarianism to Shelley's rather ostentatious "atheism." But they had a common proclivity to translate it in spiritualistic terms; their first impulse was to treat the sense of oneness it imparted as a unity of substance, and it is in this sense that we may legitimately speak of Wordsworth's "pantheism" or of Shelley's "idealism." The fact remains, however, that this intuition of oneness clashed not only with certain assumptions which they were not always eager to shed, but also with the most compelling data of everyday experience. I shall argue that the structure of Coleridge's *The Eolian Harp*, for example, is commanded by a sense of the contradiction between his personal "mystical" insight and the dualistic outlook of orthodox Christianity, and that part of his purpose in elaborating his definition of the symbol was to find a satisfactory way out of this dilemma. However, while this ontological preoccupation was of the utmost importance to Coleridge, it would seem that the problem which weighed most heavily on the minds of the English romantics was connected with what Keats called "the lore of good and ill."

In response to the *Sehnsucht*, the poetic experience apprehends the world as a sort of matter-spirit continuum. Unlike some of their continental contemporaries, the romantic poets of England did not remain content with the rather facile forms of monism, with the amateurish pantheism and Neoplatonism, to which they were undoubtedly attracted, and which consist chiefly in denying or in deifying the sensuous world. Nature, they came to think, was a *tertium quid* born of the meeting and interaction of two opposite forces: the chaotic diversity of original matter and the unifying and organizing (or, as Coleridge termed it, "esemplastic") power of an omnipresent, purposive Spirit. From such a conception of God's pervasive, all-powerful, and loving action in the created universe, it was but a short step to the familiar notion that this world is the best of all possible worlds. The intensity of the romantics' ideal dream (or vision) made all the more acute their perception not only of man's inhumanity to man, but also of a kind of cosmic cruelty which seemed to revel unhampered in ruin and destruction. They were thus brought face to face with the perennial problem of the purpose of evil and suffering in a universe which is conceived as essentially meaningful and benevolent. Coleridge, as I shall have occasion to recall, adhered for a while to the usual theological casuistry which claims that grief and evil have their hidden function in the general scheme of things. But usually, the romantics were not satisfied with such unconvincing, abstract, lifeless quibbling. Their perception of the discrepancy between the ideal and the actual does not seem to have prompted them to any sizable amount of systematic theorizing. But the anguished puzzlement which it aroused imbues their early major works with a poignancy and an ambiguity which account for much of their appeal to the modern reader. It also endows them with a dialectical quality which reverberates in their structure. Poems like *The Eolian Harp* and *Tintern Abbey*, *The Thorn* and *Alastor*, or the *Epistle to John Hamilton Reynolds* may express the despair born from the impact of experience upon innocence; they may illustrate the bafflement of the poet when faced with the contradiction between traditional faith and personal intuition; they may reflect the tragic recognition that the dream of perfection could, after all, be mere delusion. But they all manifest, in the thought and in the structure, the oscillations of the poet's mind as he wavers between opposite sets of equally compelling experiences, and desperately seeks to integrate them into a coherent outlook not manufactured by abstract sophistry, but felt in the blood.

It is a distinguishing feature of romanticism that its major representatives did not shrink away from the philosophical anxieties which, in most men, vanish as soon as the sclerosis of adulthood sets in, and which—for that very reason, perhaps—the previous century had seldom considered suitable topics for recognized poetry. The doubt and the anguish in their early poems—however unobtrusive and, at times, deliberately veiled—provided the psychological and intellectual starting point for the process of reappraisal and reconciliation out of which the romantic ethos was to grow as it gradually emerged from the will, and the need, to come to terms with the actual condition of man without betraying the ideal conveyed through the visionary experience. Such poems as *Resolution and Independence*, the *Ode to the West Wind*, and the *Ode on a Grecian Urn* communicate an exceptional sense of wholeness and assurance. They are endowed with an equipoise both emotional and ethical, which derives from a mature acceptance of man's limitations and from a strenuously acquired ability to reconcile the divergent claims of the actual and the ideal. Such poise, we may note, has always been the very essence of Western wisdom.

There seems to be something inherently Hegelian in the way the romantic mind functions. To the mature thought of the romantic poets, it will be remembered, living nature is the product of the infinite Mind working upon unorganized matter to give visible shape to His ideas. In this perspective, nature's "beauteous forms" appear to be neither an obstacle to the mystical vision, nor the ultimate object of poetic vision. Their harmony and their vitality are immediately felt as the stamp of a higher force which remains transcendent.

The romantic theory of knowledge is built on a similar triadic pattern. The romantic poets reject the doctrines of rationalism, empiricism, and associationism, and claim that all true knowledge is an act of genuine creation. Even at the lowest level, perception is a *tertium quid* resulting from the action of the mind on sensory data, that is, from a merging of subjective and objective, in the course of which the percept becomes integrated into the substance of the percipient's mind. This is why Wordsworth often used such metaphorical terms as "drink," "eat," "absorb," "nourish," and "feed" to describe the relationship which genuine knowledge establishes between the thinking subject and the external world. To the romantic mind, cognition was of two kinds: the dead and the vital. In the *Biographia Literaria*, Coleridge explains how his reading of the mystics gave him "an indistinct, yet stirring and working presentiment, that all the products of the mere *reflective* faculty partook of DEATH," and how he became convinced that "the notional understanding itself is but the shadowy abstraction of living and actual truth";[1]

---

[1] S. T. Coleridge, *Biographia Literaria*, ed. J. Shawcross (Oxford, 1907), II, 98 and 168. Unless otherwise specified, references to the *Biographia Literaria* are to this edition.

elsewhere he claims that "the man of healthful and undivided intellect uses his understanding in this state of abstraction only as a tool or organ." [2] To this definition of the understanding, he opposed what he called "vital knowledge." Admittedly, the phrase is vague and lends itself to loose rhapsodic uses. But for Coleridge it had a very definite meaning, which is conspicuous everywhere in his writings on the subject. The products of genuine knowledge are not simple mental representations, stored and sterilized in the watertight warehouses of memory, to be taken out and played with as fancy chooses. Indeed, they have something of what Matthew Arnold was to call "high seriousness": they deserve being taken earnestly and being acted upon. As they are the product of an "undivided intellect," so they affect the whole mind, they bring "the whole soul of man into activity." They are knowledge, not conceptual and discursive, not depending on accurate (and cold) reasoning, but immediate and intuitive, "stirring and working," carrying in itself the evidence of its own truth, a fountainhead of inspiration and a powerful incentive to action.

It is highly revealing that, in spite of the huge temperamental differences between Coleridge and Keats, the latter's theory of knowledge, however unsystematic its formulation, should be closely akin to the former's. The distinction between dead and vital knowledge is implicit in Keats's oft-quoted letter to Bailey of 22 November 1817: "I have never yet been able to perceive how any thing can be known for truth by consequitive reasoning—and yet it must be—Can it be that even the greatest Philosopher ever arrived at his goal without putting aside numerous objections—However it may be, O for a Life of Sensations rather than of Thoughts." [3] A truth worthy of that name can only be immediate and self-

[2] S. T. Coleridge, *The Statesman's Manual* in *Biographia Literaria*, Bohn's Standard Library (London, 1905), p. 343.
[3] *The Letters of John Keats*, ed. H. E. Rollins (Cambridge, Eng., 1958), I, 185. Further quotations from the *Letters* are identified in this chapter by the volume and page numbers in parentheses.

evident. In vital knowledge, there is no cleavage between truth and emotion. The heart's affections are holy, and the thoughts that excite them must be true. The foundation of belief is the inner certainty which can only come from personal experience. As Keats wrote in a letter to Reynolds: "We find what [Wordsworth] says true as far as we have experienced and we can judge no further but by larger experience—for axioms in philosophy are not axioms until they are proved upon our pulses: we read fine—things but never feel them to thee [sic] full until we have gone the same steps as the Author" (I, 279). Or again, in a letter to his brother and sister-in-law: "Nothing ever becomes real till it is experienced—Even a Proverb is no proverb to you till your Life has illustrated it" (II, 81).

It would appear, therefore, that Keats's famous exclamation "O for a Life of Sensations rather than of Thoughts" goes much further than de Sélincourt suggested when he wrote: "The word *intuition* would express his meaning far more truly than *sensation*. He is obviously contrasting what Milton calls the discursive and intuitive reason—or the manner of attaining the truth characteristic of the philosopher—by consecutive reasoning, and the poet's immediate apprehension of it."[4] In Keats's crucial passage, much more is at stake than the philosophy of poetry or the psychology of the poetic character: nothing less, in fact, than a philosophy of knowledge and of life. In the context in which those words are set, there is nothing to suggest that the writer was thinking primarily of the poet as opposed to the philosopher. What we do find in the letter is rather a Keatsian version of Coleridge's distinction between dead and vital knowledge. Nor does Keats state that "consequitive" knowledge refers to philosophy and sensation to poetry. "Sensation" is presented as, so far as he can conceive, the only means of attaining the truth, not only in poetry, but in practical life ("proverbs") and in philosophy

[4] *The Poems of John Keats*, ed. with an Introduction and Notes by E. de Sélincourt (London, 1905), p. xxxviii.

("axioms"). Keats's "sensation" is not an immediate intuition of truth with which the poet alone is favored: it is the lived experience of reality, on the physical, moral, and metaphysical planes; this experience, in which the personality is totally involved, with its intellectual, emotional, and volitional faculties, is the fundamental act by which a man deepens and grows toward the fullness of wisdom.

It was clear that the type of knowledge glorified by the romantics must belong to a faculty other than the ratiocinative. Imagination was traditionally associated with poetry, although generally in a deprecatory way. The romantics, however, glorified it as the queen of the cognitive faculties and the very organ of truth. By so doing, they gave a formidable impetus to research into the psychology of art. But they also unwittingly tended to confine the new concept of vital knowledge to the field of aesthetic creation. This was not at all their purpose. For Coleridge, the aesthetic faculty was only the secondary imagination. But the primary imagination was "the living power and prime agent of all human Perception, and . . . a repetition in the finite mind of the eternal act of creation in the infinite I AM." [5]

There is as close a connection between the romantics' conception of vital knowledge and their theory of creative art as there is between their ontology and their epistemology. Although the secondary imagination, as Coleridge defined it, "dissolves, diffuses, dissipates" the data of experience, it does so "in order to re-create them" into new wholes; and it always "struggles to idealize and to unify." In other words, the poetic imagination uses the immediate data of experience, disintegrating and recasting its elements in order to create a *tertium quid* which is an analogue and a symbol of natural creation because it too reveals the ideal unity of the thought underneath the diversity of its sensuous appearances.

[5] *Biographia Literaria*, I, 202.

The romantic notion of the symbol has nothing in common with the vague power of hazy suggestion which Cazamian once described as "tout ce qui peut être la source d'un rayonnement significatif indirect."[6] More recently, David Perkins, in his perceptive study of recurrent motifs in romantic poetry, was content to define the symbol "as a key image which taps and summarizes a dense and often fluid complex of doubts, intuitions, emotions, preoccupations, and the like."[7] But the truth is that, for the English romantics, the symbol is something much more definite: it is a synthesis, a fusion of polarities. It is characterized, says Coleridge, "by the translucence of the special in the individual, or of the general in the special, or of the universal in the general." But Coleridge carefully avoids any tendency to emphasize the universal at the expense of the concrete. In a rather unexpected comparison between poetry and geometry, he points out that "in geometry, it is the universal truth itself, which is uppermost in the consciousness, in the poetry, the individual form in which the Truth is clothed." In art, "the ideal consists in the balance of the generic with the individual. The former makes the character representative and symbolical, therefore instructive; because *mutatis mutandis* it is applicable to whole classes of men. The latter gives it *living* interest; for nothing *lives* or is *real*, but as definite and individual."[8] In the symbol, the vehicle, which is concrete and singular, and the meaning, which is universal and general, are indissociable and equally essential. They determine each other. Their unity is total and indivisible. This is why the symbol-making act of the secondary imagination could be said, like the cognitive act of the primary imagination, to be a repetition in the poetic mind of the eternal act of creation of the infinite mind: the symbol, Coleridge goes on, "always partakes of the reality which it

---

[6] L. Cazamian, *Symbolisme et poésie* (Neuchâtel, 1947), p. 14.
[7] David Perkins, *The Quest for Permanence: The Symbolism of Wordsworth, Shelley and Keats* (Cambridge, Mass., 1959), p. 7.
[8] *Biographia Literaria*, II, 159 and 187.

renders intelligible."[9] It too is an organic whole which owes its living quality not to a mechanical operation of craft and judgment but to the organic cooperation of all the faculties: whether sensory, emotional, intellectual, or moral, they all contribute to the elaboration of the work of art, they are all necessary for unifying the particular and the universal, the concrete and the ideal, the cognitive and the emotional, and for embodying the parent idea into organic sensuous forms which are both highly individualized and capable of touching the heart of the reader.

The romantic theory of the symbol was of course a capital contribution to modern thought. In the long run, it was to shatter the very foundations of our ideas about the nature of thinking, to such a degree that it is now possible for a distinguished philosopher to claim that man is not an *animal rationale*, but an *animal symbolicum*.[10] But this new concept, as defined by Coleridge, raises at least two intriguing problems. One is of an historical order and refers to the genesis of this notion in Coleridge's mind. It is of course well known that in the 1790's Kant, Schiller, and Goethe were all preoccupied with the symbolic power of the human mind, and that the trend was later taken up by Schlegel and Schelling. But although sources and influences can and should be duly traced, we must still ask ourselves why it is that Coleridge borrowed certain ideas rather than others, submitted to certain influences and rejected others, transformed certain concepts the way he did rather than in any other way. The answer is provided by the old scholastic principle, *quidquid recipitur, recipitur ad modum recipientis*. If Coleridge borrowed from his German contemporaries for his definition of the symbol, that can only be because their ideas corresponded to a need in his own mind. There is no doubt that Coleridge picked at his own sweet will any books that might come his way for suitable ideas, but it is most likely that he appropriated formulas

[9] *The Statesman's Manual*, p. 322.
[10] E. Cassirer, *An Essay on Man* (New Haven, 1944), p. 26.

because they appeared to him to be satisfactory expressions of thoughts of his own, which had been forming in the recesses of his mind, without yet taking their final shape. Indeed, I shall try to document the view that his conception of the symbol was part of his overall strategy to abolish the eighteenth-century assumption of an unbridgeable qualitative difference between the opposite poles of the cosmos and of human knowledge: finite and infinite, spirit and matter, subject and object.

The other problem raised by Coleridge's description of the symbol is of a critical, rather than an historical, nature. His definition is certainly clear and coherent in the abstract. But it cannot be fully understood until it has been tested by a thorough analysis of the way symbolism functions in actual poems. A major trend of present-day criticism is the study of myth and symbol in literary works, and although most theorists are of course perfectly aware that equal importance must be given to the concrete and the universal aspects of the symbol, critics of the symbolic school often yield to the almost inevitable temptation to emphasize the latter at the expense of the former, thus turning what was originally the product of symbolic creativeness into examples of allegory. The distinction is not always clear-cut. Such poems as *Alastor* or *Endymion* are certainly allegorical in intent, although they contain much that is demonstrably symbolic.

The final criterion of truly symbolic value may well have been provided by Coleridge himself when he said that the symbol "always partakes of the reality which it renders intelligible." It is not only a correlative of the meaning to be conveyed: it must be, as T. S. Eliot realized, an *objective* correlative. A symbol must be a real object, a real person, a real process, so that its wider meaning is not superimposed upon, but is contained in, its own concrete and individual reality. To unravel the complex cluster of relations between vehicle and tenor, concrete and universal, naturalistic description and indirect significance, which accounts for the symbolic value of many romantic poems, is another major concern of this book.

Not that it should be expected that startlingly new interpretations will be thus produced: the techniques of modern criticism have been abundantly brought to bear on the romantic masterpieces in the course of the last few decades, and little could be added to the impressive body of explication already in existence. But we still want to know why it was that Wordsworth, for example, felt impelled to seize on an old tree, or an old man, as symbolic, or Shelley on the west wind, or Keats on an urn or a bird. And it may well be that something remains to be said about the bewildering intricacy of the poetic devices through which they managed to express and to communicate the universal significance of concrete objects and occurrences.

Georg Brandes echoed the common belief of his day when he wrote that "according to the romantic doctrine, the artistic omnipotence of the self and the poet's will should not submit to any law." We now know, of course, that the romantic poets never advocated lawlessness in any field. Nature, for them, was not that "quelque chose d'énorme, de barbare et de sauvage" which Diderot prized so highly. On the contrary, they frequently emphasized the "laws" which bring order into the universe, and which thus manifest the divine idea that animates the created world. When Shelley forgot that he was an atheist, he was apt to insist that God is "the overruling Spirit of the collective energy of the moral and material world," "something mysteriously and illimitably pervading the frame of things."[11] In the same way Wordsworth had been impressed by the visible world "as ruled by those fixed laws/ Whence spiritual dignity originates."[12] and Coleridge had observed that "nature . . . would give us the impression of a

[11] *The Complete Works of Percy Bysshe Shelley*, ed. R. Ingpen and W. E. Peck (London, 1965), VI, 230–231.

[12] William Wordsworth, *The Prelude or Growth of a Poet's Mind*, ed. from the manuscript with an Introduction, Textual and Critical Notes by E. de Sélincourt, second edition revised by Helen Darbishire (Oxford, 1959), Bk. XIII, ll. 372–373. Unless otherwise specified, references to *The Prelude* are to this edition.

work of art, if we could see the thought which is present at once in the whole and in every part." [13] If a work of art, being a symbol, is an analogue of nature, it follows necessarily that it too should have its laws. To quote Coleridge once more: "The spirit of poetry, like all living powers, must of necessity circumscribe itself by rules, were it only to unite power with beauty." [14] But to the romantic mind these rules were not mechanical precepts imposed from outside and blindly obeyed: they were organic laws built into the very creative process by which the germinal idea shaped itself into adequate sensuous forms.

The romantic conception of form, therefore, is at once expressive and functional. What matters is the idea, and the experience from which it arises. Everything which does not derive from the experience, everything which does not help to express the idea, everything ornamental, gratuitous, and superfluous must be rigorously proscribed. Paradoxically, it was in the name of this central principle of genuine classicism that the romantics banished the conventions of pseudo-classical poetic diction with its mythological allegories, its beribboned pastorals, and its pathetic fallacies. Such devices, and many others in the fields of prosody, imagery, and dramatic structure, were uncompromisingly condemned as belonging to mechanic form, that is, "when on any given material we impress a predetermined form, not necessarily arising out of the properties of the material." [15] Some time after 1811, Coleridge discovered in Schlegel's *Vorlesungen über dramatische Kunst und Literatur* the phrase he needed [16] to express his idea of the peculiar shaping power of the imagination, and the con-

---

[13] S. T. Coleridge, "On Poesy or Art," in *Biographia Literaria*, II, 255.
[14] S. T. Coleridge, *Shakespearean Criticism*, ed. T. M. Raysor (London, 1960), I, 197.
[15] *Ibid.*
[16] This has now been established beyond any possible doubt by G. N. G. Orsini in "Coleridge and Schlegel Reconsidered," *Comparative Literature*, XVI (1964), 97–118.

cept of organic form has been an indispensable ingredient of literary theory ever since.

"Organic form," however, is but an empty phrase as long as we cannot specify what kind of formal structures result from the organic processes involved. What is now needed is a detailed examination of the way it applies in romantic poetry. It is of course increasingly acknowledged that it should not be taken as a gentle euphemism for shapelessness, and that the romantic inspiration, however emotional in its origin, worked itself into recognizable structural patterns which combine the spontaneity of the creative impulse with the orderliness of the valid poetic artifact. The reason behind the once commonly held notion that romantic poetry is rambling, diffuse, and invertebrate is that its patterns are rather unobtrusive—perhaps deliberately so.

The composition of an Elizabethan ode is usually as obvious as that of a Renaissance painting: it has—if we may borrow Wölfflin's term—a tectonic structure. All the parts that form the whole are clearly distinguishable. As the poem moves from stanza to stanza, the reader can rejoice in the unhampered perception of the poet's thematic progress from topic to topic. In retrospect, the work can be aesthetically enjoyed in the exquisite symmetry of its constituent sections. Romantic poetry, on the other hand, often deserves the epithet used by Wölfflin for baroque art: it is atectonic. It is true that the outward design of Shelley's *Ode to the West Wind*, for example, is easily perceptible and even, with regard to rhyme scheme and stanza form, exceptionally rigid; but close attention reveals an intricate network of cross-references which point to an underlying design that is far more complex. In most cases, however, the structure of a romantic poem is not immediately discernible. It seems to flow and uncoil itself in a spontaneous, haphazard, and rambling way as the poet's mood dictates. And in a sense, that is precisely what it does. But within the poetic mood itself there is an inborn orderliness whose discreet operation is revealed to the watchful reader. The number of recent learned articles dealing with design, structure, and patterning in romantic poetry attests to the growing recognition of this basic fact. In analyzing *The Eolian Harp, Tintern Abbey, The Thorn, Resolution and Independence,* and the curiously asymmetric structure of the *Ode on a Grecian Urn,* I have attempted to bring out the patterns which control those poems, not only because of their intrinsic interest, but also for the light that such patterns throw on the workings of the romantic mind.

We no longer need to demonstrate that romantic poetry is truly philosophical poetry in the sense that its purpose is both the accurate rendering and the searching interpretation of significant experiences through the imaginative use of speech. To analyze the philosophy of the romantic poets is therefore a legitimate object for scholarly study, although it has often proved difficult to resist the temptation to concentrate on the more eloquent and more explicit statements contained in their finest poems. It is easy to overemphasize the more memorable lines in *The Eolian Harp* or in *Tintern Abbey* or the obvious cyclical symbolism in the *Ode to the West Wind.* By lifting these elements out of their contexts, however, we grievously oversimplify both the creative and the intellectual processes of which the poem is the outcome, and at the same time we risk missing its genuine subtlety. A poem may contain more or less direct statements: these are but component parts, the import of which can only be grasped in reference to the whole. It is only the whole poem that *is* the poet's final statement, and this is the main reason why this book offers close readings of a number of individual pieces ranging from the apparent—but deceptive—straightforwardness of Coleridge's effusions to the multilayered complexity of *The Thorn* and to the seeming confusion of Keats's *Epistle to John Hamilton Reynolds.* The romantic inspiration is fundamentally dialectical since it springs forth from an acute perception of incongruity; if the rhythm of a poem derives in a truly organic way from this germinal insight, it should also follow a dialectical pattern, as the writer's attention shuttles back and forth between the opposite poles of self and non-self, vision and reality, particular and universal, concrete and ideal, between the dream of perfection and the apprehension of sorrow and wickedness. In a way, then, it may be claimed that structural analysis is necessary to bring together our three central themes. For it is not solely concerned with a descriptive elucidation of the formal designs into which the spontaneous overflow of powerful feelings more or less spontaneously organizes itself. Structure also provides the key to the total symbolism of any particular poem because our perception of it enables us also to perceive the relation that the poet has wished to establish between the various experiences, images, metaphors, symbols, and statements which are the material of the poem's fabric. Finally, it is perhaps not altogether unreasonable to hope that the convergence of characteristic patterns may point to the specific nature of the romantic outlook and lead to a more refined understanding of the puzzlement and anguish that beset the romantic poets while they stayed in the uncomfortable "space between" that separates the great expectations of youth from the virile acceptance of maturity.

2 The Discordant Harp:
THE STRUCTURE OF COLERIDGE'S CONVERSATION POEMS

On 31 December 1796, Coleridge casually mentioned to Thelwall that *The Eolian Harp* was "my favorite of *my* poems."[1] Without the slightest doubt it was the best poem he had written so far. Indeed, it can be considered the first romantic piece to stand on its own merits as a poem. It is also the first really worthy sample of a genre which was particularly suited to Coleridge's disposition and which G. M. Harper has termed "conversation poems":[2] a personal effusion, a smooth outpouring of sensations, feelings, and thoughts, an informal releasing of the poetic energies in Coleridge's capacious mind and soul. *The Eolian Harp* set a pattern which he was to use time and again during his *annus mirabilis* (*Reflections on Having Left a Place of Retirement, This Lime-tree Bower my Prison, Frost at Midnight, Fear in Solitude, The Nightingale*) and again in 1802 (*Dejection*) and in 1805

---

[1] *Collected Letters of Samuel Taylor Coleridge*, ed. E. L. Griggs (Oxford, 1956), I, 295.

[2] G. M. Harper, "Coleridge's Conversation Poems," *Quarterly Review*, CCXLIV (1925), 284–298. Reprinted in *Spirit of Delight* (London, 1928) and in *English Romantic Poets: Modern Essays in Criticism*, ed. M. H. Abrams (New York, 1960). On the origin of the phrase and the novelty of the genre, see R. H. Fogle, "Coleridge's Conversation Poems," *Tulane Studies in English*, V (1955), 103–110.

(*To a Gentleman*). Together with *This Lime-tree Bower my Prison* and *Dejection*, it ranks among the most delicate, the most sensitive of Coleridge's personal poems.

The Eolian Harp was first printed in 1796, in the volume entitled *Poems on Various Subjects* and, like thirty-six of the poems collected there, it was styled an "effusion," "in defiance," Coleridge claimed in his Preface, "of Churchill's line: 'Effusion on Effusion pour away.' " [3] The writer was perfectly aware that this kind of poetry was likely to give offense to those readers who had been bred in the traditional taste for impersonality. Indeed, the whole of the Preface focuses on the question of egotism in a way which is alternately aggressive and defensive: "Compositions resembling those of the present volume are not unfrequently condemned for their querulous egotism. But egotism has to be condemned then only when it offends against time and place, as in a History or an Epic Poem. To censure it in a Monody or Sonnet is almost as absurd as to dislike a circle for being round." The arguments adduced by Coleridge to justify his proclaimed egotism may sound shallow and peculiarly subjective, although one of them, at least, deserves to be quoted, as it anticipates some important considerations which Wordsworth was to expound in the Preface to the second edition of *Lyrical Ballads*: "The communicativeness of our nature leads us to describe our own sorrows; in the endeavour to describe them, intellectual activity is exerted; and by a benevolent law of our nature, from intellectual activity a pleasure results which is gradually associated and mingles as a corrective with the painful subject of the description." [4]

[3] *The Complete Poetical Works of Samuel Taylor Coleridge*, ed. E. H. Coleridge (Oxford, 1912), II, 1136.

[4] Cf. Wordsworth: "All good poetry is the spontaneous overflow of powerful feelings: . . . poems to which any value can be attached were never produced . . . but by a man who, being possessed of more than usual organic sensibility, had also thought long and deeply. . . . The emotion . . . is qualified by various pleasures, so that . . . the mind will, upon the whole, be in a state of enjoyment." *Poetical Works of William Wordsworth*, ed. E. de Sélincourt and Helen Darbishire (Oxford, 1962), II, 387–388, 400–401.

As this probably did not sound quite convincing, Coleridge, in the edition of 1797, added a paragraph calling upon his own experience:

> If I could judge of others by myself, I should not hesitate to affirm, that the most interesting passages in our most interesting Poems are those, in which the Author developes his own feelings. The sweet voice of Cona [Ossian] never sounds so sweetly as when it speaks of itself; and I should almost suspect that man of an unkindly heart, who could read the opening of the third book of the *Paradise Lost* without peculiar emotion. By a law of our Nature, he, who labours under a strong feeling, is impelled to seek for sympathy; but a Poet's feelings are all strong. Quicquid amet valde amat. Akenside therefore speaks with philosophical accuracy, when he classes Love and Poetry, as producing the same effects:
> > "Love and the wish of Poets when their tongue
> > Would teach to others' bosoms, what so charms
> > Their own."—PLEASURES OF IMAGINATION.[5]

This paragraph enlarges upon a characteristic observation penned down in a notebook some time in 1795 or 1796: "Poetry without egotism comparatively uninteresting."[6]

Coleridge's defense of egotism in this Preface is of course a manifestation of the usual romantic emphasis on feeling or emotion as the mainspring of poetry. For feelings are entirely personal and, unless the poet has that Shakespearean gift of dramatic sympathy which enables a writer to identify himself with other persons—and with this gift the English romantics most assuredly had *not* been favored—it is only of his own emotional life that a poet is fully aware: it is therefore only his own feelings that he can convey poetically. But does this imply that he is cut off from everything that is not his own self? Does this mean that romantic poetry is necessarily confined to subjectivism, self-exploration and self-discovery?

---

[5] *Complete Poetical Works of Coleridge*, II, 1144.
[6] *The Notebooks of Samuel Taylor Coleridge*, ed. K. Coburn (London, 1957), I, entry number 62.

Twentieth-century critics of romanticism, conditioned to reserve their praise for impersonal poetry, emphatically answer that it does. In a study on egotism, F. G. Steiner goes so far as to assert that "it is precisely the dissociation between individual and universal which characterizes Romantic egotism and distinguishes it from Classical or Renaissance introspection."[7] It is perhaps a little unfortunate that Steiner does not explain what he means by "universal," especially in view of the fact that he quotes a remark of Hazlitt to the effect that "Mr. Coleridge talks of himself, without being an egotist, for in him the individual is always merged in the abstract and the general."[8] To Hazlitt, it would appear, the first romantic upholder of egotism was himself no egotist. Clearly, the word is in need of some precise definition, for Hazlitt did not use it with the same meaning as Coleridge did.

The term "egotism" as it is used in romantic criticism covers at least two different concepts. First, it can denote an attitude of total absorption in the self, with utter disregard for the outside world; this can be combined with verbal impersonality, as Coleridge sarcastically observed in the Preface of 1796:

With what anxiety every fashionable author avoids the word I!—now he transforms himself into a third person—"the present writer"—now multiplies himself and swells into "we"—and all this is the watchfulness of guilt. Conscious that the said *I* is perpetually intruding on his mind and that it monopolizes his heart, he is prudishly solicitous that it may not escape from his lips.

This disinterestedness of phrase is in general commensurate with selfishness of feeling: men old and hackneyed in the ways of the world are scrupulous avoiders of Egotism.

But in legitimate romantic usage, "egotism" denotes interest in the self as the necessary starting point for the poet's explora-

[7] F. G. Steiner, "'Egoism' and 'Egotism,'" *Essays in Criticism*, II (1952), 449.
[8] *The Complete Works of William Hazlitt*, ed. P. P. Howe (London, 1930–1934), XI, 31.

tion of the universe and of the soul of man, for his endeavor to understand his own position in relation to the world of otherness. Coleridge describes himself as an egotist in the latter sense, and Hazlitt states that Coleridge is no egotist in the former. While the ego, then, is the primary source of romantic poetry, it is by no means its essence and sole aim, its center and its circumference. Romantic poetry is egotistic in its origin, but it is not altogether subjective. A detailed analysis of the structure of *The Eolian Harp* will help to show what romantic egotism really is, not as an abstract concept, but as a living source of inspiration.

The poem begins with an apostrophe to Coleridge's future wife, Sara, and offers a very concrete and particularized picture of the two sitting in their garden at dusk. But it soon goes beyond that initial stage of concrete immediacy: the description widens gradually until it encompasses not only the two young people and their garden, but also the sky ("clouds," "star"), the earth ("bean-fields"), and the "distant" sea, so that by the end of this section the stage is set for the word "world." It was not the first time that Coleridge used this image of a widening perspective leading to a sort of cosmic view. Such a conceit provided the main motif for his sonnet on *Life* (1789), the structure of which is based on a simile between widening *sensory* perspective and growing *spiritual* insight:

> As late I journey'd o'er the extensive plain
>   Where native Otter sports his scanty stream,
> Musing in torpid woe a Sister's pain,
>   The glorious prospect woke me from the dream.
>
> At every step it widen'd to my sight—
>   Wood, Meadow, verdant Hill, and dreary Steep,
> Following in quick succession of delight,—
>   Till all—at once—did my eye ravish'd sweep!
>
> May this (I cried) my course through Life portray!
> New scenes of Wisdom may each step display,
>   And Knowledge open as my days advance!

The Discordant Harp

   Till what time Death shall pour the undarken'd ray,
     My eye shall dart thro' infinite expanse,
   And thought suspended lie in Rapture's blissful trance.

In *The Eolian Harp* as in *Life*, Coleridge tries to go beyond the immediacy of sensory experience: the jasmin, the myrtle, and the star appear as "emblems" of Innocence. The allegorizing is clumsy,[9] but at least it shows the poet groping for something that has clearly nothing to do with "egotism," reaching out toward some spiritual value which is rooted in his own experience but not limited to it.

Between the first and second sections of *The Eolian Harp*, a process of contraction takes place. After his flight into the wide expanse of nature, the poet reverts to a single definite object within his immediate experience: the lute. (Incidentally, we must notice how skillfully the reader is prepared for the melody of the harp by the auditory imagery at the end of the first section: "a world *so* hush'd," "stilly murmur," "silence.") But here again, the immediate datum of personal experience is only a starting point from which the poet soon departs, not, this time, to explore the frontiers of the perceptual world, but to allow free play to his fanciful imagination:

                    And that simplest Lute,
Placed length-ways in the clasping casement, hark!
How by the desultory breeze caress'd,
Like some coy maid half yielding to her lover,
It pours such sweet upbraiding, as must needs
Tempt to repeat the wrong!

The epithet "desultory" sets the mood, and the poem's imagery proceeds desultorily. Free association is at work in the two similes which the harp's melody calls up in the poet's mind. The first simile (harp = coy maid; breeze = lover;

---

[9] In the third edition of his poems (1803), Coleridge dropped lines 5 and 8, but later changed his mind, and they remained part of the final version.

melody = sweet upbraiding) may not sound very adequate, but then, the mood is obviously playful. The second simile is both more intricate and more intriguing:

> And now, its strings
> Boldlier swept, the long sequacious notes
> Over delicious surges sink and rise,
> Such a soft floating witchery of sound
> As twilight Elfins make, when they at eve
> Voyage on gentle gales from Fairy-Land,
> Where Melodies round honey-dropping flowers,
> Footless and wild, like birds of Paradise,
> Nor pause, nor perch, hovering on untam'd wing!

We observe how the perspective again widens as the poet's imagination leaves the concrete object to dream of Fairy-Land, the harp's "sequacious notes" evoking both the "witchery of sound" made by Elfins voyaging on the gales and the (personified) Melodies that float untiringly round the flowers of Fairy-Land.

This second comparison seems to carry out with greater subtlety a purpose similar to that of the allegorizing in the first section of the poem: it dematerializes, as it were, the beauty of the harp's melody. The process is accomplished by the introduction of ghostly beings (Elfins) and of an abstract personification (Melodies); besides, Coleridge uses that swift motor imagery ("footless and wild," "nor pause, nor perch," "hovering," "untam'd wing") which was to become one of Shelley's favorite devices. Different though those two similes are, they have a definite connection which becomes clear in lines 30–31:

> Methinks, it should have been impossible
> Not to love all things in a world so fill'd;

that is, filled with beauty. The parallelism of the phrases "and the world *so* hush'd" (l.10) and "in a world so fill'd" (l.31), identical in rhythm and similarly situated at the end of the antepenultimate line of the stanza, is cleverly designed to recall the first part of the poem, and thus to clarify the meaning of "so fill'd": Coleridge is alluding both to the objective beauty of the landscape delineated in the first part, and to the beauty of the products of his own fancy, now at its most Keatsian. The artful symmetry in the fall of the first two parts is enhanced by the note of silence on which they both end ("hush'd," "silence," "stilly murmur"; "mute still air," "Music slumbering on her instrument"). Nor is this silence devoid of further significance: the final advice the poet will give to himself at the end of the poem is to bid his unregenerate mind keep silent.

The transition between sections two and three is as skillfully and unobtrusively contrived. The general impression of a fanciful *rêverie* built up in part two is summed up in the word "slumbering"; the daydreaming image glides over to the next part, although in a more naturalistic key, in the picture of the poet stretched out on the hillside, "musing" and looking at the world through "half-closed eye-lids." Such shifting devices are the equivalent in imagery of the run-on technique in prosody; by maintaining a continuity of mood and imagery as the poet passes from one topic to another, they blur the line which separates the various sections of the poem and thus create the impression of living, organic unity, with which the romantic writers were so much preoccupied.

But between parts two and three, a swift systolic movement of contraction has again occurred: the poet has left Fairy-Land and turns back to his own self, not as he is at the moment when the experience so far described takes place, but when he is lying on a hill slope at noon. This time, panoramic vision is quickly suggested in a few strokes (the earth: "yonder hill"; the sky: "sunbeams"; the sea: "the main"). But the process of expansion develops in yet another direction: after the sensory apprehension of nature (part one) and the fanciful excursion into Fairy-Land (part two), the poet's mind now indulges in speculations of a more intellectual order. Simultaneously, the harp's catalytic power to precipitate images gains in complexity. Here, as in the second part, the harp is the origin of two comparisons. To begin with, the "brain" of the poet is visited by "thoughts" and "phantasies" as the lute is caressed by the gales:

> Full many a thought uncall'd and undetain'd,
> And many idle flitting phantasies,
> Traverse my indolent and passive brain.

The word "phantasies" refers back to the playful and delicious images called up by the harp in the second section, while "thought" anticipates the famous image of lines 44–48:

> And what if all of animated nature
> Be but organic Harps diversely fram'd,
> That tremble into thought, as o'er them sweeps
> Plastic and vast, one intellectual breeze,
> At once the Soul of each, and God of all?

This second image, which comes nearer to metaphor and points to an intimation of symbolic, rather than allegorical, significance, refers to the coalescence of matter and spirit. The panoramic perception of part one has now made room for the cosmic vision.

 The last section of the poem, like the others, is characterized by a double process of contraction and expansion. Once more, Coleridge reverts to immediate experience and addresses Sara; and once more, he departs from this starting point to explore wider regions—this time, the realm of Faith. The effect of this section upon the reader is distinctly anticlimactic. The embarrassed diction (especially the double negative in ll. 50–51), the most unattractive portrait of Sara as—to borrow Humphry House's description—a rather "narrow and governessy" kind of person ("serious eye," "mild reproof," "meek daughter"), and the Sunday-school undertone of self-abasement in the phrasing provide a tame conclusion after the impressive imagery of lines 44–48. Nevertheless, there can be no doubt that Coleridge intended this section to be climactic: he repudiates his flights of fancy under Sara's "more serious eye"; he speaks of God and Christ, of holiness and faith. This, clearly, should be the culmination of a pilgrimage that has led him from sensory experience, through fanciful *rêverie* and intellectual speculation, to deeper awareness of God's greatness and of the overriding importance of faith. Whereas the sense of anticlimax that we experience has important bearings on our understanding of Coleridge's spiritual predicament in 1795, the realization that the last section was climactic in intent gives us a clearer view of the structure of the poem.

One of the earliest critics to pay any attention to the construction of romantic poems was G. M. Harper. In his 1925 discussion of *Reflections on Having Left a Place of Retirement,* he noted that "the poem begins with a quiet description of the surrounding scene and, after a superb flight of imagination, brings the mind back to the starting-point, a pleasing device which we may call 'the return.'" Harper observed other examples of this "pleasing device" in *Frost at Midnight* and in *Fears in Solitude.* It is rather strange that he should not have mentioned it in connection with *The Eolian Harp.* What Harper called "the return" is certainly a favorite pattern in romantic poetry, but it is less simple and straightforward than he suggested. It is far more than a mere pleasing, formal device. Indeed, because of its complexity, which results from the simultaneous development, the interplay, and the perfect integration of three different rhythmic processes, it casts a most useful and pertinent light on the workings of the romantic mind.

The foregoing analysis has perhaps made it clear that *The Eolian Harp* is characterized by a widening and ascending movement which carries the poet from nature to God: from sensory perception to fanciful *rêverie*, and thence, through intellectual speculation, to an assertion of his religious faith. But within this general framework, we can observe a heartbeat rhythm of systole and diastole, of contraction and expansion, in which the poet's attention is wandering to and fro between his concrete immediate experience and the wide, many-faceted world of the non-self: from the self to the forms of nature apprehended in the panoramic perception; from the self to the poetic Fairy-Land created by Fancy; from the self to an intellectual vision of cosmic unity; from the self to humble contemplation of God.

It is the combination of the pulsating rhythm and the ascending trend which creates what Harper called the "return"—only, it is not a return, for the self to which the poet finally reverts is not the same self from which he had started: he has been enriched, heightened, and uplifted by the various inner and outer experiences to which he has submitted and from which he now emerges with what the poet considers to be a deeper and more accurate knowledge of the universe and of his place in it.

The reason why *The Eolian Harp* does not succeed in the end is that the diction, the thought, and the feeling fail to live up to this high level of structural integration. In other words, when we reach the highest point in the rhythmic development of the poem, the other elements break down, not, in this case, out of any insincerity on the part of the writer, but because he is caught between an exhilarating sense of oneness, which he discards, and a depressing sense of intellectual impotence, which he upholds. While the poet's conscious aim is to end on an image of inward peace and harmony, he is in fact struggling with thoughts and feelings which are insufficiently realized and which clash with each other.

It is to a similar reason that we must ascribe the failure of *Reflections on Having Left a Place of Retirement*. In this poem, as Harper said, the imagination "seeks not . . . a metaphysical, but an ethical height." Coleridge is concerned with personal happiness and humanitarian action. In spite of its egocentric design, it is more than a mere elegiac effusion on

Coleridge's reluctance to leave Clevedon for Bristol.[10] The variant title, *Reflections on Entering into Active Life*, used in the *Monthly Magazine* for October, 1796, makes it obvious that the poem has a twofold theme as well as a twofold mood, which has been aptly described as "a blend of regret and resolution."[11] Its overall design is based on the interplay of the themes of retirement and action, and results from the intertwining of three distinguishable patterns which must be disentangled if we are to grasp its wider significance and to trace the reason for its failure.

Ostensibly, the poem falls into two main parts, each of which justifies one of the alternative titles: the theme of retirement is dealt with in the first forty-two lines, while from line 43 to line 62 Coleridge treats with belabored enthusiasm the theme of active life; the end of the poem is rounded off by the "return" device. Coleridge had good reason to change his title: the theme of retirement takes up more than twice as much space as the theme of active life, and it is treated with greater skill and more genuine feeling. This is in itself significant: romantic poetry is rooted in the poet's subjective experience, and, at its worst, it stays there.

Underneath this thematic design, there is a second structural pattern visible in the typographical arrangement, which manifests the poet's deep-rooted impulse to overcome in three different ways the limitations of pure subjectivity. Like *The Eolian Harp*, *Reflections* begins with a description of Coleridge's "Cot" and of the "Dell" in which it is located. Whether this place is taken to resemble "the abode of Man unfallen," as W. H. Marshall has claimed, or as a new version of the *locus amoenus* convention, or, what is more likely, as a faithful description of Clevedon cottage, it is certainly the unit of

[10] For modern interpretations of *Reflections*, see the notes by M. F. Schulz and by W. H. Marshall in *Notes and Queries*, CCIV, n.s. VI (1959), 143–144 and 318–321.
[11] R. W. Armour and F. R. Howes, *Coleridge the Talker* (Ithaca, 1940), p. 43.

experience nearest to the poet's heart. But with the end of line 9 and the introduction (however inadequate and ludicrous) of Bristowa's sauntering citizen, a noteworthy attempt is made to widen the range of the poem by generalizing the poet's own response to nature and by illustrating the favorable influence of natural scenery on even a gold-thirsty son of commerce.

The best section of the poem is the second, which develops according to the same movement of expansion. The "Dell" is briefly mentioned at the outset, but immediately the vista expands as the poet climbs a neighboring "Mount" and enjoys a panoramic perception which is explicitly presented as an analogue of infinite vision:

> Oh! what a goodly scene! *Here* the bleak mount,
> The bare bleak mountain speckled thin with sheep;
> Grey clouds, that shadowing spot the sunny fields;
> And river, now with bushy rocks o'er-brow'd,
> Now winding bright and full, with naked banks;
> And seats, and lawns, the Abbey and the wood,
> And cots, and hamlets, and faint city-spire;
> The Channel *there*, the Islands and white sails,
> Dim coasts, and cloud-like hills, and shoreless Ocean—
> It seem'd like Omnipresence! God, methought,
> Had built him there a Temple: the whole World
> Seem'd *imag'd* in its vast circumference.

As in *The Eolian Harp*, the discrepancy between spontaneous impulse and deliberate elaboration is apparent in the fact that this section is the poetic and emotional climax, although it is not the climax on the level of conscious thought.

The third section has likewise the dell, the cot, and the "Mount sublime" for its starting point:

> Ah! quiet Dell! dear Cot, and Mount sublime!
> I was constrain'd to quit you. Was it right,
> While my unnumber'd brethren toil'd and bled,
> That I should dream away the entrusted hours
> On rose-leaf beds, pampering the coward heart
> With feelings all too delicate for use?

The process of expansion moves in a new direction: it no longer consists in a generalization of the theme of natural piety, or in a transition from sensuous perception of nature to analogical intuition of the divine, but in the poet's own decision to give up private enjoyment for humanitarian action. It is interesting to observe that both natural piety and the cosmic vision are dismissed as "feelings too delicate for use": in *The Eolian Harp*, the pantheistic intuition of lines 44–48 had likewise been rejected as "shapings of the unregenerate mind." Such afterthoughts are characteristic of Coleridge's intellectual conflicts and of his lack of confidence in the quality of the inner experiences that moved him most. Moreover, while the intrusion of "Bristowa's citizen" in the first section was ominous enough, the bombastic phraseology of the third part, contrasting with the delicate naturalistic description of the second, inevitably suggests that Coleridge is doing his best to work himself up into a frenzy of humanitarian feeling, just as in the final section of *The Eolian Harp* he was trying to formulate an attitude which he believed to be right, although it clashed with his deep-felt experience. The difference is that the statement contained in *Reflections* is palpably untrue: Coleridge did not leave Clevedon in order to

> join head, heart, and hand,
> Active and firm, to fight the bloodless fight
> Of Science, Freedom, and the Truth in Christ,

but mainly, as Cottle dryly tells us, to be nearer Bristol, its libraries and printing presses.[12]

[12] J. Cottle, *Reminiscences of Samuel Taylor Coleridge and Robert Southey* (London, 1847), pp. 64–65: "Inconveniences connected with his residence at Clevedon, not at first taken into the calculation, now gradually unfolded themselves. The place was too far from Bristol. It was difficult of access to friends; and the neighbours were a little too tattling and inquisitive. And then again, Mr. Coleridge could not well dispense with his literary associates and particularly with his access to that fine institution, the Bristol City Library; and in addition, as he was necessitated to submit to frugal restraints, a walk to Bristol

All this is immensely revealing. Coleridge was certainly very much concerned, in his own way, with social inequality and political oppression. To him, as to Wordsworth, the problem of evil and misery in a benevolent universe was an urgent one. But whereas Wordsworth, at twenty-two, did sail for France with some idea of joining the "fight for freedom" even though it might not be altogether "bloodless," Coleridge at the same age was content to sit at his desk and pour out the torrential oratory of his *Religious Musings*. There is no ground for supposing that he was not genuinely moved at the thought of the

> numberless
> Whom foul Oppression's ruffian gluttony
> Drives from Life's plenteous feast,

as he had chosen to describe them in that work (ll. 276–278). But the verse reveals that the emotion, however eloquent and, perhaps, intense, was distinctly inferior in quality and depth. *The Eolian Harp* is spoiled by Coleridge's dogmatic adherence to one aspect of Christian doctrine which could not but obliterate his heartfelt experience. Likewise, his attitude toward social evil, as expressed in *Reflections*, sounds both rhetorical and conventional because of an underlying and somewhat mechanical acquiescence to the usual theological casuistry on that problem. At that particular stage in his evolution, Coleridge, it would seem, found facile relief in the comfortable view that evil somehow, sometime, *must* be "ultimately subservient to good." [13] This kind of sophistry came to

---

was rather a serious undertaking; and a return the same day hardly to be accomplished, in the failure of which, his 'Sara' was lonely and uneasy; so that his friends urged him to return once more to the place he had left; which he did, forsaking, with reluctance, his rose-bound cottage, and taking up his abode on Redcliff-hill."

[13] J. Priestley, *Disquisitions Relating to Matter and Spirit*, 2nd ed. (Birmingham, 1782), quoted by H. W. Piper in *The Active Universe: Pantheism and the Concept of Imagination in the English Romantic Poets* (London, 1962), p. 47, where Coleridge's concern with the problem of evil is discussed from a doctrinal viewpoint.

him all the more naturally since it harmonized with his monistic proclivities. Already in the *Religious Musings*, the notion that "There is one Mind, one omnipresent Mind, / Omnific" and that "His most holy name is Love" (ll. 105–106) had apparently enabled him to infer that "Creation's eyeless drudge, black Ruin" (l. 321) was a suitable instrument to bring about the "blest future" envisioned by his "young anticipating heart" (ll. 356–357).

The true, somewhat artificial nature of Coleridge's involvement in "the lore of good and ill" at the time is perhaps best illustrated in the *Ode to the Departing Year*. There is indeed genuine pathos in the opening lines of that poem:

> Spirit who sweepest the wild Harp of Time!
>   It is most hard, with an untroubled ear
>   Thy dark inwoven harmonies to hear!
>   (ll. 1–3)

But the first stanza as a whole sounds as if the poet were less indignant at the unpleasant events of 1796 (duly listed in the "Argument" and in the footnotes) than querulously resentful of the fact that they prevented his contemplative eye from remaining "fix'd on Heaven's unchanging clime" (l. 4), and the construction of the poem is highly suggestive of Coleridge's real outlook at the time. After a long, turgid account of the workings of "Strange-eyed Destruction" (l. 146), liberally sprinkled with exclamation marks and allegorizing capital letters, the poet ultimately turns back with relief to his own gentle, meditative soul:

> Now I recentre my immortal mind
>   In the deep Sabbath of meek self-content;
> Cleans'd from the vaporous passions that bedim
>   God's Image, sister of the Seraphim.
>   (ll. 158–161)

Even the images of evil in *The Ancient Mariner* have an allegorical aspect which points to deliberate contriving rather than spontaneous immediacy, and it is this peculiar—although ethically meritorious, no doubt—kind of insincerity that spoils *Reflections*. As in *The Eolian Harp*, there is a discordance between his genuine interest and the beliefs and attitudes which he feels he must uphold.

But if we disregard poetic quality to concentrate on structure, we observe that the unfortunate third section of *Reflections* fits nicely into the general rhythm of the poem. In the first part, the passage on the Bristol merchant is succeeded by a short effusion to Sara on the nature of their own happiness; in the second part, the description of the landscape is rounded off with a brief personal comment: "It was a luxury—to be!" Likewise, after the initial description of his own divided mood at the beginning of the third section, Coleridge again widens the scope with generalities on the nature of true charity, and then reverts to his own self and to his alleged decision to enter into active life.

This pattern of expansion and contraction, which exemplifies the romantic preoccupation with the relationship between the personal and the impersonal, is combined with a third structural device: the ascending, spiral-like movement which we found in *The Eolian Harp*—and which, incidentally, also commands the architecture of Wordsworth's "I wandered lonely as a cloud." *Reflections* closes on a new description of the "Cot," not as it actually is, but as seen through the poet's memory and modified by his enriching experience. As a result, the remembrance of the place blends with the humanitarian ideal: "And that all had such!" This design illustrates the characteristic romantic concern with the theme of psychological continuity and ethical growth—a concern which should not be underestimated, for to it we owe *The Prelude*.

The main reason for the failure of the poem is to be found in the poem itself. *Reflections* was clearly intended to develop in a continuously ascending direction, passing from natural piety through nearly mystical contemplation of nature to humanitarian action. But Coleridge's performance does not live up to his intention: far less space is devoted to the intended climactic stage (action) than to the initial and intermediary stages (piety and contemplation); besides, the humanitarian section is bombastic in both rhythm and diction, capital letters having to make up for the lack of genuine inspiration. Poetic emphasis and conscious emphasis do not coincide: while Coleridge consciously wanted to extol humanitarianism in *Reflections* and fideism in *The Eolian Harp,* the best sections in both poems are those that express an intuition of infinity through the panoramic perception of the vast expanse of nature.

It was not until June, 1797, with *This Lime-tree Bower my Prison*,[14] that Coleridge achieved the perfect blending of feeling and thought, imagery and structure, for which he was obviously groping. In this poem, too, the heartbeat rhythm is the fundamental pattern. It starts with Coleridge querulously complaining that he is obliged to stay at home as a result of Sara accidentally emptying a skillet of boiling milk on his foot. The process of expansion takes place as the poet's imagination follows his friends on the heath and up the hill, from the top of which they can rejoice in the by now familiar panoramic perception ("wide Heaven," "the many-steepled tract magnificent," "the sea"). Then occurs the systolic beat, as Coleridge focuses his attention on Charles Lamb; obviously, he is identifying with his friend, since what he says of the latter is also true of himself:

> thou hast pined
> And hunger'd after Nature, many a year,
> In the great City pent, winning thy way
> With sad yet patient soul, through evil and pain
> And strange calamity!

[14] For an extended analysis of this poem, see "Coleridge's 'This Lime-Tree Bower My Prison'" by A. W. Rudrum, *Southern Review* (Adelaide), I (1964), ii, 30–42.

Following this passage, the panoramic perception is briefly recalled ("glorious sun" and "clouds," "heath-flowers" and "distant groves," "blue Ocean") and is transmuted into a cosmic vision of the landscape as a living thing revealing the presence of God. In the third section, Coleridge turns back to himself, noting that his mood has changed from melancholy to delight, and his attention immediately expands to a minute description of the lime-tree bower, which now appears to him as a microcosm in which the presence of the spirit of nature can be as intensely felt as it is in the "wide landscape." The poem closes with a "return" to Coleridge himself, blessing "the last rook," "black" and "creeking," in the same spirit that the Ancient Mariner blesses the "slimy water-snakes."

It may be futile to speculate about the part played by the conscious mind and the unconscious in the establishment of this complex pattern, which often recurs in romantic poetry. While the overall spatial movement of expansion and ascension may have been premeditated, one feels inclined to believe that the inner rhythm of systole and diastole originates spontaneously in the deeper layers of the romantic mind: it derives from an urgent need to restore, between the self and the world around and above, the organic links which the romantic poets felt had been severed by eighteenth-century neoclassicism. At any rate, the structure of *The Eolian Harp* and of the other "conversation poems" illuminates the nature of romantic egotism. Although Coleridge's Preface to the 1796 edition of his *Poems* may appear to be a defense of egotism, it should be clear that this apology is no more than a tactical move designed to justify one particular aspect of his poetry. But "egotism" in the sense of a total and exclusive concentration of attention upon the self is certainly no part of the romantic view of poetry; nor is it an important element in romantic poetry itself. The rhythm of contraction and expansion to which Coleridge's inspiration spontaneously shaped itself in the poems that have just been considered shows that, to him, the ego was primarily a starting point for philosophical speculation and for poetic meditation. It was what it has been for many thinkers ever since Descartes uttered his *Cogito, ergo sum*: the basic certainty in which all else is rooted. Romanticism was concerned with the ego, not in and for itself, but as an element in a wide, complex network of relationships which also embraces the fundamentals of human thought and experience: nature, man, and God.

Furthermore, if it is permissible to consider the quality of the poetry as a key to the emotional urgency of the inspiring idea, it will be readily perceived that the topic which most powerfully fired Coleridge's imagination in those, his formative years, was not of an ethical but of an ontological order. However sincere he may have been in his denunciation of oppression and in his proclamation of man's duty to man, his feelings in this connection only found expression in inflated diction and artificial allegory. The truly impassioned lines, the truly convincing images, are those which attempt to translate and convey his sense of the essential oneness that gives life and meaning to the diversity of things. And it is in order to provide an accurate definition of this cosmic unity, without at the same time obliterating the distinctions which, as a Christian, he felt bound to maintain, that Coleridge was driven to frame a new concept of the symbol.

3 Counterfeit Infinity:
COLERIDGE AND THE SYMBOL

The *Eolian Harp* has long enjoyed pride of place as the first expression of the grand romantic idea of the One Life. No student of Coleridge's thought or of romantic philosophy in general can dispense with, nor perhaps even refrain from, quoting its two most impassioned passages:

> O! the one Life within us and abroad,
> Which meets all motion and becomes its soul,
> A light in sound, a sound-like power in light,
> Rhythm in all thought, and joyance every where—
> (ll. 26–29)
>
> And what if all of animated nature
> Be but organic Harps diversely fram'd
> That tremble into thought, as o'er them sweeps
> Plastic and vast, one intellectual breeze,
> At once the Soul of each, and God of all?
> (ll. 44–48)

It may be impertinent, but it is certainly not untrue, to observe that many a scholar seems to have focused his attention on these lines without casting more than a desultory glance at the whole poem, the greater part of which is presumably considered irrelevant, since it contains little that can be construed as a philosophical statement. Consequently, the implications of the last section of the poem, which clearly indicates the conscious trend of Coleridge's thought at the time of writing, were for a long time overlooked, ignored, or grossly misunderstood. Nevertheless, throughout the history of *Eolian Harp* criticism, it is possible to trace a growing awareness of the revealing light (or, rather, shadow) which the last section throws on the better-known passages. G. M. Harper has already observed that the end of the poem shows how Coleridge, "out of consideration for Sara's religious scruples, and in obedience to his own deep humility, apologized for these shapings of the unregenerate mind." Stallknecht, although more concerned than Harper with Coleridge's philosophy, does not make much of the inner contradiction which characterizes the poem: "The Coleridge of *Religious Musings* and the 'Eolian Harp' approaches pantheism of an extreme type. As time passed, he seems to have grown more and more cautious in these matters, although we must remember that even in the 'Eolian Harp' itself he voices some hesitation concerning this speculation."[1] Kenneth Burke, for his part, shrewdly observes that "the aesthetic is presented in terms of 'temptation'—and the poem closes with apologies to his wife, as the poet promises to reform."[2] So far as I know, Humphry House was the first to devote more than passing attention to this important point, which has a bearing on the whole meaning of the poem. More recently, however, Marshall Suther expressed the opinion that the structure of the poem rests on an opposition between "the storm of imagination," "the poetic trance," and what he chooses to call "domestic peace," "domestic contentment," "domestic responsibility."[3]

In examining *The Eolian Harp* as a landmark in the devel-

[1] N. P. Stallknecht, *Strange Seas of Thought* (Durham, N.C., 1949), p. 144.
[2] Kenneth Burke, *The Philosophy of Literary Form* (Baton Rouge, La., 1941), p. 93.
[3] Humphry House, *Coleridge* (London, 1953), p. 76. Marshall Suther, *The Dark Night of Samuel Taylor Coleridge* (New York, 1960), pp. 86–89, and *Visions of Xanadu* (New York, 1965), p. 69.

opment of Coleridge's thought, we must recall that lines 26–33 were not added until 1817, when the poem was reprinted with *Satyrane's Letters*. As Humphry House convincingly pointed out, they destroy the balance and unity of the poem by triumphantly confirming the pantheistic view expressed in lines 44–48, a view which, at the time of writing—during the summer and fall of 1795—certainly did not represent any final, firmly held conviction; indeed, in the last section of the poem, Coleridge summarily dismisses this view as "shapings of the unregenerate mind." I do not mean to say that the students of romantic thought are wrong in pointing to these appended lines as a reliable, or even felicitous, expression of an important aspect of Coleridge's mature cosmology. But from a historical point of view, the poem ought to be analyzed as it was originally written: lines 26–33 will therefore be excluded from our present consideration. Further, the pantheistic statement of lines 44–48 must be interpreted within the framework of that early version, not in the light of later accretions: full awareness of their contextual position will clarify their relation to other parts and to the total meaning of the poem at the time of writing. Moreover, close attention to the overall structure of *The Eolian Harp* is bound to illumine the nature of an antinomy which is central to Coleridge's poetic and philosophical endeavor: the antinomy between his pious adherence to Christian transcendentalism and his irrepressible intuition of oneness. Finally, after the poet's attitude in 1795 has been ascertained, it will be possible to discuss the intellectual evolution which prompted him to restate, in later years, an idea which he had uncompromisingly rejected when he composed the poem.

The Eolian Harp is a conversation poem in more senses than one. Not only is it an "effusion" to Sara Coleridge, *née* Fricker. It is also a dialogue of the poet with himself. Coleridge allows an idea to emerge freely in his mind, then picks it up for consideration, finally makes up his mind about it, and drops it as irresponsible and dangerous to the salvation of his soul. The meaning of the harp metaphor, which crystallizes this idea, is perhaps clearer in one of the early drafts:

> Thus *God* would be the universal Soul,
> Mechaniz'd matter as th' organic harps
> And each one's Tunes be that, which each calls I.[4]

One of the aims of the romantics was to find a substitute for the outdated and, to them, unsatisfactory philosophy that sees the world as a mechanism and God as the great watchmaker, and so emphasizes the dualism of matter and spirit. They were deeply aware of the unity of the cosmos and simply refused to believe in the watertight pigeonholes of traditional philosophy. As a result, they were trying to express this intensely felt unity, either through poetic images or in philosophical statements. It is, then, by no means surprising that Coleridge should have been attracted to some form of monism, and particularly to a notion of God as a plastic spirit identifying himself with material forms to organize and shape them from within and to endow them with their own living identity. That some such view preoccupied Coleridge's mind at an early date is apparent from his sonnet to Bowles (1794), in the final couplet of which he unexpectedly and rather extravagantly compares Bowles's poetic genius to God himself:

> Like that great Spirit, who with plastic sweep
> Mov'd on the darkness of the formless Deep!

It is precisely this particular trend in Coleridge's multifarious thinking that received climactic utterance in *The Eolian Harp*.

We can only speculate as to what prompted Coleridge so explicitly to identify the God of all forms of animated nature with the soul of each. H. J. W. Milley is probably right in saying that "Coleridge, in 'The Eolian Harp' for the first time,

---

[4] *The Complete Poetical Works of Samuel Taylor Coleridge*, ed. E. H. Coleridge (Oxford, 1912), II, 1022–1023.

for himself discovered the countryside." [5] Marrying and becoming the owner of a house have always been, for a young man, rather thrilling experiences, and, as we know, Coleridge had a definite tendency to enthusiasm. Newly wed as he was, he was not yet aware of the less attractive sides of Sara's personality. He must have felt in himself an irrepressible upsurge of his emotional nature that brought him to cast a hyperbolically benevolent look on his surroundings and to feel most emphatically the presence of God all around him. We remember that he significantly used the word "Omnipresence" (not, for instance, "Omnipotence") for God a little later, in *Reflections;* so the Neoplatonic pantheistic conceit of lines 44–48 may have sounded, for one short moment, the right way to interpret and express the kind of feeling that he was experiencing.

But we fail to catch the actual mood of the poem in its original form if we allow the ambiguity of this passage to pass unnoticed. No doubt, there is a suggestion of finality and more than an intimation of certainty or at least high seriousness in the magnificent wording, the ample rhythm so finely suited to the greatness of the thought, the perfect adequacy of the metaphor. On another plane, however, the passage is surrounded with connotations of diffidence: it formulates one of the thoughts, "uncall'd and undetain'd," which, together with the "idle flitting phantasies" of an earlier section, are

> As wild and various as the random gales
> That swell and flutter on this subject Lute!

Moreover, the phrasing is distinctly hypothetical: "And what if . . . ?" This notion that God and Nature are one, Coleridge seems to imply, is not a statement, but merely a speculation not to be taken too seriously. Too little attention is usually paid to the note of diffidence, or at least of cautious tentativeness, that often creeps into the utterances of the romantics when they try to formulate the essence of their experience

---

[5] H. J. W. Milley, "Some Notes on Coleridge's 'Eolian Harp,'" *Modern Philology*, XXXVI (1939), 359–375.

and the nature of the oneness they experience. This prudent attitude toward any kind of speculation that might smack of pantheism is a frequent feature of Coleridge's poetry in those early years. It is conspicuous in a passage of *Religious Musings* where the poet apostrophizes the organizing spirits which are supposed to act as intermediaries between God and the created world, and evokes—in a characteristic what-if clause—the possibility that they might be components of the divine substance:

> And ye of plastic power, that interfused
> Roll through the grosser and material mass
> In organizing surge! Holies of God!
> (And what if Monads of the infinite mind?)
> (ll. 405-409)

This last suggestion is expanded in the first draft of *The Destiny of Nations*, where Coleridge does not speak in his own name, but describes the same idea—which may or may not be true—as a "dream" of "others":

> But properties are God: the Naked Mass
> (If Mass there be, at best a guess obscure,)
> Acts only by its inactivity.
> Here *we* pause humbly. *Others* boldlier *dream*
> That as one body is the Aggregate
> Of Atoms numberless, each organiz'd,
> So by a strange and dim similitude
> Infinite myriads of self-conscious minds
> Form one all-conscious Spirit, who controlls
> With absolute ubiquity of Thought
> All his component Monads: linked Minds
> Each in his own sphere evermore evolving
> Its own entrusted powers—*Howe'er this be,*
> Whether a *dream presumptious,* caught from earth
> And earthly form, or *vision veiling Truth,*
> Yet the Omnific Father of all Worlds,
> God in God immanent, the eternal Word,
> That gives forth, yet remains—[6]

---

[6] *Complete Poetical Works of Coleridge,* II, 1025; italics mine.

This lengthy, eloquent development of the idea of pantheistic immanence testifies to its attractiveness, while the sharp contrast between "we" and "others," as well as the note of suspended judgment at the end, makes plain the uneasy mixture of attraction and revulsion in Coleridge's mind.[7]

As we turn back to *The Eolian Harp* and to the poet's indirect appraisal of his own speculations, we observe that, in the last section, Samuel gives way to Sara—a sad anticlimax, one feels inclined to say. Surely, however, Sara is but a mouthpiece for something in Coleridge himself. At any rate, the last sentence of the poem provides evidence that he agrees with her in considering such thoughts to be "dim" and "unhallow'd,"

> shapings of the unregenerate mind;
> Bubbles that glitter as they rise and break
> On vain Philosophy's aye-babbling spring.

The thought expressed in lines 44-48 was not—in 1795—a firmly held belief, but little more (and Kenneth Burke's term is the right word for it) than a temptation, albeit a strong one. It is not possible to agree entirely with Humphry House, who says that in the last section Coleridge "utterly repudiates the experience he has just had": how can one repudiate one's experiences? What Coleridge repudiates is not the experience, but the thought, the interpretation he has just given of his experience. Seen in this light, the poem appears to be a document in the age-old contest between Faith and Philosophy, and the conclusion reached by Coleridge, at this early stage in the growth of his mind, is that God is "incomprehensible," to be thought and spoken of only in terms of the "Faith that inly feels." We remember that less than a year before, Coleridge in his notebooks had reminded himself of "the

---

[7] Other revealing examples are to be found in Wordsworth: "If this / Be but a vain belief . . ." (*Tintern Abbey*, ll. 49-50): "If this be error . . ." (*Prelude*, Bk. II, l. 419). See A. Gérard, *L'Idée romantique de la poésie en Angleterre* (Paris, 1955), pp. 158-159.

superiority of the knowledge which we have by faith to the knowledge which we have by Natural Philosophy." [8]

The Eolian Harp, then, is a dialectical poem. And the whole argument springs from the romantic *Sehnsucht*, from the romantic dissatisfaction with the commonly accepted view of God and the world, from the romantic desire to probe and feel and understand the deep, puzzling network of relationships that underlies the unity of the cosmos. The interpretation of this unity provided by lines 44–48 is strongly tinged with a pantheism which could not but clash with Coleridge's religious beliefs. As a result, the poet found himself guilty of the "misty rather than mystic confusion of God with the world" with which he was, at a later date, to charge Wordsworth.[9] And he was driven to a pious position of medieval fideism which, though it might satisfy Sara's elementary mental needs, would not indefinitely suffice for a man of Coleridge's intellectual stature.

[8] *The Notebooks of Samuel Taylor Coleridge*, ed. K. Coburn (London, 1957), I, entry number 6.

[9] S. T. Coleridge, *Biographia Epistolaris*, ed. A. Turnbull (London, 1911), II, 195. I am convinced that this charge was utterly unjustified. Most of the time, Wordsworth was as careful as Coleridge was to maintain the ontological distinction between God and the world, or at least to convey his uncertainty about their true relationship. An early example of that distinction, which is all the more interesting because it is based on the panoramic perception which so often inspired Coleridge, is to be found in MS. B of *The Ruined Cottage*:

> Oh! then what soul was his when on the tops
> Of the high mountains he beheld the sun
> Rise up and bathe the world in light. He looked,
> The ocean and the earth beneath him lay
> In gladness and deep joy. The clouds were touched
> And in their silent faces did he read
> Unutterable love . . .

The concluding lines of the passage clearly exclude any confusion of God with the world:

> In such access of mind, in such high hour
> Of visitation from the living God,
> He did not feel the God; he felt his works.
>   (ll. 122–137)

The dialectical argument of the poem is thus seen to develop through three stages: first, there is the experience itself, or rather a cluster of experiential units deftly fused together, which involves the poet's love for his wife, his perception of nature, the free play of his fancy, the feeling of oneness, and the harp's melody; second, there is the philosophical interpretation of this experience, couched in metaphorical language and with a pantheistic bias; third, we have the repudiation of this interpretation in the name of religious orthodoxy. But a fourth stage was to come, finding utterance in the lines added in 1817. This final stage might be described as a recantation of the repudiation of the philosophical interpretation! Obviously, between 1795 and 1817, Coleridge had changed his mind about this interpretation. This does not mean that he had become a pantheist, but rather that he had evolved a philosophy of nature in which the metaphor of lines 44–48 did make sense within the framework of orthodox Christianity. The question that we now have to answer, therefore, is: when and how did this development take place?

Three factors in particular contributed to Coleridge's intellectual predicament in the year 1795: his revulsion against the "Newtonian" cosmology; his attachment to Christianity; and the intensity of his newly felt experience of nature. It may be useful to go into this last, which provides, of course, the experiential foundation for much of his later thinking.

One of the first of Coleridge's poems to use the nature motif in a significant way is the sonnet on *Life*. In the octet, it will be remembered, the poet describes himself journeying "o'er the extensive plain"; "at every step" "the glorious prospect" "widen'd," the climax being reached when his "ravish'd" eye ultimately embraced the whole landscape. There is a regrettably mechanical parallel between this natural description and the tercets, which purport to delineate Coleridge's "course through Life" as he expects it to develop: he hopes that "each step" will display "new scenes of Wisdom," that his "knowledge" may "open" more and more, with the climax taking place at death, when

> My eye shall dart thro' infinite expanse,
> And thought suspended lie in Rapture's blissful trance.

Coleridge's sedulous craftsmanship is exemplified in the many equations of the poem: life is an extensive plain, the course of life is a journey, sensory perception is compared to gradually widening knowledge, the prospect of the whole landscape is an analogue to the infinite knowledge that is Death's greatest gift. What is chiefly conspicuous, however, is Coleridge's concern with infinity conceived in terms of the spatial metaphor. A moment of delightful ecstasy occurs at the end of the octet as the poet rejoices in his total apprehension of the landscape: "Till all—at once—did my eye ravish'd sweep!" Similarly, at the end of the sestet, "Rapture's blissful trance" results from a flash of spiritual insight into "infinite expanse."

In this poem, the link between spiritual knowledge and what I have called the "panoramic perception" is of an allegorical character. Besides, Coleridge's attention was focused on the tenor of the simile, more than on the vehicle: nature is described in vague and general terms ("Wood, Meadow, verdant Hill, and dreary steep"), and Coleridge does not hesitate to make use of artificial and conventional diction ("Where native Otter sports his scanty stream"). He is chiefly interested in the workings of his own mind, and his only concern in looking at nature is to discover there an analogue for what goes on in his mind.

The situation is quite different in *The Eolian Harp*. Here, it is the experience of nature that is central and, indeed, the origin of the poem. And the landscape is more than an analogue of spiritual infinity: lines 44–48 show us Coleridge toying with the notion that the relationship between nature and spirit might be one, not of similitude, but rather of identity, the forms of nature being one with the spiritual energy that gives them life. The rejection of this notion at the end of the poem could not solve the problem: it only shelved it, as it turned out, for future consideration.

As we know, the panoramic perception recurs in *Reflections*, where the "goodly scene" is described in far greater detail than it was in *Life*. As in *The Eolian Harp*, the poet's apprehension of nature brings to his mind the thought of God:

> It seem'd like Omnipresence! God, methought,
> Had built him there a Temple: the whole World
> Seem'd *imag'd* in its vast circumference.

In this passage, the distinction between God and nature, which is basic to Christian orthodoxy, is firmly maintained. The key words are "seem'd like," "methought," "seem'd *imag'd*": they remind the reader of the hypothetical phrasing of line 44 in *The Eolian Harp*. Coleridge is again at pains to emphasize that this thought is a subjective speculation, and no light is thrown on the actual nature of the relation between God and the universe.

That Coleridge was deeply preoccupied—and in a more vitally committed way than might be expected—with this problem of romantic thought is evident from a notebook entry of November or December, 1796, which ends as follows:

> inward desolations—
> an horror of great darkness
> great things that on the ocean
> counterfeit infinity—[10]

These are the last lines of what J. L. Lowes rightly called "one of the most wildly incoherent pages of the Note Book."[11] M. H. Abrams attributes both the incoherence and the colorful intensity of the whole entry to the effect of opium; according to him, the last two lines exhibit a peculiar aspect of Cole-

---

[10] *Notebooks of Coleridge*, I, entry number 273.
[11] J. L. Lowes, *The Road to Xanadu* (Boston, 1927), p. 191.

ridge's intoxication: "in the 'great things' and 'counterfeit infinity' of the ocean, space once more undergoes its limitless expansion."[12] Although opium may have played a part in the chaotic imagery of the entry, it should be clear from the foregoing explication of *Life* that this is by no means the whole story: the image of limitless expansion held a definite appeal for Coleridge at a date when he was not yet addicted to the drug. If it is at all possible to devise an explanation for the lines that have just been quoted, I would suggest that "inward desolations" must refer to a complex cluster of feelings from which, given Coleridge's intense intellectual interests, philosophical uncertainty is probably not absent. It might well be that this philosophical element is more particularly hinted at in the phrase "great darkness." The mention of the ocean will remind the reader of the "Shoreless ocean" in *Reflections;* in both instances, the ocean is a climactic image of endless expansion. And I feel inclined to believe that the striking phrase "counterfeit infinity" refers to Coleridge's mental predicament as exemplified in *The Eolian Harp*, that is, to the temptation to confuse God with the world. The word "counterfeit" indicates that he is aware of the falsity of any such notion, but the tormented mood of the entry ("inward desolations," "horror," "great darkness") would likewise suggest that, as yet, he had found no way out of the dilemma in which he was caught—committed to the certainty of faith on the one hand, and yet unable to ignore the almost inescapable implications of his personal experience of nature on the other.

Some such interpretation would seem to be confirmed by a passage in a letter written to John Thelwall on 31 December 1796, presumably a very short time after the notebook entry. In this letter, Coleridge quotes lines 44–48 as a paraphrase of the opinion of Alexander Monro, the author of *Observations on the Structure and Functions of the Nervous System* (Edin-

[12] M. H. Abrams, *The Milk of Paradise* (Cambridge, Mass., 1934), p. 31.

burgh, 1783), who "believes in a plastic immaterial Nature—all-pervading." This passage belongs to a paragraph in which Coleridge draws up a list of various philosophical interpretations as to the nature of life:

Dr Beddoes, & Dr Darwin think that *Life* is utterly inexplicable, writing as Materialists—You, I understand, have adopted the idea that it is the result of organized matter acted on by external Stimuli. . . . Monro believes in a plastic immaterial Nature—all-pervading . . . Hunter that the *Blood* is the Life—which is saying nothing at all . . . & Ferriar believes in a *Soul*, like an orthodox Churchman—So much for Physicians & Surgeons—Now as to the Metaphysicians, Plato says, it is *Harmony* —he might as well have said a fiddle stick's end—but I love Plato—his dear *gorgeous* Nonsense! And *I, tho' last not least*, I do not know what to think about it—on the whole, I have rather made up my mind that I am a mere *apparition*—a naked Spirit!—And that Life is I myself! which is a mighty clear account of it.[13]

"I do not know what to think about it!" In a flippant but scholarly mood, Coleridge conveys to Thelwall the perplexity, the "darkness" he is in, as well as his despair of finding the light of truth in the heavy fog generated by so many conflicting opinions. We may well believe that when he was not "joking"—as, further in the letter, he said he was—the sheer intricacy of the problem, added to its intellectual urgency, left him gasping in "inward desolations."

In early July, 1797, the panoramic perception reappears in *This Lime-tree Bower my Prison*, where Coleridge identifies himself with Charles Lamb, hoping that his friend may stand

> Silent, with swimming sense; and gazing round
> On the wide Landscape gaze till all doth seem
> Less gross than bodily, a living Thing

---

[13] *Collected Letters of Samuel Taylor Coleridge*, ed. E. L. Griggs (Oxford, 1956), I, 294–295.

Counterfeit Infinity 53

> Which acts upon the mind, & with such Hues
> As cloath th'Almighty Spirit, when he makes
> Spirits perceive his presence! [14]

It is worth noting that here again Coleridge stresses the subjective character of his observation ("seem"), although such a device might be deemed unnecessary in view of the palpable fact that there is not the slightest trace of pantheism in his utterance: things are not described as emanations of the Spirit, as they were to some extent in *The Eolian Harp;* the beauty of the forms of nature is compared with the "hues" that "cloath" (in the printed version: "veil") "th'Almighty Spirit, when he makes / Spirits perceive his presence"; God is not "one intellectual breeze," nor even "Omnipresence," but omnipotence, "th'Almighty Spirit"; and the world is not described as essentially spiritual but as "less gross than bodily," that is, less inert than alive.[15]

On 14 October 1797, Coleridge cited these lines from *This Lime-tree Bower my Prison* in another letter to John Thelwall, which, although well known, must be quoted at some length because it establishes a clear and explicit connection between the panoramic perception and the obscure phrase "counterfeit infinity" used in the notebook a year before:

> I can *at times* feel strongly the beauties, you describe, in themselves, & for themselves—but more frequently *all things* appear little—all the knowledge, that can be acquired, child's play—the universe itself—what but an immense heap of *little* things?—I

---

[14] I am quoting here an early version (*Letters of Coleridge*, I, 350) of this passage. In the later printed texts, the clause "a living thing which acts upon the mind" has been deleted, not, I think, for any ideological reason, but because the sentence as it stood was somewhat awkward, grammatically and stylistically.

[15] An additional reason for quoting from the early version is that it is more explicit than the printed text. A "thing," we may presume, would be "gross"; a "living thing," on the contrary, is "bodily." It is probably unnecessary to remind the reader of the significant reappearance of the phrase "living thing" in *The Ancient Mariner*. It also occurs frequently in Wordsworth's poetry.

can contemplate nothing but parts, & parts are all *little*—!—My mind feels as if it ached to behold & know something *great*—something *one & indivisible*—and it is only in the faith of this that rocks or waterfalls, mountains or caverns give me the sense of sublimity or majesty!—But in this faith *all things* counterfeit infinity—!

After quoting the above lines from *This Lime-tree Bower my Prison*, Coleridge goes on to say: "It is but seldom that I raise & spiritualize my intellect to this height." [16]

I do not think it has ever been pointed out that this passage describes two widely divergent attitudes to nature. First, Coleridge speaks of natural objects seen "in themselves, & for themselves"; sometimes they seem to him beautiful, but more often they appear as "parts" at which he can only cast a disparaging and disappointed glance. On the other hand, the objects of nature can also be seen in the light of the faith that there exists "something *great*—something *one & indivisible*"; contemplated from this second vantage point (and not in and for themselves), "*all things* counterfeit infinity." It should *not* be assumed that the words "*all things*" refer to the panoramic perception. Indeed, *This Lime-tree Bower my Prison* shows that Coleridge had outgrown the stage when insight into the "one life" could be brought about only through his all-embracing apprehension of a wide landscape. The meaning of the poem is clearly expressed in line 61: "No plot so narrow, be but Nature there." Whether independently, or under the influence of Wordsworth, Coleridge had learned by now that

> the meanest flower that blows can give
> Thoughts that do often lie too deep for tears.

The important point about the letter to Thelwall, however, is that the phrase "counterfeit infinity" is here set in a context entirely different from, indeed, distinctly antipodal to, that of the notebook entry of the previous year. The dominant mood of the notebook entry is one of chaos, puzzlement, horror, and

---

[16] *Letters of Coleridge*, I, 349–350.

Counterfeit Infinity

despair, and the phrase implies deceit and fraud. On the contrary, in the letter, Coleridge's perception of things as counterfeiting infinity is described as a raising and a spiritualizing of his intellect to heights seldom reached.

The difference in mood between the utterances of 1796 and those of 1797 can only be accounted for, it seems to me, by the hypothesis that Coleridge had somehow found a way of reconciling his intuition of nature with the central tenet of Christian transcendentalism. Nature is not infinity: nature merely counterfeits infinity. But this does not imply that our experience of nature is illusory and deceptive and, at all events, utterly meaningless. On the contrary, if we look at nature, not with the eyes of the "unregenerate mind," but in the faith that there does exist, beyond and above nature, "something *great*—something *one* & *indivisible*," then our feeling of infinity while contemplating nature is indeed endowed with positive significance: it raises and spiritualizes the intellect (for which, at a later date, Coleridge would probably have used the word "imagination"), so that the mind, while acknowledging the littleness of the things of nature, can still receive from them an intimation of infinity.[17]

---

[17] The process is rather similar to the workings of superstition as Coleridge describes them in *The Destiny of Nations*. The legends of Lapland having, for some recondite reason, caught his imagination, Coleridge records some of them in a passage introduced as follows:

> And what if some rebellious, o'er dark realms
> Arrogate power? yet these train up to God,
> And on the rude eye, unconfirmed for day,
> Flash meteor-lights better than total gloom.

He then proceeds to define the positive value of superstition, which, however false, provides at least an intimation of spiritual being:

> For Fancy is the power
> That first unsensualises the dark mind,
> Giving it new delights; and bids it swell
> With wild activity; and peopling air,
> By obscure fears of Beings invisible,
> Emancipates it from the grosser thrall

This process of spiritual intuition is described in the first draft of *The Destiny of Nations*, where it is associated with the harp motif:

> Seize then, my Soul, from Freedom's trophied dome
> The harp which hanging high between the shields
> Of Brutus and Leonidas, oft gives
> A fitful music, when with breeze-like Touch
> Great Spirits passing thrill its wings: the Bard
> Listens and knows, thy will to work by Fame.
> For what is Freedom, but the unfetter'd use
> Of all the powers which God for use had given?
> But chiefly this, him first to view, him last,
> Thro' shapes, and sounds, and all the world of sense,
> The changes of empires, and the deeds of Man
> Translucent, as thro' clouds that veil the Light.[18]

For the printed version (1817) Coleridge, among other changes, condensed the last three lines to make it clearer that he was referring to man's immediate perception of natural objects and natural events as a heap of little things which can only counterfeit infinity:

> Through meaner powers and secondary things
> Effulgent, as through clouds that veil his blaze.
> (ll. 16–17)

But the occurrence of the image of translucence in the first draft is interesting because it will become central to Coleridge's full-blown definition of the symbol in *The Statesman's Manual*: "A symbol . . . is characterized by a translucence of the special in the individual, or of the general in the especial, or of the universal in the general. Above all by the translucence of the eternal through and in the temporal."

> Of the present impulse, teaching Self-control,
> Till superstition with unconscious hand
> Seat Reason on her throne.
> (ll. 60–88)

[18] *Complete Poetical Works of Coleridge*, II, 1024.

And, of course, the complementary metaphors of the veiled light and of the translucent veil belong to the most significant recurring themes in Shelley's imagery.

In his attempt to account for his sense of cosmic unity without at the same time yielding to the temptation of pantheism, Coleridge was working his way toward a conception of nature as symbolic. But this conception had two important implications. First, it entailed a reappraisal of the relationship between God and the created universe. And second, it led to a redefinition of the word "symbol," which was to crystallize the main orientation of poetry and poetic theory for more than a century.

The conventional meaning of the word "symbol" in the theological language of the time can be exemplified through a passage of Priestley, to whom Coleridge's early thought was heavily indebted:

> The idea which the scriptures give us of the divine nature is that of a being, properly speaking, *everywhere present,* constantly supporting, and, at pleasure, controlling the laws of nature, but not the object of any of our senses: and that, out of condescension, as it were, to the weakness of human apprehension, he chose, in the early ages of the world, to signify his peculiar presence by some *visible symbol,* as that of a supernatural bright cloud, or some other appearance which could not but impress their minds with the idea of a real local presence.[19]

Plainly, Priestley's cloud, qua symbol, has only what Herr Teufelsdröckh was later to call "extrinsic significance." It is, as the *Oxford English Dictionary* puts it, "a material object representing or taken to represent something immaterial or abstract," "not by exact resemblance, but by vague suggestion, or by some accidental or conventional relation" (in this case, presumably, brightness, altitude, eerie aspect, ghostly insubstantiality, and so forth). It is a mere appearance arbitrarily

---

[19] J. Priestley, *Disquisitions Relating to Matter and Spirit* (Birmingham, 1782), p. 148.

chosen by God to become for a while his "local habitation" and an outward token of his presence, which is not perceptible to human senses. It might stand under the same category as Carlyle's "stupidest heraldic Coats-of-arms; military Banners everywhere; and generally all national or other sectarian Costumes and Customs; they have no intrinsic, necessary divineness, or even worth; but have acquired an extrinsic one." [20] In connection with the relationship between God and nature, overemphasis on divine transcendence would seem to preclude any other definition of the symbol, in the same way that overstressing divine omnipresence tends to abolish any real distinction between the Creator and the created world.

However much Coleridge may have been influenced by Priestley's *Disquisitions Relating to Matter and Spirit* while writing his *Religious Musings*, he could hardly have any use for such a mechanical, emblematic conception of the symbol.[21]

[20] Carlyle's discussion of the symbol is to be found in Book III, Chapter iii of *Sartor Resartus* (London, 1833).

[21] H. W. Piper (*The Active Universe* [London, 1962], p. 57), however, claims to find in the following passage from the first printed version of *Religious Musings* (*Complete Poetical Works of Coleridge*, I, 109), an example of a symbol which is "a little similar but much subtler" than Priestley's bright cloud:

> Yet thou more bright than all that Angel Blaze,
> Despised GALILEAN! Man of Woes!
> For chiefly in the oppressed Good Man's face
> The Great Invisible (by symbols seen)
> Shines with peculiar and concentred light,
> . . . .
> Who thee beheld thy imag'd Father saw.

Yet, the paradoxical statements that "the Great *Invisible*" can be "*seen*" and "*shines*" in Christ's face, and that to behold Christ is to *see* his "*imag'd* Father," suggest that this particular symbol (Christ and his face) does not merely "signify" what it means (as does Priestley's cloud), but in some way contains it, *is* it. In Carlyle's phrasing, we might say that Christ, for Coleridge, is "an embodiment and revelation of the Infinite; the Infinite is made to blend itself with the Finite, to stand visible, and as it were, attainable there." Indeed, the passage is of special interest in that it clarifies this blending of finite and infinite

More congenial and fruitful, no doubt, was Berkeley's view of the relation between God and nature in human perception. Indeed, Berkeley's description of the growth of the mind in this respect sets a theoretical pattern which seems to have been faithfully reflected in Coleridge's and Wordsworth's experience:

Sense at first besets and overbears the mind. The sensible appearances are all in all: our reasonings are employed about them: our desires terminate in them: we look no farther for realities or causes; till the intellect begins to dawn, and cast a ray on this shadowy scene. We then perceive the true principle of unity, identity, and existence. Those things that before seemed to constitute the whole of Being, upon taking an intellectual view of things, prove to be but fleeting phantoms.[22]

There is, then, a first stage, in which the sensible appearances are "all in all"; Wordsworth, we recall, used the same

---

which so often sounds like a hollow and rhapsodic commonplace in romantic poetry and in romantic theory. Considerable emphasis is placed on Christ as a finite being: he is a "Galilean," a "Man," and the light radiating from his face is "peculiar and concentred." The light imagery is handled in a way that anticipates Coleridge's later theoretical definition of the symbol as "translucence" of the infinite through the finite. The description of Christ as "more bright" than "Angel Blaze" announces the direction in which the symbolism is going to proceed, for what can be brighter than "Angel Blaze" except God's own radiance? And the tenor of the light metaphor, that is, the intrinsic meaning of the symbol, becomes obvious when the absolute selflessness of Christ's sacrifice, most conspicuous in his mourning for his persecutors, appears to be the "chief" manifestation of God's all-embracing love:

> When all of Self regardless the scourg'd Saint
> Mourns for th' oppressor.

H. W. Piper has refrained from quoting these two lines, but they are essential for comprehending the difference in kind (and not only in subtlety) between the extrinsic symbol as exemplified in Priestley's cloud and the intrinsic symbol of the romantics.

[22] *Siris*, In *The Works of George Berkeley*, ed. A. C. Fraser (Oxford, 1871), II, 478.

phrase in *Tintern Abbey* to describe a bygone phase in his apprehension of the created world: "For nature then (. . .) / To me was all in all" (ll. 72–75). The "romantic" exaltation of nature with its inherent proclivity to pantheism is the logical outcome of this assumption that "things . . . constitute the whole of Being."

But when what Berkeley calls the intellect begins to dawn, the mind realizes that there are not one but two orders of Being, the sensible and the spiritual: "as sure . . . as the sensible world really exists, so sure is there an infinite omnipresent Spirit, who contains and supports it." [23] This insight, in its turn, can conceivably lead to two antinomic attitudes. One is based on the depressing notion that nature is but a "shadowy scene," a deceitful counterfeit of infinity, a heap of little things, a veil that clouds the bright face of eternity, a conglomeration of "fleeting phantoms." But there is another approach, which was intimated by Berkeley himself in his assertion that in the "boundless extent" and the "glittering furniture" of the created world, the human mind can actually perceive, though not God himself, "the energy of an all-perfect Mind displayed in endless forms." [24] In such a view, intimations of divinity do not flow forth from single privileged objects such as Priestley's cloud, arbitrarily endowed with extrinsic, emblematic meaning: they are diffused throughout visible nature, whose lineaments really bear the stamp of their creator's unending action. As Berkeley said, God is "to all created beings the source of unity and identity, harmony and order, existence and stability"; [25] consequently, man's perception of those corporeal properties is also an intimation of their "true principle," of their necessary cause, the divine mind, transcendent, yet, by his creative action, omnipresent.

This was what Coleridge had in mind when he wrote, in *The Destiny of Nations*:

[23] *Three Dialogues between Hylas and Philonous*, in *ibid.*, I, 304.
[24] *Ibid.*, p. 303.
[25] *Siris*, in *The Works of George Berkeley*, II, 478–479.

> For all that meets the bodily sense I deem
> Symbolical, one mighty alphabet
> For infant minds; and we in this low world
> Placed with our backs to bright Reality,
> That we may learn with young unwounded ken
> The substance from its shadow.
>
> (ll. 18–25)

Symbolic value is no longer the extrinsic quality, the super-added privilege of arbitrarily chosen objects, as it was in conventional theological parlance. *All things* now appear symbolical. The whole of nature and each of its parts are genuine symbols endowed, in Carlyle's phrase, with "intrinsic meaning." The ascription of substantial oneness to the forms of nature may be a literal untruth ("counterfeit"), since corporeal objects, being mere shadows, cannot have substance. It is nevertheless valid and valuable, since their shapes and harmony, their organization and the laws which they obey actually derive from the workings of the divine mind and provide visible evidence of God's invisible design, to which they refer the beholder. Wordsworth did not mean anything else when he wrote that the outward forms of the Alpine landscape

> Were all like workings of one mind, the features
> Of the same face, blossoms upon one tree,
> Characters of the great Apocalypse,
> The types and symbols of Eternity,
> Of first and last, and midst, and without end.[26]

In developing this new definition of the symbol, Coleridge freed the romantic perception of nature from its pantheistic suggestions, and reinstalled it in the orthodox tradition of Christian transcendentalism. It should be added that he was also joining one of the most pregnant trends of early European romanticism. In Germany, the most sensitive minds of the time were trying to overcome the crude dualism of the *Aufklärung* along similar lines. As early as 1787, in a section

---

[26] *Prelude*, Bk. VI, ll. 636–640.

of *Philosophische Briefe* known as "Theosophie des Junius," Schiller had done so in terms that anticipate Coleridge: in their organized multiplicity, the forms and the laws of nature appeared to him as "symbols," as "hieroglyphics," as "the alphabet" through which the mind could communicate with God.[27] In the very year when Coleridge wrote *This Lime-tree Bower my Prison*, Goethe was trying to account for the peculiar impression which certain objects made upon him by describing them as "symbolic," as representative of a "totality" which is included in them and which conveys a feeling of the One and the Whole.[28] At a later date, Baudelaire, in France, was to insist on the capacity of the mind to perceive familiar objects as symbolic of the hidden depths of life [29]—an idea forcefully expressed in the well-known *Correspondances* sonnet:

[27] *Schillers Werke*, ed. L. Bellermann (Leipzig, 1895), XV, 141: "Also gibt es für mich nur eine einzige Erscheinung in der Natur, das denkende Wesen. Die grosze Zusamensetzung, die wir Welt nennen, bleibt mir jetzt nur merkwürdig, weil sie vorhanden ist, mir die mannigfaltigen Äuszerungen jenes Wesens symbolisch zu bezeichnen. Alles in mir und auszer mir ist nur Hieroglyphe einer Kraft, die mir ähnlich ist. Die Gesetze der Natur sind die Chiffern, welche das denkende Wesen zusammenfügt, sich dem denkenden Wesen verständlich zu machen—das Alphabet, vermittelst dessen alle Geister mit dem vollkommensten Geist und mit sich selbst unterhandeln." For an account of the growth of the symbol concept in Germany, see J. Rouge, "La Notion du symbole chez Goethe" in *Goethe: Etudes publiées pour le centenaire de sa mort* (Paris, 1932), pp. 285–310.

[28] Letter of 16 August 1797, in *Briefwechsel zwischen Schiller und Goethe*, ed. P. Stein (Leipzig, n.d.), II, 115: "Ich habe daher die Gegenstände, die einen solchen Effect hervorbringen, genau betrachtet und zu meiner Verwunderung bemerkt dasz sie eigentlich symbolisch sind, das heiszt, wie ich kaum zu sagen brauche, es sind eminente Fälle, die, in einer charakteristischen Mannigfaltigkeit, als Repräsentanten von vielen andern dastehen, eine gewisse Totalität in sich schlieszen, eine gewisse Reihe fordern, ähnliches und fremdes in meinen Geiste aufregen und so von auszen wie von innen an eine gewisse Einheit une Allheit Anspruch machen."

[29] C. Baudelaire, "Fusées, XVII" in *Oeuvres Complètes* (Paris, 1935), II, 634: "Dans certains états de l'âme presque surnaturels, la profondeur de la vie se révèle presque tout entière dans le spectacle, si ordinaire qu'il soit, qu'on a sous les yeux. Il en devient le Symbole."

La Nature est un temple où de vivants piliers
Laissent parfois sortir de confuses paroles;
L'homme y passe à travers des forêts de symboles
Qui l'observent avec des regards familiers.

The discordance between structural emphasis and imaginative intensity in *The Eolian Harp* was not due to a lack of technical skill, but rather to the fact that, at the time of writing, the poet was as yet unable to reconcile two divergent outlooks to which he felt equally committed, although for different reasons. One was the Christian view of what Kierkegaard was to describe as the infinite qualitative difference between God and the created world; the other was the romantic vision itself, the sense of the cosmic unity of being, the felt intuition of the world as a continuum in which spirit and matter, self and non-self are fused into a living totality.

The systolic rhythm provided a satisfactory structural correlative for the "unremitting interchange" between man and nature. As M. F. Schulz says, "these expansions and contractions of awareness, imaged in a series of scene-shifts, give structural actuality to the subject-object opposition by representing it as a centrifugal-centripetal action."[30] But with regard to the relationship between spirit and matter, God and the created universe, Coleridge, in the conversation poems, was still tentatively groping for a way out of the apparent antinomy between the Christian doctrine and the romantic experience, or rather, for a way of accounting for the latter in terms that would not entail a repudiation of the former. The outcome was the elaboration of the symbol concept, through which the intuited oneness of the cosmos is seen to reside, not in any monistic unity of substance, but in a relational pattern of causation and consequent analogy. This symbolic conception of nature, which Coleridge shared with his German contemporaries, was of course the necessary prerequisite for the development of a symbolist theory of literature.

[30] M. F. Schulz, "Oneness and Multeity in Coleridge's Poems," *Tulane Studies in English*, IX (1959), 53–60.

4 Emblems of Misery:
WORDSWORTH'S *THE THORN*

THERE is considerable truth in Keats's observation, in one of his letters, that Coleridge was "incapable of remaining content with half knowledge."[1] The conversation poems fail to reach the highest order of poetry not only because of the discrepancy between the intentional meaning revealed through structural gradation and the dazzling visionary flashes of insight expressed in isolated passages, but also because of Coleridge's tendency toward explicit philosophical statement rather than symbolic indirection. He cannot refrain from striving to give us both the symbol and its interpretation. The same could be said of much romantic poetry, especially of the kind dealing with the cosmic insight. But the symbolic conception of nature also involves less ambitious applications than this overall intuition of universal oneness: natural forms and occurrences can also symbolize emotional states and human destinies because they illustrate the very same creative or destroying processes to which man too is submitted. And although even Baudelaire found it necessary to explicate the *morale* of his fine poem, *L'Albatros*, it is nonetheless true that when they use natural forms as emblems of human inward-

---

[1] *The Letters of John Keats*, ed. H. E. Rollins (Cambridge, Eng., 1958), I, 194.

ness rather than of cosmic unity, the romantic poets generally feel that they can leave the symbol to speak for itself. In this respect, one of the most successful of the early romantic poems of England is Wordsworth's *The Thorn*, which was written in March, 1798, and appeared in *Lyrical Ballads*.

O. J. Campbell and P. Mueschke have noted that the curious oxymoron of this title was "a kind of public announcement" that the joint authors were to use the ballad "not so much for purposes of pure narrative as for the vehicle of personal emotion."[2] Although it may sound perverse to describe T. S. Eliot, in any respect whatsoever, as a latter-day romantic, there is no doubt that what the Lake poets set out to do in 1798 corresponded closely to the purpose he assigned to art in his famous essay on *Hamlet*: "The only way of expressing emotion in the form of art is by finding an 'objective correlative'; in other words, a set of objects, a situation, a chain of events which shall be the formula of that *particular* emotion; such that when the external facts, which must terminate in sensory experience are given, the emotion is immediately evoked." Even Hemingway, in *Death in the Afternoon*, described his greatest difficulty and his highest endeavor as the will to put down "the real thing, the sequence of motion and fact which made the emotion." In the lyrical ballads of Wordsworth and Coleridge, too, the "situation," the "chain of events," the "sequence of motion and fact," is not there for its own sake but for the sake of the emotion it produced, which at the time would have been called feeling.

But *The Thorn* is of peculiar interest because of the precocious skill with which the poet has woven into a highly complex, yet, as I hope to show, fully unified pattern several "objective correlatives" which belong to various orders of poetic being: the descriptive, the narrative, and the psychological. Its immediate emotional impact upon the reader is certain

---

[2] O. J. Campbell and P. Mueschke, "Wordsworth's Aesthetic Development, 1795–1802," *Essays and Studies in English and Comparative Literature*, X (1933), 23–26.

and perfectly clear. The way this effect is created can only be elucidated by disentangling the intricate interplay of the three imaginative elements which are the raw materials of its texture: the thorn and its setting, the story of Martha Ray, and the attitude of the narrator.

This complex organization accounts for the uncommon amount of critical dissension which characterizes interpretations of *The Thorn*. Not only are critics unable to agree whether the poem is good or bad and for what reasons, but there is a puzzling variety of views concerning such an apparently straightforward point as its very subject matter: whether it is about a man or a woman or a tree! By focusing his detailed analysis of the poem on the narrator's style, Coleridge seems to have assumed (at least for the purpose of the discussion) that the central element is the narrator,[3] a view which was later adopted by Wordsworth's editor, E. de Sélincourt,[4] and which has been fully developed by S. M. Parrish; the latter, indeed, after summarily dismissing the dozens of earlier critics who commented on *The Thorn*, makes out a powerful case for his reading of the poem as a "dramatic monologue" and a "psychological study" designed to bring out the narrator's superstitious character.[5] Mary Moorman takes her cue from the Fenwick note and considers the narrator and his story the "device"—a not very successful one, she thinks—invented by Wordsworth to convey to the reader the powerful impression made by the thorn upon him.[6] Most commentators,

[3] *Biographia Literaria*, ed. J. Shawcross (Oxford, 1907), I, 36–38.

[4] *The Poetical Works of William Wordsworth*, ed. E. de Sélincourt and Helen Darbishire (Oxford, 1962), II, 513. Wordsworth himself, at one place, defined his purpose as to present "some of the general laws by which superstition acts upon the mind" (*ibid.*, p. 512).

[5] S. M. Parrish, " 'The Thorn': Wordsworth's Dramatic Monologue," *Journal of English Literary History*, XXIV (1957), 153–163, and "Dramatic Technique in the *Lyrical Ballads*," *PMLA*, LXXIV (1959), 85–97. Such is also the interpretation of W. J. B. Owen in *Wordsworth's Preface to Lyrical Ballads* (Copenhagen, 1957), p. 87.

[6] M. Moorman, *William Wordsworth: A Biography. The Early Years, 1770–1803* (Oxford, 1957), pp. 386–388.

however, have brought their attention to bear on the Martha Ray story as yet another treatment of the theme of undeserved suffering and of the motif of the abandoned mother; the latest exponent of this point of view is John F. Danby, for whom, although "the narrator's role is important for transmitting the total experience of the poem . . . , he is . . . a means to the poem, not an end in itself"; nothing, therefore, "could be more misleading" than to assume that the "main interest" is "the psychology of the narrator." [7]

Given this anarchy of interpretative views, it is small wonder that critical valuation should range widely and wildly from Helen Darbishire's appreciation of *The Thorn* as "a great and remarkable poem" [8] to Campbell and Mueschke's condemnation of it as an awkward attempt to transform "intractable and embarrassing autobiographical material into impersonal art," and to D. Ferry's summary statement that the poem is "probably not worth examining." [9] Obviously, a new attempt should be made to assess the possible connection and interdependence of the three main motifs and to appraise the degree of unity in mood and structure achieved in this poem. Wordsworth himself, we may recall, wrote in 1805 that "the poem is a favourite with me," [10] and in 1809 he classified it as one of the best of the poems "relating to human life." [11]

On 19 March 1798, Dorothy Wordsworth entered the following note in her diary: "Wm. and Basil and I walked to the hill-top, a very cold bleak day. We were met on our return by

[7] J. F. Danby, *The Simple Wordsworth: Studies in the Poems, 1797–1807* (London, 1960), pp. 57–72. The same view had been offered by R. Sharrock in "Wordsworth's Revolt Against Literature," *Essays in Criticism*, III (1953), 396–412.
[8] H. Darbishire, *The Poet Wordsworth* (Oxford, 1950), pp. 36–44.
[9] D. Ferry, *The Limits of Mortality: An Essay on Wordsworth's Major Poems* (Middletown, Conn., 1959), p. 98.
[10] *The Early Letters of William and Dorothy Wordsworth*, ed. E. de Sélincourt (Oxford, 1935), p. 490.
[11] *The Letters of William and Dorothy Wordsworth: The Middle Years, 1806–1820*, ed. E. de Sélincourt (Oxford, 1937), p. 308.

a severe hailstorm. William wrote some lines describing a stunted thorn." [12] The lines Wordsworth wrote on that day are probably the rough draft to be found in the Alfoxden manuscript. They read like an objective description of the tree, although most of the outer features which the final version invests with symbolic value are already present.[13] In the Fenwick note, Wordsworth himself tells us that he composed the poem "with great rapidity." In any case, it must have been finished by 20 April, when, according to Dorothy, he began *Peter Bell*. By then, the thorn and what the poet had made of it had become a familiar household matter, for on that very day Dorothy wrote in her diary: "Came home the Crookham way, by *the* thorn, and the 'little muddy pond.' " [14] The time of the year undoubtedly provided Wordsworth with part of his inspiration. Although Dorothy, in the course of that month, dutifully jots down her notes about hailstorms and showers and green grass and luscious flowers, observing that "the Spring advances rapidly," we notice that the first part of the poem oscillates between bitter winter imagery and colorful spring-flower imagery.

Dorothy's diary is the only contemporaneous documentary evidence we have of the circumstances surrounding the composition of the poem. What little it contains confirms Wordsworth's own reminiscences in the Fenwick note: "Alfoxden, 1798. Arose out of my observing, on the ridge of Quantock Hill, on a stormy day, a thorn which I had often passed in calm and bright weather without noticing it. I said to myself, 'Cannot I by some invention do as much to make this Thorn permanently an impressive object as the storm has made it to my eyes at this moment?' I began the poem accordingly, and composed it with great rapidity." [15] There is no warranted

---

[12] *Journals of Dorothy Wordsworth*, ed. E. de Sélincourt (London, 1952), I, 13.
[13] *Poetical Works*, II, 240 n.
[14] *Journals*, I, 16; italics mine.
[15] *Poetical Works*, II, 511–512.

Emblems of Misery 69

reason to doubt the accuracy of Wordsworth's memory on this particular point, and in the present state of our knowledge, the only possible basis for an analysis of the poem as a whole is the assumption that its primary theme is the tree, and that the Martha Ray story and the narrator belong to the "invention" devised by Wordsworth to impress the thorn on the imagination of his readers.

The problem is whether this device is a success or a failure. Both opinions have been put forward, although with few critical arguments to back them apart from the critics' own tastes. It may therefore be fruitful to approach this controversial poem from a purely aesthetic angle, which can be summed up in the following question: Has Wordsworth succeeded in fusing into a satisfactory and convincing unity the three main elements of the poem, that is, the thorn, the narrator, and the story? In order to answer this question, however, we must first make up our minds on a preliminary problem: Why is it that the storm made the thorn an "impressive object" in Wordsworth's eyes? Or, to put it in a slightly different way: Which are the elements, in the poet's description of the thorn, that point to the nature of the impression it made upon him?

Clearly, the thorn, as suddenly revealed by the storm to the poet's eye and imagination, is not just any old tree. It is that, of course, and also something more, the clue to which is given by various phrases that are not purely descriptive. In the first draft of the Alfoxden manuscript, Wordsworth had used a rather daring and somewhat comical image: "a toothless thorn." We can see in what sense a thorn may be said to be toothless; yet toothlessness is mainly an attribute of human old age, hence the choice of such an epithet intimates that the thorn had, in the poet's view, a quasi-human quality, or rather, that it appeared to him to be a living natural metaphor for something human. This is no pathetic fallacy. Wordsworth hardly ever reads human feelings into the forms of nature. His is the symbolic perception, which sees in natural forms analogues of human attitudes. We note that the comparison of the thorn with "rock or stone" anticipates an image that will recur in *Resolution and Independence,* and associates the thorn with the immovability and imperviousness of extreme old age.

There are other connotations which link the thorn with Wordsworth's solitaries. In his imagination, the thorn has undergone cruel experiences: exposed on the top of the mountain, it is the victim of the "stormy winter gale." Moreover, the mosses that grow over it are felt to be malignant forces consciously striving to destroy it:

> you'd say that they are bent
> With plain and manifest intent
> To drag it to the ground;
> And all have joined in one endeavour
> To bury this poor Thorn for ever.
> (ll. 18–22)

All this creates around the small ("Not higher than a two years' child") helpless tree an atmosphere of wretchedness, of isolation ("forlorn"), of "melancholy," and accounts for the pity of the narrator as expressed in the phrase "this poor Thorn."

At this point, it is useful to quote another example of Wordsworth's use of landscape.[16] On 5 March, thus about a fortnight before Wordsworth embarked on the composition of *The Thorn,* Dorothy sent to Mary Hutchinson a copy of part of *The Ruined Cottage.* It is likely that William had his say in the choice of the passage. That they should have elected the episode dealing with the sorrow of Margaret may therefore be significant of Wordsworth's obsession with the theme of derelict womanhood. In this extract, when the Wanderer comes back to the cottage to visit Margaret after she has lost

[16] Another highly successful instance, as we shall see, is to be found in the first section of *Tintern Abbey.*

Emblems of Misery 71

her elder child, he gives the following description of the house and garden:

> Her cottage in its outward look appeared
> As chearful as before, in any shew
> Of neatness little changed, but that I thought
> *The honey-suckle crowded round the door,*
> And from the wall hung down in heavier tufts,
> And knots of worthless stone-crop started out
> Along the window's edge and grew like weeds
> Against the lower panes. I turned aside
> And strolled into her garden. It was changed.
> The unprofitable bindweed spread his bells
> From side to side, and with unwieldy wreaths
> *Had dragged the rose from its sustaining wall*
> *And bent it down to earth.* The border tufts,
> Daisy, and thrift, and lowly camomile,
> And thyme, had struggled out into the paths
> Which they used to deck.

This manipulation of the setting is highly characteristic of Wordsworth. On the literal level, the neglect into which the house and the garden have fallen is a result of the derangement of Margaret's mind:

> In every act
> Pertaining to her house affairs appeared
> The careless stillness which a thinking soul
> Gives to an idle matter.[17]

But on another plane, the honeysuckle encroaching upon the door, the window's edge gnawed by the stonecrop, the rose dragged from the wall by the bindweed, all appear as objective correlatives of a mind in the process of being gradually overwhelmed and degraded by sorrow and suffering. The image of the rose is especially pregnant with symbolic possibilities, and although Wordsworth later rewrote these lines to a considerable extent, he kept its essentials in the 1814 version:

[17] *Early Letters*, pp. 183-185; italics mine.

> The cumbrous bind-weed, with its wreaths and bells,
> Had twined about her two small rows of peas
> *And dragged them to the earth.*[18]

The wording is closer to that of *The Thorn* and confirms the view that the little tree too is endowed with symbolic significance: it is the emblem of a being overcome by the suffering inflicted by outside forces.[19]

An entirely different aspect of the symbolism of the thorn is revealed in the phrase "It stands erect," which is repeated twice in the first stanza. One must of course make allowance for the repetitive style of the narrator. But one should not forget either that Wordsworth, in the 1800 Preface, was careful to repudiate any accusation of tautology. Throughout the poem, repetitions are meant to be functional:

An attempt is rarely made to communicate impassioned feelings without something of an accompanying consciousness of the inadequateness of our own powers, or the deficiencies of language. During such efforts, there will be a craving in the mind, and as long as it is unsatisfied the speaker will cling to the same words, or words of the same character. . . . Further, from a spirit of fondness, exultation and gratitude, the mind luxuriates in the repeti-

---

[18] *The Excursion,* I, ll. 728–730, in *Poetical Works,* V, 33; italics mine.

[19] The comparison between *The Ruined Cottage* and *The Thorn* is perhaps even more pertinent than here specified. In Southey's *Commonplace Book,* there is a brief note which runs as follows: "The ruined cottage has matter for a best poem. The path overgrown—the holyhock blooming amid weeds. It shall be related to a friend whom I have purposely led there in an evening walk." J. S. Lyon, who quotes this passage, goes on to comment that "The striking parallels between these specifications and Wordsworth's story in *The Excursion* lead one to suspect that there was either a common source or some exchange of ideas" (*The Excursion. A Study* [New Haven, 1950], p. 47). But the particular nature of those specifications leads us, in our turn, to wonder whether the germinal idea of *The Ruined Cottage* is not to be found in the natural setting viewed as symbolic, just as the sight of the thorn provided the impulse for the poem of that name.

tion of words which appear successfully to communicate its feelings.[20]

Particular importance should therefore be attached to the repetition of words or images: they indicate the presence of "impassioned feelings" which the narrator is desperately trying to convey with inadequate means, or, conversely, his sense that he has hit on the right phrase to convey them. Such are the word "old," the stone comparison, the pictorial image of the lichens overgrowing the tree, and the repetitive ("endeavour," "intent") symbolic description of the malevolent mosses. Such too is the phrase "It stands erect." Obviously, what strikes the narrator is the resilience of the tree, so old and so small, in front of the adverse powers that conspire against it: the lichens, the mosses, the winter gales. The erectness of the thorn counteracts the general impression of wretchedness that surrounds it: it gives an intimation of stubborn stoicism.

Stoicism was to become an important trend in Wordsworth's later thought as well in the general outlook of romanticism. It is also an important part of the underlying symbolism of this poem. This appears in the way Wordsworth modified the description of the little muddy pond which is never dry, substituting

> Though but of Compass small, and bare
> To thirsty suns and parching air
> (ll. 32–33)

for the often ridiculed lines

> I've measured it from side to side;
> 'Tis three feet long, and two feet wide.

The 1798 version is perfectly justifiable in view of the psychology of the narrator, who wishes, by the cumulative effect of trivial but concrete details, to impress upon his listeners the general truth of a story which is not devoid of somewhat improbable incidents. Its main defect is that it comes too early

[20] *Poetical Works*, II, 513.

in the poem, before the reader has become familiar with the narrator's manner. But in the 1820 version, what we may perhaps describe as the pond's resistance to annihilation mirrors the resilience of the little thorn: the pond manages never to be dry in spite of its scant surface and its exposure to the dessicating power of sun and wind. Taken in conjunction with the pond, the small thorn, "so old and gray," proposes an image of persecution and misery, but also of stubborn and unobtrusive endurance. Seen in this light, the correlation between the tree and the tale becomes obvious.

But before we proceed to examine the Martha Ray story, we must consider the third item in the natural setting: the "beauteous heap." As the narrator reaches this point in the description, there occurs a sudden reversal of mood and imagery; at the same time, however, the continuity of the whole is ensured, and Wordsworth skillfully manages a remarkable coalescence of contrast and unity because he resorts to the very element—the mosses—which had been put to quite different uses in his description of the thorn and of the pond.

The thorn is "aged"; the mound is "a fresh sight." The thorn is "gray"; the mound is covered with lovely tints

> Of olive green and scarlet bright,
> In spikes, in branches, and in stars,
> Green, red, and pearly white!
> (ll. 46–48)

The combination of contrast and similitude is so subtly contrived as nearly to defy analysis. The mound is a "hill of moss": the mosses which closely clasped round the thorn in a predatory netlike way are now described as "mossy network" beautifully "woven" in "all colours that were ever seen." The objective comparison of the thorn with a "two years' child" (which, however, connotes smallness and helplessness) is now echoed by the unexpected comparison of the "beauteous heap" with an "infant's grave," which, in the midst of the luxuriant flower imagery suddenly recalls the gloomy atmosphere surrounding the thorn. It is difficult to agree with J. F. Danby's statement that "the mound is grotesquely prettified in order that what is said should echo gruesomely against what might be feared or suggested." Nor can one help wondering how many readers have sensed what he calls "dramatic irony" in this description.

On the contrary, it would seem that the mound fulfills other, and quite straightforward, functions. The infant motif makes its first appearance in stanza I, where the thorn is compared to a two years' child in size. The mound introduces the suggestion of a dead baby in stanza v. It is not until we reach stanza XII that the story is definitely seen to deal with an actual infant; and in stanza XIV, we learn that the child has disappeared—whether it was stillborn or, as intimated for the first time in stanza XIX, killed by its mother. The mound, therefore, is a link in the chain that leads slowly and by graded steps to the most gruesome suggestion of all, one before which the narrator recoils. This is an example of the slow and devious but highly effective way in which the narrator approaches his own subject: the story of Martha Ray.

On the other hand, the colorful loveliness of the mound, in its sharp contrast to the dereliction of the nearby thorn, is one of what we might roughly call the "positive" elements of the poem. It is in a way related to the resilience of the thorn and of the pond. All in all, however, the positive elements operate on different levels. The beauteous heap is an image of natural beauty and joy and benevolence; in its association with infancy, it is suggestive of innocence. The thorn and the pond, on the other hand, are related to the world of experience and of endurance.

Such, it would seem, are the components of the cluster of impressions that flashed upon Wordsworth's imagination when he observed "this Thorn" he had never noticed before. The storm, with its inherent connotations of trials and ordeals, of elemental fury and malevolent power, was undoubtedly the event that suddenly brought into sharp relief the symbolic potentialities of the small old tree and of its natural setting.

The Alfoxden manuscript version contains only a description of the thorn, with embryonic suggestions of its symbolic value. We have no indication concerning the creative process through which the poem reached its full-blown maturity. But there is no reason to distrust Wordsworth's statement that he set out to find some device by means of which he could make the tree "permanently an impressive object." Nor is it surprising that the first element of "invention" that occurred to him at the time should have been the association of the thorn with the theme of abandoned womanhood. At least three possible sources have been unearthed for the story of Martha Ray.[21] But no poet of Wordsworth's stature has ever been influenced by mere literary sources unless he was ready, because of his own experience, to receive their influence. And Wordsworth's silence on his interest in the Martha Ray story—while he expatiated at great length on the narrator—is eloquent. Speaking of other poems in *Lyrical Ballads*, such as *The Mad Mother* or *The Complaint of a Forsaken Indian Woman*, and also of the beggar-woman in the earlier *Evening Walk*, Mary Moorman rightly argues that "the thought of Annette and of his own desertion of her, and of his unknown child, gave to these poems, and to many others, a sharpness of realism that they would otherwise not have possessed." *The Thorn* is undoubtedly one of those "many others," and it is surprising that Sir Herbert Read, in his psychological study of Wordsworth's inspiration, should not have availed himself of this poem instead of dismissing it casually as "objective to a pointless degree." [22] Campbell and Mueschke are certainly right in pointing out that its "subject-matter remains dangerously close

---

[21] *Ibid.*, pp. 513–514, and H. Darbishire, *The Poet Wordsworth*, p. 37.
[22] H. Read, *The True Voice of Feeling* (London, 1954), p. 200.

Emblems of Misery

to [Wordsworth's] own personal experiences. It continues to betray his emotional excitement over the situation of the seduced and abandoned mother." That the material, as they say, was "embarrassing," is not open to doubt; whether it was "intractable" as well is another matter, to be dealt with in our discussion of the narrator.

Meanwhile, let us observe that there is a similar relationship between the thorn and the Martha Ray story on the one hand, and the ruined cottage and the Margaret story on the other: the thorn and the cottage provide both a setting and a symbolic correlative for the tales and the human situation they illustrate. Throughout the poem we find words and images that point to the symbolic value of the thorn: the tree and the woman are both solitary in a mainly hostile environment ("mainly," because their dereliction is alleviated by the beauteous heap and by the narrator's sympathy); the action of the mosses and the gales can be equated not only with the woman's abandonment by her lover but also with the enmity of the villagers claiming what they think is justice. The tree is "wretched" (l. 9) and so is the woman (l. 68). The thorn is "like a stone" (ll. 10 and 12); Martha Ray crouching on the hill in the storm offers the appearance of a "jutting crag" (stanza XVII). That this is the symbolic nexus linking the thorn and Martha Ray was obliquely made clear by Wordsworth himself at the end of *The Prelude:* turning back to the memorable days of 1798, he selects among his and Coleridge's achievements of that period *The Ancient Mariner, Christabel, The Idiot Boy,* and also *The Thorn,* described as the tale of

> her who sate
> In *misery* near the *miserable* Thorn.
> (Bk. XIII, ll. 402–403; italics mine)

As J. F. Danby has noted, "The woman is first related to the three things of the setting, then (suddenly) to a wider Wordsworthian context of day and night, wind and stillness, sky and star." The tale is thus raised to a plane where the whole cosmos is involved in a manner which anticipates the Lucy poems. But with Martha as with the thorn, the atmospheric imagery is predominantly of a winter-like character. True, the "blue delight" is mentioned, but the imagery is mainly concocted of "wind" and "whirlwind," of "frosty air" and "rain" and "snow" and "tempest" (stanzas xii and xiii). And it is during a heavy storm that the narrator meets the woman for the first time (stanzas xvi and xvii). In this way, the bereaved mother becomes imaginatively associated with the thorn, and a contrast is established between her and her infant's grave, similar to that which was delineated in the first part of the poem between the thorn and the hillock.

This is part of the overall polarity of positive and negative elements that constitute the structural axis of the poem. On the negative side, we may list the general appearance of the thorn and the dereliction of the abandoned woman. On the positive side, we find the endurance of the thorn and of the pond, and the paradoxically festive aspect of the ground. If we concentrate for the moment on the negative aspects, it is obvious that Wordsworth has indeed achieved his primary purpose: by being associated with Martha Ray's story, the thorn becomes a permanently impressive object because it is seen to be an objective correlative of human suffering. But the positive elements we have discovered point to several levels of meaning. The erectness of the thorn, in spite of the hostile forces that torment it, suggests a stoic ideal of acceptance and endurance which will become a permanent trend in Wordsworth's (and also in Keats's) view of life. The mound itself, on the other hand, appears to be an image of nature's tenderness to man. For one thing, its luscious colors tone down the horror of the woman's predicament: there is nothing lurid about the infant's grave. Moreover, through the agency of the mound, nature plays an active part in the poem. Before we consider the implications of this, however, it is necessary to analyze more closely the structure and the purpose of the story itself.

Emblems of Misery 79

The facts are scanty. Twenty years before the telling, Martha Ray fell in love with Stephen Hill, who promised to marry her but absent-mindedly brought another girl to the altar. Six months later, it became obvious that Martha was pregnant; somehow, the child was never seen. Since that time, Martha has been in the habit of climbing the mountain and sitting between the thorn and the mound, crying "Oh misery! Oh misery!" This is about all the narrator is personally prepared to vouch for. But he also faithfully reports the village gossip, which accuses Martha of killing her baby. Furthermore, he reports three supernatural incidents, to which we shall revert in due course, for they mark the main stages in the development of the narrative.

We slowly discern, from the narrator's rambling discourse, that the factual aspect of the story hinges on the death of the child. As J. F. Danby says, "There is in the poem the possibility of a betrayed mother murdering her child," but the point, surely, is that it is never more than a possibility. In the eyes of the narrator—as we shall see when dealing with this third factor in the poem—it is a remote possibility. And in the eyes of Wordsworth, it is an uninteresting possibility. The narrative systematically diverts the reader's attention from the factual aspect of this central element. In stanza xiv, the narrator stresses the general ignorance about this, but evokes the possibility that the child might have died; then comes the first supernatural episode: the eerie voices many thought were "voices of the dead" (stanza xv); if this belief were justified, it would imply that the child was killed by his mother. But the narrator, without denying that the voices, if any, were of the dead, expressly repudiates such an interpretation—

> I cannot think, whate'er they say
> They had to do with Martha Ray
> (ll. 164–165)

—and turns back, in stanza xvi, to a matter of experienced fact.

The detective problem of the child's death is raised again, with greater explicitness and urgency, in stanzas XIX and XX. Again, the narrator, without denying that Martha may have killed her child, expressly dissociates himself from the notion that she might have resorted to bloodshed:

> But kill a new-born infant *thus*
> I do not think she could!
> (ll. 212–213; italics mine)

Again these conjectures are associated with a supernatural occurrence: the vision of the dead baby's face looking up from the pond. And again the reader's attention is diverted to a matter of plain fact: the villagers' decision to bring the mother to public justice.

But when the villagers undertake to dig for the baby's corpse,

> instantly the hill of moss
> Before their eyes began to stir!
> And, for full fifty yards around,
> The grass—it shook upon the ground!
> (ll. 225–228)

This third supernatural event is in itself as improbable as the other two. Yet the narrator does not describe it with his usual diffidence. There is no such phrase as "I've heard many swear" (l. 162), or "Some say" (l. 214). The episode is reported as a fact. I shall come back to what this tells us about the alleged superstitious character of the narrator. Meanwhile, I want to stress the function of this incident in the general narrative pattern. For this function is quite different from that of the previous supernatural episodes. Those, indeed, were damning for the mother and—presumably for that very reason—are presented by the narrator as a mere report of gossip. The third episode, on the contrary, records an intervention of nature to the benefit of Martha Ray and—for that reason too—is presented as fact. For the last action of nature prevents the villagers from reaching factual truth. They cling to their opinion, of course, and remain convinced that Martha has killed her baby. But they are unable to prove it and consequently to bring the woman to public justice. In other words, the purpose of nature is to protect Martha Ray against human judgment; she does not become an accused and a culprit; she remains what she has been throughout the poem: a miserable woman toward whom, in the absence of proof, judgment must remain suspended. This, we must insist, is achieved through the third supernatural episode, which effectively counterbalances the other two: that is probably the reason why it captures the imagination of the narrator in such a way that he feels impelled to present it as fact. Here indeed is where the trend of the whole poem is perceptible. Nature points to the right attitude toward Martha Ray, an attitude of pity and sympathy, focused on the woman's misery—not on the facts, which might show her to be guilty in the eyes of mere "public justice"—because what matters is not guilt and punishment but sorrow and compassion. Herein, too, lies the cathartic effect of the poem, the transmutation of evil into good through the overcoming of horror by pity—an effect which is also achieved through the personality of the narrator, whose attitude counteracts in the same way the attitude of the villagers.

Wordsworth's purpose in telling the story of Martha Ray in the words of a narrator was partly to hide the autobiographical character of the situation and emotions described in the poem. This is indirectly revealed by the rather naïve warning in the Preface to the first edition of *Lyrical Ballads:* "The poem of The Thorn, as the reader will soon discover, is not supposed to be spoken in the author's own person; the character of the loquacious narrator will sufficiently show itself in the course of the story." [23]

Wordsworth was so dismayed by Coleridge's criticism of

[23] *Poetical Works,* II, 512.

the device on literary grounds that he felt the need, first to justify himself at considerable length in the Preface to the second edition, and later to bring a number of alterations to the text. He even entertained the strange notion that *The Thorn* "ought to have been preceded by an introductory essay," in which, presumably, he would have conveyed more explanations about the narrator's character. Yet, in the laborious description of the Preface, there is little that could not easily be inferred from the poem. That the narrator is "talkative" and a man of "slow faculties" is surely obvious from the manner of his speech. That he is an elderly man who had something to do with the navy appears when he describes himself climbing the mountain

> with my telescope
> To view the ocean wide and bright,
> (ll. 170-171)

a notoriously favorite occupation of retired sailors. That he was living in "some village or country town of which he was not a native, or in which he had not been accustomed to live," is apparent from the time scheme of the poem: the events related occurred twenty years before the telling (stanza x) and when the narrator came to "this country," he had never heard of Martha Ray. Moreover, the narrator is careful to disclaim any personal knowledge of the events he relates. Such phrases as "they say," "I've heard many swear," "I cannot tell," "some will say," "I've heard," "all aver," and the like are scattered throughout the poem. The effect is to increase the psychical distance and to facilitate the willing suspension of disbelief on the part of the reader; the narrator does not claim to be reporting events of which he is personally cognizant: his is mainly a record of public rumor.

But the problem that faces us is whether the narrator is necessary to the poem, and whether he harmonizes with the other elements in it. In our endeavor to assess the significance and the reciprocal relationship of the story and the natural environment, we have been obliged more than once to argue on the basis of the narrator's way of telling his tale; this in itself suggests that the narrator is organically essential. In order to understand the full extent of his contribution to the poem, however, it is necessary to probe somewhat deeper into his character.

In the 1800 Preface, Wordsworth makes much of the old man's credulity and proneness to superstition: "Such men, having little to do, become credulous and talkative from indolence; and from the same cause, and other predisposing causes by which it is probable that such men may have been affected, they are prone to superstition." [24] But when we compare this assertion with the actual character of the storyteller as it appears in the poem, we begin to feel that Wordsworth has overstated his case. Indeed, the narrator shows a critical sense which discriminates between the various degrees of truth of the events he reports. The only fact within his own experience is to be found in stanza XVI:

> But that she goes to this old Thorn,
> The Thorn which I described to you,
> And there sits on a scarlet cloak
> I will be sworn is true.
> (ll. 166–169)

Then, there are a number of occurrences of which he knows only by hearsay, but which are presented as equally true: these deal with the events that led to Martha's tragedy in stanzas X and XI, and also with nature's intervention to protect the woman against the villagers. All the rest is gossip and presented as conjecture, the narrator insisting on everybody's ignorance, and then hiding himself behind the collective "they" of the village community. It is clear that his credulity operates within limited boundaries.

His superstitiousness is equally selective. That he accepts to some extent the superstitions of the village is apparent from

[24] *Ibid.*

the very fact that he does tell the story, and also from his acceptance of the miraculous intervention of nature at the end. But his participation is not equal at all points, and more than once he pronounces negatively on the rumors he is reporting. This is particularly obvious in the matter of Martha's possible guilt. The narrator carefully stresses the general ignorance on this point; he emphasizes the conjectural character of the villagers' accusation; he points out that the report of the first two supernatural episodes is based on gossip; and he dissociates himself from such gossip in a manner calculated to divert the reader's attention from all idea of moral guilt while preserving the sense of appalling horror which surrounds the woman. Since Wordsworth felt it necessary to build up an aura of supernatural terror [25] before releasing the full force of pity, undoubtedly a somewhat superstitious narrator was necessary as well, and his insistence on what is after all a minor point was probably unavoidable in view of the strictures to which the poem had been submitted; but it tends to blur the ultimate critical issue. For what is of real interest is the way in which the old man's superstitiousness functions.

In a passing remark on this poem, A. E. M. Conran asserts that "in *The Thorn*, society had been represented by the village gossips—among whom, for this purpose, we can include the story-teller; they are impotent to affect or ameliorate the central tragedy." [26] On the contrary, the superstition of the narrator and the superstition of the village people are biased in utterly opposite directions. The villagers are malevolent: they are bent on discovering what they believe to be the facts in order to bring Martha Ray to public justice, whereas the

---

[25] Whether he did so successfully or not is a matter of personal appreciation in individual readers. J. F. Danby reports the reaction of Swinburne, who, he says, "was right to record 'the dreadfulness of a shocking reality' in his response to the poem, 'an effect of unmodified and haunting horror'" (*The Simple Wordsworth*, p. 70).

[26] A. E. M. Conran, "The Dialectic of Experience: A Study of Wordsworth's *Resolution and Independence*," PMLA, LXXV (1960), 67.

narrator brings the poem back into a focus of his own choosing by repeatedly driving the reader's attention away from the "facts" in order to concentrate on the woman's predicament. In other words, the narrator fulfills the same function as nature does. In speaking of Martha Ray, Helen Darbishire says that "Nature seems to sympathise with her love and suffering. She has covered with beautiful mosses the little mound where the child lies buried." This points to a more complete poetic truth. As we have seen, nature's sympathy also manifests itself in a more active way, at least to the old man's imagination. And it is highly significant of his bias that the third supernatural event should prove more acceptable to him than the other two. On the plane of the poem's fiction, Martha is rescued from the hostility of the villagers by the miraculous intervention of nature. On the plane of the story's morale, she is rescued by the narrator's attitude, which makes itself felt in his manner of presenting his tale. It appears, therefore, that Wordsworth's device of interposing a narrator between the story and the reader is both necessary and successful. The story could not have been made as impressive if it had been told in the name of an omniscient author: the mystery surrounding the facts could not have been plausibly maintained; the impression of horror could not have been built up with the same credibility; the purpose of the story could not have been achieved with anything approaching the same ease and smoothness. Indeed, the beautifully managed convergence of nature's intervention and of the narrator's bias leads effortlessly to the intense realization of sheer human suffering which—as embodied in the thorn—formed the starting point of the poem. In the last stanza, the narrator's final statement of ignorance—"I cannot tell how this may be"—follows the lead given by nature in protecting Martha against the villagers' fact-finding obsession. The attention is therefore brought back to the woman's emotional predicament, which is now clearly identified with that of the thorn, thus rounding off the poem through the device of the "return." The narrator's imagination has penetrated to the core of human misery, which is the actual theme of the poem, and which lies beyond the realms of fact and guilt and justice.

In a way, *The Eolian Harp* and *The Thorn* can be regarded as representing the opposite poles of the romantic outlook. While Coleridge's object was to reach, through ruminative self-exploration, some sort of insight into the ideal unity of the cosmos and the metaphysical relationship between man, nature, and God, the main source of Wordsworth's inspiration in this poem was the stark, unpalatable facts of man's actual experience. Under the controlling principle of the symbolic vision, the poem integrates into a unified whole the writer's perception of human misery and human endurance, and his conception of the right attitude toward evil and suffering: the tree and Martha Ray are emblems of misery; in contrast to the village people, nature and the narrator exemplify an attitude of moral sympathy in which there is no room for the harshness of judicial appraisal. We need only recall the rhetorical lines devoted by Coleridge to the theme of social injustice to become aware that Wordsworth's mind was working at a far deeper level of imaginative insight. What stirred his poetic faculty had nothing to do with the shallowness of concrete facts, of legal guilt, of class struggle, or of institutional abuses: his theme was the fallen condition of man.

In *The Thorn*, there are no such inner contradictions as make havoc of the structural unity of several of Coleridge's conversation pieces. In Wordsworth the dialectical nature of romanticism reveals itself in a different way, although it refers basically to the same ambiguous apprehension of the world. Coleridge, it will be recalled, had not been able to reconcile the humility which is implied by traditional Christian faith with the pride involved in his glorious insight into the divine oneness of the cosmos. Torn between his belief in man's inherent inferiority and the pantheistic temptation induced by

Emblems of Misery 87

his visionary intuition, Coleridge rather incongruously found himself faced with Pope's dilemma: "In doubt to deem himself a god, or beast"! That the same dichotomy between ideal man and actual man was present in Wordsworth's mind as well can be inferred from a comparison between the poet's comments on his ballads in the Preface of 1800, and the ballads themselves.

In his endeavor to justify on psychological grounds his choice of country bumpkins as suitable material for poetic treatment, Wordsworth proceeded to an idealization of rural experience, feelings, language, and manners, which Coleridge was at no pains to refute:

Low and rustic life was generally chosen because, in that situation, the essential passions of the heart find a better soil in which they can attain their maturity, are less under restraint, and speak a plainer and more emphatic language; because in that condition of life our elementary feelings exist in a state of greater simplicity, and consequently, may be more accurately contemplated, and more forcibly communicated; because the manners of rural life germinate from those elementary feelings, and, from the necessary character of rural occupation, are more easily comprehended and are more durable; and, lastly, because in that condition the passions of men are incorporated with the beautiful and permanent forms of nature.[27]

Here as elsewhere,[28] Wordsworth is at pains to convince his readers that his cherished rustics are the living impersonation of Ideal Man:

> Man free, man working for himself, with choice
> Of time, and place, and object; by his wants,
> His comforts, native occupations, cares,
> Conducted on to individual ends
> Or social, and still followed by a train

[27] *Poetical Works*, II, 386–387. For Coleridge's refutation, see *Biographia Literaria*, II, 31–32.
[28] Most notably the well-known letter to John Wilson of June, 1802 (*Early Letters*, pp. 294–295).

> Unwoo'd, unthought-of even, simplicity,
> And beauty, and inevitable grace.[29]

As a matter of fact, they are nothing of the kind. Although the ballads are peopled with characters conspicuous for their "simplicity," there is little of "beauty and inevitable grace" about most of them. The majority of the tales deal with evil, violence, and suffering. As so often happens, the poet's own comments have little relevance to the real depth and amplitude of his achievement. While the Preface suggests that Wordsworth was consciously intent on giving expression to a vision of ideal harmony and happiness, the ballads themselves reveal that, as a poet, he was chiefly moved by the evil present in the human condition.

[29] *The Prelude* (1805), Bk. VIII, ll. 152–158.

5 Dark Passages:
WORDSWORTH'S *TINTERN ABBEY*

At the end of his definition of the symbol in *The Statesman's Manual*, Coleridge says that the symbol "always partakes of the reality which it renders intelligible." This rather obscure statement is of decisive importance because it is the one element in the definition which establishes a fundamental distinction between symbol and allegory. After all, allegory too "is characterized by a translucence of the special in the individual, or of the general in the especial, or of the universal in the general." But allegory is contrived artificially, whereas the true symbol must grow organically: as Coleridge further says, "it abides itself as a living part in that unity, of which it is the representative." The allegorical imagination is essentially idealistic: it searches the world of natural forms for parables or emblems of that which, to it, is alone important, the world of spirit; it seeks to render the ideal world intelligible by means of materials which, in themselves, are of no value; to quote Coleridge again, "Allegory is but a translation of abstract notions into a picture-language which is itself nothing but an abstraction from objects of the senses." The symbolical imagination must be both idealistic and naturalistic: to it, the natural forms are alive and significant in themselves; they are intrinsically valuable because they partake of the One Life which they illustrate or exemplify.

This inherent ambivalence of all great art comes out neatly in the phrase "concrete universal" coined by W. K. Wimsatt, Jr., in the mid-twentieth century,[1] and it is an essential part, and perhaps the very foundation, of the romantic theory of poetry as expression. Goethe did not mean anything else when he claimed that true poetry resulted from a spontaneous and often unconscious apprehension of the universal in the particular, whereas in allegory the particular serves only and intentionally as instance of the general.[2] In the romantic symbol, the individual is as alive, as genuine, and as real as the ideal which it manifests, and the purpose of symbolic art is to reveal its microcosmic character. "Man's mind," Coleridge says, "is the very focus of the rays of intellect which are scattered throughout the images of nature. Now so to place these images, totalized, and fitted to the limits of the human mind, as to elicit from, and to superimpose upon, the forms themselves the moral reflexions to which they approximate, to make the external internal, the internal external, to make nature thought, and thought nature—this is the mystery of genius in the Fine arts."[3] But the point is that the "rays of intellect" are actually there; they are not read into the images of nature. The symbol, therefore, is, in this sense, the appropriate medium of poetic expression for an age which believes as intensely in the physical world as it believes in the metaphysical world, and which wants to convey its acute sense of their oneness.

Although it is not very difficult to define the symbol as a theoretical concept, we need to know how the processes it implies work out in concrete poetic practice. Such testing is by no means easy, for the critic is tempted to emphasize either the universal at the expense of the particular, or the concrete

[1] W. K. Wimsatt, Jr., *The Verbal Icon: Studies in the Meaning of Poetry* (Lexington, 1954), pp. 69–83.
[2] See J. Rouge, "La Notion du symbole chez Goethe," in *Goethe: Etudes publiées pour le centenaire de sa mort* (Paris, 1932), p. 303.
[3] "On Poesy or Art," in *Biographia Literaria*, ed. J. Shawcross (Oxford, 1907), II, 257–258.

at the expense of the ideal, thus wrecking the delicate equipoise, the intimate fusion of polar qualities, which marks the symbol at its most complex and most successful. An interesting example of this is provided by some fairly recent discussions of the landscape setting in *Tintern Abbey*.

In *The Unmediated Vision*,[4] G. H. Hartman, commenting on the description of the Tintern landscape, shows himself convinced that "its mood is not surprise or exultation, but an intense matter-of-factness"; and he goes on to complain that the poet "does not tell us about the reason why this valley in particular, these waters, and these hedgerows have exerted such an influence on him," observing that "even the smoke that ascends from among the trees awakens poetic delight and for no apparent reason." Hartman's central view of *Tintern Abbey* is that Wordsworth was "trying to convey a disproportion between his high feelings and the visible character of the scene." In such a perspective, it is almost inevitable that the critic should emphasize the matter-of-factness of the description: the landscape is regarded as having no further significance apart from "the intrinsic and unfictional loveliness of the Wye valley." "This valley," Hartman says, "these waters and cliffs, these pastoral farms never, even at the most intense, convey more than the suggestion of a *possible sublimity*. This is the basic experience. The objects do arouse a sense of beauty, but the emotion of the mind in beholding them is far too strong to make this evident beauty its explanation, and far too sincere to make this independent beauty its function." One of the conclusions of Hartman's analysis is that there is to be found in the poem a "strict separation of the statement of emotion from the description of object, so that no facile nexus of cause and effect may be found between them, and so that, if associated, they are so without explanation, inevitably." In other words, Hartman views the landscape description at the

[4] G. H. Hartman, *The Unmediated Vision: An Interpretation of Wordsworth, Hopkins, Rilke and Valéry* (New Haven, 1954), pp. 3–9.

beginning of *Tintern Abbey* as so perfectly naturalistic, so empty of any further meaning, that there is nothing in it to account for the high intellectual tenor of the strong emotion it is alleged to awaken in the soul of the poet. It is beautiful in itself, it is described for its own sake, and it has no ulterior, symbolic meaning.[5]

Hartman's reading seems to be at variance with Wordsworth's own interpretation of his experience. After all, Wordsworth, in 1798, does make the landscape the starting point of a mental process which leads him to lofty heights of mystical speculation. On the other hand, Hartman's view would appear to tally with the experience that occurred to Wordsworth in 1793: as the poet recollects his earlier stay near Tintern Abbey, he acknowledges that nature *then* was "all in all"; the intrinsic beauty of the natural forms was fully satisfying; it kindled purely aesthetic emotions and had

> no need of a remoter charm,
> By thought supplied, nor any interest
> Unborrowed from the eye.
> (ll. 81–83)

The appeal of the natural setting was purely to the senses and the emotions, as described in the fourth section of the poem. If Hartman's interpretation is accepted, Wordsworth's perception of the landscape in 1793 and his poetic description of it in 1798 are perfectly identical; in that case, indeed, there is nothing, in the experience or in the poem, to account for the mystical speculations at the end of sections two and four, and one is bound to agree with F. W. Bateson, that *Tintern Abbey* is fundamentally contradictory and embodies "a series of concessions to irrationality." [6]

[5] It should be noted, however, that Hartman departs from his main argument when he admits the presence of symbolic elements in lines 6–7 and also in the final lines of the section, where he finds "a transcendental image, a supernatural suggestion."

[6] F. W. Bateson, *Wordsworth: A Re-interpretation* (London, 1954), p. 141.

From Hartman's analysis of the Tintern landscape as a self-sufficient piece of matter-of-fact reality, we now turn to another interpretation, worked out on quite different lines by J. Benziger in 1950.[7] In Benziger's opinion, Wordsworth found in the Wye landscape "the 'objective correlative' for his philosophy of that period" and is thus "presenting to us a *paysage moralisé.*" Eliot's phrase is certainly more appropriate than the French one, which somehow suggests that Wordsworth deliberately modeled the landscape into an equivalent of his moods and thoughts. It is not likely that Wordsworth tried to do anything of the sort. We are not so well documented on the genesis of *Tintern Abbey* as we are on that of *The Thorn*, but there is no reason why the creative process should not have been of the same kind in both poems. In all likelihood, the poet was struck by certain objective features of the landscape, which set in motion the train of thought that constitutes the body of the poem. It was therefore suitable that the landscape should be described objectively, in the naturalistic terms stressed by Hartman. But this does not prevent a detailed examination from showing that it contains in itself "rays of intellect," an intrinsic significance which goes beyond mere "possible" sublimity, and which makes it truly symbolic in Coleridge's sense of the term. Indeed, Benziger has elucidated some of those intrinsic and objective elements which point to a level of meaning above themselves. In *Tintern Abbey,* he observes, "the world of man, of pastoral farms and plots of cottage ground, merges gently, through orchard and hedgerow, into nature's copse and woodland. And the world of organic nature, by way of the lofty cliffs, merges gently with the inorganic quiet of the sky—with what is surely a symbol of the Divine Quiet." In other words, "to Wordsworth the landscape of the Wye declared the unity of the universe."

If we follow Benziger's view, we cannot fail to conclude that the Tintern landscape as seen in 1798 was a suitable

[7] J. Benziger, "Tintern Abbey Revisited," *PMLA*, LXX (1950), 154–162.

starting point for the philosophical meditation developed in the poem. There is thus an absolute contradiction between Hartman's reading and Benziger's. Yet a more glaring example of the potentialities of *Tintern Abbey* as a bone of critical contention is provided by John F. Danby. At one point, Danby makes use of the very elements on which Benziger based his interpretation, and concludes in the following terms: "The itemizing of the landscape detail at the beginning of 'Tintern Abbey' is strangely inert. The plots of cottage-ground, with their hedgerows . . . , the orchard-tufts and wreaths of smoke, are scarcely central to the mood and matter of the poem, scarcely in fact relevant." Yet, a few pages further, he quotes the same opening lines of the poem to support his contention that "whenever Wordsworth is at his best the natural scene he stands before is assimilated to something other. It ceases to be merely external and becomes what may be called a mental landscape, a state of being the mind partakes of with the object and the object with the mind." [8]

This whirlpool of interpretative contradiction suggests that there is something inherently ambiguous in the first section of *Tintern Abbey*. Indeed, it corresponds to an essential duality in Wordsworth's genius, a duality of which Coleridge was perfectly aware. Coleridge, it will be remembered, would lament that "there was a something corporeal, a *matter-of-factness*, a clinging to the palpable" [9] in much of his friend's poetry, while on the other hand he would appreciate "above all the original gift of spreading . . . the depth and height of the ideal world around forms, incidents, and situations, of which, for the common view, custom had bedimmed all the lustre, had dried up the sparkle and the dew drops." [10]

[8] J. F. Danby, *The Simple Wordsworth: Studies in the Poems, 1797–1807* (London, 1960), pp. 97 and 109.
[9] Quoted in W. Hazlitt, "My First Acquaintance with Poets," *The Plain Speaker, Complete Works*, ed. P. P. Howe (London, 1933), XVII, p. 116.
[10] *Biographia Literaria*, I, 59. For J. K. Stephen's satirical account of this duality, see "A Sonnet" in *Lapsus Calami* (Cambridge, Eng., 1891), p. 83.

These two opposite properties are Wordsworth's "two voices" caustically referred to in a sonnet by J. K. Stephen; and with regard to the first section of *Tintern Abbey*, the views put forward by Benziger and by Hartman suggest that there must be a tendency in the critic's mind to hear only the one of the two voices to which his ear is attuned: either the vatic voice "of the deep," of the prophetic imagination, of the visionary soul, or that which Stephen chose to describe as the voice

> of an old half-witted sheep
> Which bleats articulate monotony,
> And indicates that two and two are three,
> That grass is green, lakes damp, and mountains steep.

But if we can find out whether and how the two voices are correlated in that passage, we shall account for and explain away the critical contradiction which has just been pointed out and, at the same time, foster a richer and more accurate understanding of the poem as a whole. That Hartman should be able to emphasize the self-sufficient matter-of-factness of the landscape shows how naturalistic it is, how much it partakes of reality; it shows that Wordsworth was truly "clinging to the palpable." And that Benziger should be able to view the same description as a *paysage moralisé* shows in which way it is significant of the reality of which it partakes. The views are complementary, for only that which is genuinely naturalistic can also be genuinely symbolic: it is just because it is self-contained and matter-of-fact that the Wye landscape appears to be "a living part in that unity of which it is the representative." It is thus necessary to probe more deeply into the nature of landscape symbolism in *Tintern Abbey*.

As most critics have acknowledged, the first section of the poem is a beautifully constructed description of the Wye landscape. It develops through four sentences in which the key word "again" keeps recurring, thus linking past and present indissolubly; this effect is enhanced by the reiteration of "these"; it is highly important to keep in mind that Wordsworth is dealing with a revisited setting. Concerned as he is with the growth of the mind, memory necessarily plays an important part in his outlook.[11] One of the characteristic elements in the total rhythm of the poem is the shuttling to and fro in time, the poet looking back to his own past (and to Dorothy's present as the reenactment of his past) and searching his past evolution and his present thoughts and experiences for the seeds of the future.

Although this stanza gives an impression of organic unity, which will be discussed further on, its formal arrangement is remarkable. It begins with an auditory impression ("I hear") which is recalled, near the end, in the word "silence." The central picture, however, is mainly visual ("I behold," "I view," "I see"). But here again a fine symmetry is created by the contrast of the two upward movements at the beginning ("lofty cliffs") and the end ("smoke sent up") with the horizontal, panoramic sweep of the main description. There is nothing vague or haphazard about this: not only is the landscape beautiful in itself, but its description by Wordsworth is a masterpiece of artistic organization. This observation may help us understand why Wordsworth was impressed by that particular landscape, and the way he chose to render it points to those elements that struck him as significant. In fact, there is little in the whole poem that cannot be brought back to something in the landscape as Wordsworth viewed it.

In her detailed account of Wordsworth's early years, Mary Moorman casually observes that if *Tintern Abbey* "was composed, as Wordsworth says 'upon leaving Tintern' on July 13th, the scene of its composition must have been not 'above' Tintern, but below it."[12] But although one may feel entitled to conclude with Mary Moorman that the elaborate title "is not quite accurate" with regard to the actual place of composi-

[11] On this point, see J. C. Smith, *A Study of Wordsworth* (London, 1946), pp. 15–20.
[12] M. Moorman, *William Wordsworth: A Biography. The Early Years, 1770–1803* (Oxford, 1957), p. 402. This particular point had been made earlier in J. B. McNulty, "Wordsworth's Tour of the Wye: 1798," *Modern Language Notes*, LX (1945), 291–295.

tion, one must also acknowledge that it is in perfect harmony with the situation described. This is not without importance, for the romantic apprehension of cosmic unity appears to have often been the result of what I have ventured to call the panoramic perception, in the course of which the poet's glance seems to encompass the whole visible world. Within the panoramic perception, many variations are conceivable. Coleridge's conversation poems exemplify an expansion of the self, a widening of vision, which extends to the horizon and thus turns the landscape into a spatial analogue of infinity. Wordsworth, as is well known, has a marked preference for valleys, which, being enclosed from all sides, constitute a small-scale universe and are thus endowed with a microcosmic character. We need hardly recall that one of the fundamental premises of romantic nature symbolism is the notion that, as Coleridge put it, "in Nature there is a tendency to respect herself so as to attempt in each part what she has produced in the Whole." [13]

With regard to the intuition of universal oneness, the seclusion of the valley turns it into a microcosm; with regard to human inwardness, it impresses "thoughts of a more deep seclusion." Here we find one of those indeterminate comparatives that have an irritating effect upon William Empson. It is also the only passage in the section that points to an ulterior, inner significance. It has been discussed by Hartman with a view to ascribing a clear denotative meaning to it. But we should do well to remember that those "thoughts" are impressed by the "steep and lofty cliffs." The passage is admittedly vague, and it would be difficult to provide an interpretation that could be fully substantiated. Yet it is hard to escape the impression that Wordsworth is here making the external ("cliffs") internal ("more deep seclusion") and that he is thinking of his own fecund solitude, in which his recollections of natural beauty prompt him to "elevated thoughts."

The correspondence between man's inwardness and the outwardness of nature, which is a corollary of the romantic

[13] MS. *Semina Rerum,* quoted in J. H. Muirhead, *Coleridge as Philosopher* (London, 1954), p. 124.

idea of the One Life, is at work in other ways as well. It is not by mere chance that Wordsworth writes the line "The day is come when I again *repose*" immediately after mentioning "the *quiet* of the sky" (italics mine); more comes into play than mere association of ideas. Benziger has pointed out the elements in the poem which refer to what he calls Wordsworth's "quietism"; but the specific religious connotations of the word "quietism" are irrelevant in the present context. What Wordsworth means is exactly what he says: that the quiet harmony of the landscape has the power to induce a similar quietness in the senses and in the mind, so that the eye becomes able to pierce beyond the sensory allurements of nature's beauteous forms and to see into the life of things. The quietness of nature is no mere correlative of the quietness of the spirit: here is one of the causal relations Hartman was vainly looking for. After all, it is not the business of the poet to *tell* us why this or that landscape inspires him; his method is necessarily indirect and unobtrusive; his design is not palpable. Rather, it is the painstaking and pedestrian business of the critic to trace these "reasons" and to try to account for the effect of the landscape on the poet and of the poem upon the reader.

Benziger has emphasized one aspect of the microcosmic quality of the Wye valley, namely, how it illustrates the interconnection of the three planes of being: the natural ("grove," "copses"), the human ("cottages," "orchards," "farms"), and the divine ("sky"). This sets a basic triadic pattern which recurs throughout the poem from various angles. We find it in section two with its ascent from (a) "sensations" to (b) "acts of kindness" and (c) the "serene and blessed mood." We also find it in section four, where the poet (a) looks on "nature," (b) hears "the still sad music of humanity," and (c) has "a sense sublime of something far more deeply interfused." It controls Wordsworth's conception of the three ages of man, which is adumbrated in this poem for the first time.

The romantic perception of nature consists essentially in an intuition (which need not be mystical) of the unity that underlies the intrinsic diversity of things. Coleridge defined life as "*the principle of individuation,* or the power which unites a given *all* into a *whole* that is presupposed by all its parts."[14] This is in complete agreement with Wordsworth's encomium of the man who

>   sees the parts
> As parts, but with a feeling of the whole.[15]

Accordingly, romantic poetry strives to express that sense of wholeness and unity. And the close interlinking of various planes of being is only one of the means through which this central purpose is achieved. It will be noticed that in the first part of *Tintern Abbey* Wordsworth's wording is consistently designed to blur the outlines of things, which are not described as distinct and definite, but rather as patches (plots, tufts, copses, groves) which melt into each other. The function of hedgerows is to separate; but in the poem, this function is toned down, and the hedgerows are "hardly hedgerows" but appear as "little lines / Of sportive wood run wild."

Another element of pervasive unity is to be found in the general coloring of the landscape. The only color mentioned is green, and the word occurred three times in the first version of the poem. Lines 13-14 are the only ones with which Wordsworth tampered to any notable extent until the final version of 1845. After 1803, "green" was deleted at one place, probably as redundant, but as early as 1802 Wordsworth had hit upon the characteristic phrase "clad in *one* green hue," which was to remain in the final version. Obviously, the uniform green-

---

[14] S. T. Coleridge, "The Theory of Life," in *Miscellanies, Aesthetic and Literary,* ed. T. Ashe (London, 1892), p. 385. As J. H. Muirhead has observed, "We are apt to think of individuation as a process of separation and detachment, but Coleridge insists throughout on the opposite tendency to interconnection as an inseparable element in it" (*Coleridge as Philosopher,* p. 128).

[15] *The Prelude* (1805), Bk. VII, ll. 711-712. There is an evident similarity between this passage and the ideas expressed by Coleridge in his letter to John Thelwall of 14 October 1797 (see supra, pp. 53-54).

ness of the whole landscape appealed to Wordsworth's imagination as a suitable emblem of the oneness he wanted to convey.[16]

Even the way prosody is manipulated tends to create an impression of organic unity—in Wölfflin's sense of the word. The consistent use of run-on lines carries the reader irresistibly forward from beginning to end of the section, and hardly allows him to distinguish the component parts which constitute the whole.

The description of the Wye landscape, then, is one of those passages where Wordsworth's two voices can be heard in unison. While it exhibits the tendency that Coleridge was later to deplore as "a strict adherence to matter of fact," [17] the passage contains the elements that will constitute the general pattern of the poem. In its insistence that the setting Wordsworth is describing is a revisited landscape, it anticipates the intricate weaving of the themes of time and memory which are central to Wordsworth's deep preoccupation with the growth of the mind. In its indirect references to the harmony of the three planes of being, it adumbrates the great romantic vision of cosmic unity. The vertical line of the cliffs and the upward movement of the smoke prepare the reader's mind for the recurring pattern of ascent toward spiritual insight which dominates the total structure of the poem. But what needs emphasizing is that this description is symbolic, and not allegorical, *because* of its very matter-of-factness. It is interesting, in this respect, to recall that few poems have been as completely given to their author. "I began it," Wordsworth tells us, "upon leaving Tintern, after crossing the Wye, and con-

---

[16] Another graphic phrase, "green to the very door," for some reason appealed to Dorothy and to Coleridge. The latter used it in his notebooks in 1803 (*The Notebooks of Samuel Taylor Coleridge*, ed. K. Coburn [London, 1957], I, entry number 1470), and we find it under Dorothy's pen as late as 1820 (*Journals of Dorothy Wordsworth*, ed. E. de Sélincourt [London, 1952], II, 34).

[17] *Collected Letters of Samuel Taylor Coleridge*, ed. E. L. Griggs (Oxford, 1956), II, 449.

cluded it just as I was entering Bristol in the evening, after a ramble of 4 or 5 days, with my sister. Not a line of it was altered, and not any part of it written down till I reached Bristol. It was published almost immediately." [18] The changes brought to it until the definitive edition of 1845 are of little consequence indeed. If anything can be inferred from the nearly extempore character of the poem, it is that Wordsworth did not consciously set out to depict a *paysage moralisé;* indeed, it is highly unlikely that he would have been articulately aware of the symbolic trends which, even now, can only be disclosed by the minutest analytical processes. On the contrary, it is probable that Wordsworth just felt that the landscape was a suitable setting for the thoughts that were filling his mind at the time: it was precisely those objective features of the landscape that he took in and subsequently described, which prompted him to those thoughts.

For the relationship between the Wye landscape and the poem is not symbolical only. It is also causal. Because of its actual objective features, which, as perceived by Wordsworth, become what Coleridge called "rays of intellect," it is natural that the Tintern landscape should have started, in the poet's mind, the ruminative process of which the poem is the record; it is natural that a revisited landscape should have prompted him to reflections on his own inner development, on his gains and his losses; it is equally natural that the quiet harmony of the landscape should have led him to think of the unity of being and, by contrast, of his own perplexities, which he endeavors to define in the next stanzas.

In this latter respect, we must observe that the landscape description of section one is less purely objective than might be thought on a superficial reading. The strong sensory assertions ("I hear," "I behold," "I see") unexpectedly lead to the somewhat dubious statement that the smoke—which the poet does see—gives

---

[18] *The Poetical Works of William Wordsworth,* ed. E. de Sélincourt and Helen Darbishire (Oxford, 1962), II, 517.

> some *uncertain* notice, *as might seem,*
> Of vagrant dwellers in the houseless woods,
> Or of some Hermit's cave, where by his fire
> The Hermit sits alone.
>
> (ll. 19-22; italics mine)

In a way, this intimation of human presence brings the landscape description to a climax. Admittedly, as F. W. Bateson rightly comments, "hermits were one of the conventional properties of late eighteenth-century landscape, and their presence guaranteed the aesthetic, non-documentary quality of the picture." So were gypsies. But thinking back on the beggar-woman in *An Evening Walk*, on *The Female Vagrant*, on *The Mad Mother*, we remember what Mary Moorman has called Wordsworth's "natural attraction to the ragged vagrant," [19] which lifts the motif above the level of mere literary convention and turns the character into an emblem of suffering mankind: within the framework of the poem, the vagrants announce "the still, sad music of humanity." And as we remember *The Old Cumberland Beggar* or *Resolution and Independence*, it becomes clear that Wordsworth has endowed the conventional eighteenth-century hermit with a significance that goes beyond the mere picturesque. His solitaries exemplify the highest form of contemplation and wisdom; they are man stripped of all inessentials, living in intimate communion with nature.[20] Thus the hermit in his cave carries a faint suggestion of the human ideal toward which Wordsworth was groping at the time, and which he was to define with greater assurance in later poems.

But seen from a different angle, this late intrusion of man into the natural landscape has an anticlimactic effect, thus setting a pattern which, as I hope to make clear, recurs throughout the poem. It is not only that the half-conventional

---

[19] *William Wordsworth*, p. 118.
[20] On Wordsworth's solitaries, see J. Jones, *The Egotistical Sublime: A History of Wordsworth's Imagination* (London, 1954), pp. 61–70.

figures of the vagrants and the hermit suggest some slackening of the poetic tension initially created by the immediate sensory presence of the natural scenery. What must be stressed is that the poet shows himself aware that he is passing from objective data to subjective inferences (as is shown by the italicized words in the above quotation), and this entails a corresponding loosening of his grasp upon the actual. There is, then, already in the first section, an implied contrast between what is observed and what is imagined, between fact and hypothesis, which is fundamental to the poem as a whole and prepares for the deeper perplexity to which Wordsworth is about to turn his attention.

To describe *Tintern Abbey* as an utterance of puzzlement may seem unduly to contradict our most cherished and time-honored assumptions about it. It should be remembered, however, that it shares with *The Eolian Harp* the dubious privilege of being one of the most lopsidedly quoted poems in the whole corpus of romantic poetry. Countless gallons of doctrinal juice have been squeezed out of lines 35–49 and 93–111. And truly, those passages are remarkable for the loftiness of the feelings and ideas they convey, and for the eloquence with which they convey them. In consequence, it is hard to resist the temptation of extending to the poem as a whole the triumphant impression they make on the reader. Thus we find F. W. Bateson confidently asserting of *Tintern Abbey* that "rhetorically it is superbly assured and persuasive." This is probably the reason why it was so dear to Victorian hearts. But our time feels a contemptuous dislike for what is superbly assured: hence the twentieth-century reaction against *Tintern Abbey*. For William Empson, it is a hopeless muddle on all planes, beginning with the grammatical; for F. W. Bateson, it "conceals a confession of failure." All the same, the two purple passages represent only thirty-nine lines out of one hundred and fifty-nine. *Tintern Abbey* is a long and complex poem, and only a close contextual scrutiny of its structure can bring us nearer its total meaning by eliciting the significance of each part in relation to the whole.

The second section deals with the interval between Wordsworth's two visits to the place, and with the effect of his remembrance of "these beauteous forms" on his mind. After the introduction, it is divided into two sentences, both of which include near their beginnings the verb "owe." As Wordsworth turns from an objective and symbolical description of external nature to an analysis of his inner self, nature appears to him as the main causal factor in his moral evolution.

Although the constant use of run-on lines creates an impression of smooth continuousness and organic unity, this stanza too has a strong structure, both grammatical and thematic. The two sentences are different in tone and in the nature of the statements they make. The first one deals with two "gifts"—"sensations" and "feelings"—which are presented as undoubtedly originating in nature. It also deals with the psychological and moral consequences of those gifts: the "sensations sweet" have wrought a "tranquil restoration" of the poet's "purer mind"; and a note of diffidence creeps in as Wordsworth passes from the psychological to the moral plane: his "feelings of unremembered pleasure" have "perhaps" led him to "acts of kindness and of love." There is thus a gradual ascent from the sensory to the psychological and the moral; on the other hand, slight undertones of doubt make their intrusion in the passage from the psychological to the ethical.

This pattern is reproduced and developed in the second sentence. Besides the sensations and the feelings, Wordsworth's recollections of nature have also kindled a "blessed mood": this mood is described as such at great length and with considerable eloquence. But in the last line, a new element is introduced, parallel to the "tranquil restoration" and the "acts of kindness" of the first sentence, in the same way that the mood itself parallels the "sensations" and the "feelings": the blessed mood is interpreted as a sort of mystical insight into the life of things.

Apart from the iterative triadic patterning, a comparison of both parts of the section reveals a threefold change in the tone and subject matter: first, a raising of the level of reminiscence, which now passes from the ethical to the mystical; second, a heightened poetic intensity, which makes the end of the passage particularly memorable and eminently quotable; third, an increase in the note of diffidence, which materializes in the words "I trust" and "may."

These last two qualities sound contradictory, yet they are equally important for a balanced understanding of the poem, and they provide the key to its meandering structure. For *Tintern Abbey* is built on a pattern of ascent and descent which is repeated twice: ascent toward the loftiest heights of mystical speculation, descent toward the firm ground of ascertained fact. The poetic—we might even say, vatic—quality of lines 37–49 shows how profoundly moving such mystical thoughts were to Wordsworth. But they are only one source of his inspiration. The other source is his experience of the actual, the matter-of-fact. If Wordsworth is probably the most perfect impersonation of the romantic spirit, he owes it to this dual character. It is the essence of romanticism to aim at the reconciliation of opposite elements, and in no other romantic poet (with the possible exception of Keats) was the duality of naturalism and idealism so strongly marked as in Wordsworth. Coleridge, as we know, saw to it that his friend was fully aware of the somewhat pedestrian character of his matter-of-fact, down-to-earth inspiration; but Wordsworth was equally aware of the subjective, hypothetical, unascertainable, character of his mystical inspiration. His great achievement is that he was able, at times, to reconcile them. But we cannot emphasize too strongly that that stage was not yet in sight when he wrote *Tintern Abbey*. In this poem, we can see his mind at work during a transitional period: taking his cue from the very objective landscape (section one), he works his way through equally matter-of-fact psychological experiences up to dizzy flights of mystical speculation (section two). But the more he rises above his actual sensory and psychological experience, the less assured he is of the truth of his speculations: hence the return, in section three, to less sublime but more factual considerations.

Norman Lacey is one of the few critics who have felt the need to see the sublime passage of section two in the context of the whole poem. He is thus driven to point out—in speaking of the transition from section two to section three—that Wordsworth "is not certain what kind of connection there is, if any, between nature and his mystical experience, and he returns to what he knows for certain, that in the fret and fever of the world he has often turned for relief to his memory of the beautiful scene in the Wye valley." [21] In fact, Wordsworth's doubt bears on two entirely different points: in the first place, as Lacey says, he is not quite sure that his "blessed mood" is actually due to the influence of the "beauteous forms" of nature; although the mood itself is an incontrovertible psychological fact, its origin is not clear: this is the point emphasized by Hartman as well. On the other hand, a far stronger doubt is cast on what might be called the cognitive content Wordsworth is tempted to assign to the mood. "This" in line 49 refers to what immediately precedes, that is, the suggestion that "we see into the life of things": it is the interpretation of the mood, which Wordsworth concedes may be "but a vain belief."

It is essential to the often unrecognized pathos of *Tintern Abbey* that as the poet soars to ever loftier heights of speculation, he feels the more in danger of losing his grasp upon the actual, which provided his initial inspiration. That is why, in section three, Wordsworth falls back on the matter of ascertained inner experience from which he took off in section

[21] N. Lacey, *Wordsworth's View of Nature and Its Ethical Consequences* (Cambridge, Eng., 1948), p. 3; the same idea is repeated on p. 63.

two: the relief wrought in him by the memory of the Wye amidst "the fretful stir / Unprofitable, and the fever of the world," a phrase which simply enlarges on the "din of towns and cities." Section three gives a definite sense of anticlimax. But this is no blemish on the poem as a whole. The anticlimax is inherent in the design of the poem, which deals with the alternate moods through which Wordsworth passes as he tentatively gropes after the meanings both certain and possible of his experience of nature.

The fourth section briefly reverts to the present of the first ("And now . . ."), only to refer to a slightly remoter past than in the second. The poet, in section two, had analyzed the effect of nature's "beauteous forms" during the interval between his two visits to Tintern Abbey; in section four he begins by trying to recapture his mood at the time of his first visit. Since he even mentions his "boyish days," the section deals with three moments in time which are neatly homologous with the three aspects of nature's action in section two: there is an unobtrusive correspondence between the "sensations," the "feelings," and the "gift of aspect more sublime" of section two on the one hand, and the "glad animal movements," the "passion," and the "other gifts" of section four on the other.

The introductory lines of the fourth section are of considerable interest in that they show the poet aware of the complexity of his mood:

> And now, with gleams of half-extinguished thought,
> With many recognitions dim and faint,
> And somewhat of a sad perplexity,
> The picture of the mind revives again.
>
> (ll. 58–60)

"Perplexity" is probably the key word to the total meaning of the poem. And Wordsworth's puzzlement has two main causes. Looking back to what precedes, we can find evidence of his uncertainty about the relationship between his "blessed mood" and the forms of nature, and also about the actual validity of the mystical thoughts which supply him with his highest inspiration. But his puzzlement is not of a merely intellectual order. His "sad perplexity" is mixed with the sense of "present pleasure" (l. 63). The word "perplexity" anticipates another kind of uncertainty, which is the subject of section four and which is concerned with his valuation of the changes—the losses and the new gifts—which time has wrought in him. In those introductory lines, past, present, and future are closely correlated; so are sadness and pleasure. The reason for the sadness and the perplexity is the plain fact that his

>   pleasing thoughts
> That in this moment there is life and food
> For future years
>   (ll. 63–65)

are less assured than the tranquil, self-possessed phrasing might suggest: they are no more than a "hope" which the poet "dares" to entertain (l. 65). Consequently, in order to disentangle the threads woven into his complex and contradictory mood, Wordsworth is driven to trace back the main trend of his own evolution.

As Campbell and Mueschke have observed, the poem develops through a process of incremental repetition. In a sustained endeavor to assess his present relationship to nature, Wordsworth first analyzes the effects which the memory of the Wye landscape has exerted upon his mind (section two); he thus reaches a glorious mystical insight, the truth of which, however, remains doubtful in his own eyes. He then tackles the problem from another angle, and retraces his own evolution from boyhood to maturity, thus encompassing a far wider stretch of time in section four than in section two: this is part of the incremental aspect of the process. Its repetitive aspect is obvious. As the poet contrasts what he is with what he was, we again notice the three-stage ascending movement already perceived in section two: from the "glad animal movements" of his boyhood through the passionate love of natural forms characteristic of adolescence, to the more thoughtful attitude of his early maturity. But in this respect too the repetition is incremental: the ascending movement, we might say, takes us higher up in section four than in section two. It takes us to a more sweeping vision of cosmic unity. In the former passage, the poet merely sees into "the life of things"; in the latter, man is included in his vision, and the life of things is seen to reside in an all-pervading presence, whose nature is described in grandiose terms with an unmistakable pantheistic slant.

The last dozen lines or so of the fourth section constitute the climax of the poem. Here, indeed, Wordsworth epitomizes the three aspects of what he is trying to convey, that is, (a) his mystical sense of the spiritual unity that brings together the mutifarious forms of the created world ("all thinking things, all objects of all thought"), (b) his conviction that the source of man's moral and spiritual growth is to be found in all the external forms of nature ("all that we behold," "all the mighty world of eye, and ear"), and (c) his correlative assurance that nature acts upon the whole of man's personality ("sense," "thoughts," "heart," "soul," "moral being").

The important point is that the two lines of approach—the static introspective line of section two and the dynamic biographical line of section four—are convergent. The main movement carries the poet from the sensory to the emotional and the mystical, from the assurance of matter-of-fact perception to a level of ideality which not only is impressive and inspiring but is also imbued with the uncertainty inherent in all metaphysical thought. For here, too, the cosmic vision of universal oneness, while couched in lines of great eloquence and convincing beauty, is embedded in a strikingly tentative context.

The note of diffidence can be felt, of course, in low-tension passages which are seldom quoted; but when due attention is paid to such phrases as "so I dare to hope" (l. 65) or "I would believe" (l. 87), the nature of Wordsworth's perplexity is clarified and its centrality to the poem becomes obvious. His return to Tintern Abbey has reconstructed the externals of the situation that was his five years before; his own inner experience appears to be all the more different because of the similarity in the setting. These two elements, similitude and difference, are basic, and they cut across the divisions of outward experience and inner feeling. In spite of the changes wrought in him in the course of the intervening years, one element of his inner experience remains constant: it is to nature that he owes what he has and what he is. The "aching joys" and "dizzy raptures" of his youth were gifts of nature; so were the "tranquil restoration" of his mind and his "little acts of kindness and of love" in the years between; so are the "serene and blessed mood" and the "sense sublime" of his present early manhood. But while this "mood" and this "sense" and the happiness they induce in him are sheer psychological facts, the value of their content is by no means a matter of certainty. We cannot help remembering that Coleridge, in *The Eolian Harp*, dismissed as "shapings of the unregenerate mind" a similarly glorious vision (with a similarly pantheistic tinge) of the One Life. The actual tone of *Tintern Abbey* is not assertive, as it is generally taken to be, but tentative and exploratory.

The beginning of the fifth section—"Nor perchance, / If I were not thus taught,"—closely parallels the negative hypothesis of section three—"If this / Be but a vain belief"—thus ushering in a second descending movement leading to a new apparent anticlimax. But this time, it would seem, Wordsworth is contemplating a deprivation more fundamental than in the earlier passage. The wording and the structure of sections two and three intimate the poet's misgivings regarding the connection between the "beauteous forms" and the "blessed mood" as well as about the mystical significance attributed to the "blessed mood." But now, Wordsworth prophetically puts forward the far more disquieting suggestion that he might become completely cut off from nature, that he might no longer be taught by nature and the language of the senses. J. F. Danby perceptively observed that "the ecstatic harmony is only a phase in a larger movement that passes on, in individual experience, to eventual loss . . . Wordsworth had had the most Nature could give, and the more, therefore, it could take away. He includes the record of the high experience in his poem but is aware of the inevitability of the loss."[22] And once again Wordsworth falls back on a matter of experiential fact, as he had done in section three. The sudden turning to Dorothy, who has not yet been mentioned in the poem, may be unexpected; yet it fits perfectly into the whole scheme, which, as should be clear by now, pulsates between the two poles of Wordsworth's inspiration: on the one hand, the matter-of-fact objectivity of his perception of nature (section one), the deep certainty of his own psychological experience (section three), and the equally objective and comforting presence of his sister (section five); on the other hand, his lofty but subjective aspiration to insight into the life of things (section two) and to an intuition of the unity of the cosmos (section four). This symmetrical pattern, with its alternating rhythm of ascent toward metaphysical intuition and descent to the bedrock of sensory and psychological certainty, is fundamental to the total meaning of the poem.

The address to Dorothy, then, is an indirect way for Wordsworth to turn back to his own self and to such assurance as he may have gained thus far. Indeed, the last stanza repeats, on a smaller scale, the ambitious time scheme of the whole poem. In his sister's present Wordsworth relives his own past as re-created in section four:

> in thine voice I catch
> The language of my former heart, and read
> My former pleasures in the shooting lights
> Of thy wild eyes.
> (ll. 116–119)

[22] *The Simple Wordsworth*, pp. 94–96.

The imaginary landscape which surrounds Dorothy, with its "misty mountain-winds" (l. 136) is reminiscent of the picturesque presentation of nature in section four rather than of the quiet harmony of section one. Likewise, Dorothy's "wild eyes" and "wild ecstasies" (l. 138) recall her brother's past "aching joys" and "dizzy raptures" rather than his present soberly meditative mood. The identification is pushed so far that Wordsworth projects his own present into his sister's future:

>   when thy mind
> Shall be a mansion for all lovely forms,
> Thy memory be as a dwelling-place
> For all sweet sounds and harmonies; oh! then,
> If solitude, or fear, or pain, or grief,
> Should be thy portion, with what healing thoughts
> Of tender joy wilt thou remember me,
> And these my exhortations.
>
>   (ll. 139–146)

Not only will her mood be one of sober pleasure, but her memory of nature and of her brother will play the same restoring role described in very similar terms at the beginning of section two and in section three: "lovely forms" and "all sweet sounds and harmonies" echo with significant precision the "beauteous forms" and the "sensations sweet" of section two; they will provide "healing thoughts"—analogous to the "tranquil restoration" of the poet's mind—to which she will be able to turn in times of "solitude, or fear, or pain, or grief," in the same way her brother now turns to his recollections of natural beauty for solace "in lonely rooms" and " 'mid the din of towns and cities," in "hours of weariness," or when oppressed by "the fretful stir / Unprofitable, and the fever of the world."

Dorothy is thus presented as a sort of duplication of her brother, and the close correspondence of their characters and interests and sensibilities may do much to account for the feeling that existed between them. But while Wordsworth, in turning to his sister, is in fact turning imaginatively back to his own self and experience, there is, in his prophecy of Dorothy's future as identical with his own present, an omission which, so far as I know, has passed unnoticed, and is both puzzling and significant.

There is hardly a line in the last section which does not refer to some earlier passage. But it contains nothing that might be considered an echo of those parts of the poem where, clearly, Wordsworth's poetic power was at its most intense: the end of sections two and four. Nor is there any reference in it to "acts of kindness and of love" or to "the still, sad music of humanity"; indeed, human society is evoked in negative terms—"The dreary intercourse of daily life" (l. 131)— strongly reminiscent of the first part of section two and of section three. In other words, all the elements which, in the poem, carry with them overtones, however slight, of diffidence and uncertainty, are left out of the concluding section. And the last description of nature's benevolence (ll. 122–134) is couched in terms as general as those of section three.

The quiet assertive tone of section five is unmistakable; yet, it is also undeniable that this section is keyed at a lower pitch of imaginative thinking than are the sublime passages of the earlier sections. The poem, therefore, ends paradoxically on a note of confident assertion which produces a sense of anticlimax. In this paradox, however, there is no contradiction such as that which mars *The Eolian Harp*. For the two contrasting movements are fused into the aesthetic unity of the rhythmic pattern. If, starting from its structural organization, we seek to define the highly complex mood of the poem, we shall find that it is one of perplexity on a background of absolute certainty. The certainty refers to Wordsworth's actual experience of nature as a thing of beauty and a source of healing thoughts; it is characteristic of Wordsworth's honesty, of his determined refusal to sacrifice truth to rhetorical flourish, that he should end his poem on this less lofty plane.

But the dynamic nucleus which gives *Tintern Abbey* its momentous impetus is of course perplexity. Wordsworth had reached the age when a man pauses for the first time to reckon up his losses and his gains. His losses were quite clear to him: he had lost the intimate emotional relationship with nature that was his five years before. The gains were not so obvious, for the "other gifts" twice mentioned in the poem are of a less ascertainable nature, dealing as they do with metaphysical intuitions. Twice in the course of the poem, Wordsworth's inspiration warms up and rockets upward to mystical summits. But although the poetic eloquence of those two passages testifies to the intensity of the accompanying emotion, Wordsworth's intellectual truthfulness prevents him from presenting as fact what is no more than surmise. Hence the perplexity. For if the "other gifts" are but vain belief, the loss, it is clear, is total and irrecoverable.

One feels bound to confess with due humility that the painstaking procedures of close textual criticism do little more than confirm Keats's brilliant flash of insight and sympathy in a passage which it is necessary to quote in full:

I compare human life to a large Mansion of Many Apartments, two of which I can only describe, the doors of the rest being as yet shut upon me—The first we step into we call the infant or thoughtless Chamber, in which we remain as long as we do not think—We remain there a long while, and notwithstanding the doors of the second Chamber remain wide open, showing a bright appearance, we care not to hasten to it; but are at length imperceptibly impelled by the awakening of the thinking principle—within us—we no sooner get into the second Chamber, which I shall call the Chamber of Maiden-Thought, than we become intoxicated with the light and the atmosphere, we see nothing but pleasant wonders, and think of delaying there for ever in delight: However among the effects this breathing is father of is that tremendous one of sharpening one's vision into the heart and nature of Man—of convincing ones nerves that the World is full of Misery and Heartbreak, Pain, Sickness and oppression—

whereby This Chamber of Maiden Thought becomes gradually darken'd and at the same time on all sides of it many doors are set open—but all dark—all leading to dark passages—We see not the ballance of good and evil. We are in a Mist—*We* are now in that state—We feel the "burden of the Mystery," To this point was Wordsworth come, as far as I can conceive when he wrote "Tintern Abbey" and it seems to me that his Genius is explorative of those dark Passages.[23]

Yet, something should be added to Keats's observation. For as we reread the first lines of section five—

> Nor perchance,
> If I were not thus taught, should I the more
> Suffer my genial spirits to decay

—we are struck by a note that anticipates later stages in the poet's development. The way the sentence is turned is suggestive of Wordsworth's stern determination—while contemplating his greatest loss—not to give himself up to the annihilating power of his sad perplexity. Faced with a vital dilemma—either to lose his grasp of the actual, or to admit the vanity of his highest intuitions—by an act of the will based on certain knowledge, Wordsworth decides to seek the meaning which his experience, past and present, holds for the future.

Lacey has expressed his surprise that Wordsworth "did not realize clearly that he was most certainly in possession of the truth when he was *'laid asleep in body'*—in other words, that his mystical experiences were the only starting point for all true insight 'into the life of things,' and that he must at all costs pin his faith to *them*, and not to the language of the sense." [24] Whether it would have been a good idea for Wordsworth to turn off one of his voices is open to doubt. The fact remains that we find no attempt, within the poem, to reconcile

---

[23] *The Letters of John Keats*, ed. H. E. Rollins (Cambridge, Eng., 1958), I, 280–281.
[24] *Wordsworth's View of Nature*, pp. 64–65; the italics are Lacey's.

insight and sensation on the ideational level. Nor is there, we must note, any explicit condemnation of the nearly pantheistic utterances of the sublime passages, as we find in Coleridge's *The Eolian Harp*. The point is that Wordsworth was not concerned with offering the final poetic statement of a fully formed philosophical creed—unlike Coleridge, who was "incapable of remaining content with half knowledge." Wordsworth, in this poem, was first and foremost concerned with expressing the complex totality of a mood which included elements both of knowledge and of half knowledge. To knowledge belong his sensory apprehension of nature, the healing power of his memory of nature, his past, and Dorothy's present, emotional involvement in nature. To half knowledge belong his speculations as to the actual content of his mystical moods and about the relationship of these moods with nature, and also his perplexity regarding the balance of loss and gain in his own evolution. This duality of the divided self accounts for the dialectical oscillation which drives Wordsworth to statements of sublimity, only to stress their hypothetical character immediately afterward.

But while the dominant mood of the greater part of *Tintern Abbey* is one of puzzlement, it was not in the nature of Wordsworth to remain satisfied with a depiction, however accurate and subtle, of his ambiguous predicament at the moment of writing. Indeed, this very ambiguity was something that he wanted to overcome. His ultimate concern, therefore, was to find in the lessons of the past and of the present some experiential certainty that might put his mind at rest by supplying a firm basis for his hopes of future development. What emerges at the outset of a reflective process remarkable both for its honesty and clear-sightedness, is the confidence expressed in the lines

> Knowing that Nature never did betray
> The heart that loved her,
> (ll. 122–123)

where the verb "knowing" carries the full force of absolute conviction. This certainty, this complete assurance of the benevolence of nature, which is the incontrovertible conclusion to be drawn from his past, is also the foundation for his "hope" and his "trust" and his determination to uphold his "genial spirits" and his "cheerful faith." At a later stage, the benevolence of nature will be seen as one form of the providential benevolence of God. Meanwhile, as Elizabeth Nitchie has observed, the last sentence of *Tintern Abbey* "echoes the beginning and completes the circle of the poem." [25] But it is not idle to note which one among the symbolic features of the Wye landscape Wordsworth chose to recall: the oneness of its green hue and the ascending line of the "steep and lofty cliffs."

[25] In *The Major Romantic Poets*, ed. C. D. Thorpe, C. Baker, and B. Weaver (Carbondale, 1957), p. 15.

6 A Leading from Above:
WORDSWORTH'S *RESOLUTION AND INDEPENDENCE*

As we have worked our way through some early romantic poetry we have found that much of it radiates from a nucleus of ambiguity. The prime mover of romantic inspiration is an intuition of the living cosmic unity which runs directly counter to the prevailing dualism of eighteenth-century thought. This is the idea of the One Life—in which man, nature, and God are felt to be somehow vitally linked in a complex network of relationships—which provides the main structural principle of romantic poetry: the process of expansion and contraction characteristic of *Tintern Abbey* as well as of *The Eolian Harp* shows that, to the romantic imagination, there is no unbridgeable gap between self and non-self, between the soul of man and the world of matter, and the finest passages in these and other poems are those that successfully translate into speech a quasi-mystical sense of universal oneness.

But on closer analysis, it appears that this latter insight is always set in a context of doubt and diffidence, as a tentative suggestion, and as an uncertain ideal, the far-off object of the romantic *Sehnsucht*. In *The Eolian Harp*, Coleridge expressly rejects it because it is liable to clash with Christian doctrine;

in *Tintern Abbey,* Wordsworth does not conceal his perplexity about its actual significance. The contradiction between the idealization of rustic life in the Preface to *Lyrical Ballads* and the actual presentation of human experience in the ballads themselves clarifies the nature of this perplexity, to which the poet is driven by the general discrepancy between his sense of the ideal and his perception of the actual. A case might be made for the notion that the writing of poetry was, for the romantics, a continuous endeavor both to express their ambivalent apprehension of the world and to overcome its dialectical antinomies.

The concept of the symbol was a satisfactory way of accounting for the felt relationship between nature, on the one hand, and the infinite and the world of man on the other. In Coleridge's conversation poems, the panoramic vision provides a spatial analogon for the spiritual infinite which created nature and still maintains it. The tectonic organization of the Tintern landscape turns it into a self-contained microcosm, which both kindles the ruminative mood of the poet and reflects his upward aspirations. The tormented shape of the old thorn-tree is a correlative of human suffering and resilience, while its natural environment underscores the healing power of nature and symbolizes Wordworth's compassionate refusal to pass judgment on human guilt.

But while the symbol concept thus offered a way out of the dilemma between an unorthodox pantheistic conception of the world and the spiritless dualism of the eighteenth-century tradition, it did nothing to remove the antinomy of ideal and experience which was so crucial to romanticism: as Keats said, "We see not the balance of good and evil." For some reason, it was not in the nature of the English poets to be satisfied with the mere statement of irreconcilables which is the basis of the *Ironie* of the German romantics. Wordsworth, in particular, always felt compelled to solve the primeval problem of evil and suffering which thus presented itself in a modified form and with renewed urgency. Indeed, the source of his lifelong interest in the growth of his own mind is probably to be found in the fascination with which he watched his own attempt, through trial and error and in the increasing light of experience and meditation, to come to terms with the reality of evil, of loss, and of pain, without giving up his idealistic insight into the nature of life and of the world.

While *Tintern Abbey* was primarily a detailed analysis of his perplexity and diffident hopes, Wordsworth's first extended attempt to effect a genuine reconciliation of fact and ideal is to be found in *Resolution and Independence*, which A. C. Bradley once declared to be "the most Wordsworthian of Wordsworth's poems, and the best test of ability to understand him."[1] Nearly half a century later, F. W. Bateson confirmed this judgment, adding that in this poem Wordsworth's "Two Voices turn out to be complementary instead of contradictory."[2] While in *Tintern Abbey* the two voices are, so to speak, juxtaposed into a dialogue, the unity of which is one of aesthetic patterning, in *Resolution and Independence* a deeper fusion is achieved because the urgent inner conflict—which forms the main theme of the work and is reflected in its motifs, its diction, and its overall structure—is genuinely solved at the end.

The starting point of the poem is an abrupt shift in mood from exaltation to despondency. "I was in the state of feeling described in the beginning of the poem," Wordsworth says in a Fenwick note, "while crossing over Barton Fell from Mr. Clarkson's, at the foot of Ullswater, towards Askam."[3] As Mary Moorman suggests, "that may have been on April 7th 1802 . . . when he left the Clarksons on foot to go into

---

[1] A. C. Bradley, *Oxford Lectures on Poetry* (London, 1904), p. 130.
[2] F. W. Bateson, *Wordsworth: A Re-interpretation* (London, 1954), p. 4.
[3] *The Poetical Works of William Wordsworth*, ed. E. de Sélincourt and Helen Darbishire (Oxford, 1962), II, 510.

Yorkshire to visit Mary Hutchinson." [4] Several plausible reasons have been adduced for Wordsworth's emotional unbalance at the time: he must have been deeply preoccupied with Coleridge's dejection; his own health was failing; and as we can see from the great *Ode*, he had become aware that his highest poetic gift, "the visionary gleam," was deserting him. All these, no doubt, are important background elements, but it seems likely that his mood was primarily affected by his relationship with Mary Hutchinson. Wordsworth's errand on 7 April 1802 could hardly be described as pleasant. On 22 March, a letter had come "from poor Annette," and, Dorothy writes, "we resolved to see Annette and that Will should go to Mary." [5] It may have been at the foot of Ullswater, on the way to Askam, that the thought of his present predicament and future responsibilities, both economic and emotional, startled Wordsworth out of his happy birthday mood and started the train of meditation and recollection that was to give birth to *Resolution and Independence.*

Although W. W. Robson, at the close of his searching analysis of the poem, forcefully asserts that *Resolution and Independence* "has a structure, and it is this structure which makes it a successful and public poem," [6] its formal design has never received the attention it deserves. Its basic pattern is again one of contraction and expansion, the poet's attention shifting back and forth from the outside world to his inner self. At the same time, an ascending movement results from the interaction of self and non-self, and the poem ends on a note of enriched self-awareness. The process of expansion and contraction occurs twice: after the objective description of

[4] M. Moorman, *William Wordsworth: A Biography. The Early Years, 1770–1803* (Oxford, 1957), p. 540.
[5] *Journals of Dorothy Wordsworth*, ed. E. de Sélincourt (London, 1952), I, 127–128.
[6] W. W. Robson, "Wordsworth: *Resolution and Independence*," in *Interpretations*, ed. J. Wain (London, 1955), p. 127.

nature in stanzas I and II, Wordsworth muses on his own self and his own problems in stanzas III to VI. Stanza VII is transitional, and vicariously self-centered in the sense that Wordsworth is here speaking of other poets; but the generalization at the end displaces the focus of his attention. The centrifugal force operates again as Wordsworth now turns his attention toward the old man, in stanzas VIII to XV. Like stanza VII, stanza XVI is transitional: it initiates the poet's return to his own inwardness, which is the main theme of the end of the poem, with a short return to objectivity in stanza XVIII.

This division of the poem into two main parts, each divided in its turn into two sub-parts, is based on the topics with which the poet is concerned at each given point. But closer attention reveals that the fundamental contrarieties on which the structure of the poem rests go further and deeper than the surface polarity of subject and object, poet and outside world. In other words, the dialectics of the poem does not lead only to the well-known romantic coalescence of the self and the world. It has another and subtler aspect, which involves moral concepts and emotions of the highest order, and we can see from *Resolution and Independence* that the problem of happiness and suffering was for Wordsworth, as it was to be for Keats, one of utmost urgency. From this second point of view, based on thematic values rather than subject matter, it will be seen that the first part formulates the problem, and the second solves it. But the thematic pattern does not coincide at all points with the pattern of the subject matter: the contrapuntal variations give some idea of Wordsworth's skill as a poet.

On both levels, the first part is divided into two sub-parts. On the topical level, the first sub-part, centered on nature, comprises stanzas I and II, while the second, centered on the poet, includes stanzas III to VII; on the thematic level, however, the dividing line comes after stanza III: the first three stanzas are devoted to the theme of joy, whereas the last four deal with distress. That the first three stanzas form a self-contained whole in spite of the change of subject from non-self to self after stanza II is shown by the close equivalence of lines 1–3—

> There was a roaring in the wind all night;
> The rain came heavily and fell in floods;
> But now the sun is rising calm and bright;

—and lines 20–21:

> My old remembrances went from me wholly;
> And all the ways of men, so vain and melancholy.

Both passages express a similar shift, one in the physical realm of nature (the end of wind and rain), the other in the mood of the poet (the forgetting of old sufferings and of human folly). The third stanza thus plays a pivotal part and ensures the organic unity in an interlocking wavelike movement, which could be represented as follows:

subject matter: nature   self

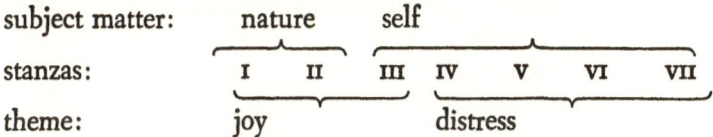

theme: joy   distress

The same pattern is repeated in the second part, which can also be considered from the point of view of subject matter and from the point of view of the moral theme. The development of the moral theme now reverses the trend of the first part, since it consists in a new shift from distress and dereliction back to joy, although joy of a different kind. The ambivalent transitional function of stanza III in the first part is now fulfilled by stanzas XVI and XVII: so far as subject matter is concerned, these deal with the poet and no longer with the old man, but with regard to the thematic values, they go on treating the motif of pain. The design is the same as in the first part:

subject matter: the old man   the poet

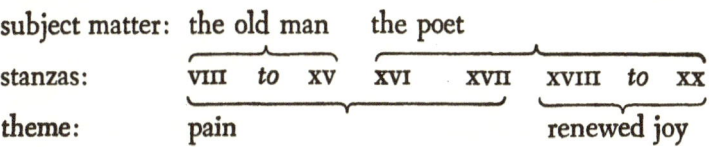

theme: pain   renewed joy

Moreover, as with stanza III, the last words of stanza XVI refer the reader back to the first stanza of the second part by repeating the idea that the old man is a messenger "from above" or "from some far region," sent "by peculiar grace" in order to give the poet "apt admonishment."

Stanza XVI resembles stanza III in yet another significant way which strengthens its focal function. Stanza III described the ecstasy of communion with nature, in which sense-awareness is changed into *Einfühlung*:

> I heard the woods and distant waters roar;
> *Or heard them not,* as happy as a boy.
> (ll. 18–19; italics mine)

Stanza XVI refers to a similar trance-like feeling of inwardness:

> But now his voice to me was like a stream
> *Scarce heard;* . . .
> And the whole body of the Man did seem
> Like one whom I had met with *in a dream.*
> (ll. 107–110; italics mine)

The stream image provides an explicit link with the "waters" of stanza III. This similarity between the two stanzas is extremely important. It shows that although the poem ushers in a new turn in Wordsworth's outlook on life, a basic continuity characterizes his belief in the unity of the cosmos and in the paramount validity of visionary knowledge.

The contest between two moods, which is the core of the problem, is deftly defined in the final lines of the first part:

> We Poets in our youth begin in gladness;
> But thereof come in the end despondency and madness.
> (ll. 48–49)

The psychological theme, therefore, is how, in the end, "despondency" succeeds the "gladness" that was at the beginning. W. W. Robson has called attention to the tense-scheme of this part, and indeed the shift from present to past is a masterstroke: the joy of the present moment ("But now the sun is rising . . .") is projected into the past in stanza III ("I was a Traveller then . . .") and does become a thing of the past in stanza IV ("To me that morning did it happen so . . ."), while the use of the present perfect in stanza VI ("My whole life I have lived in pleasant thought . . .") prepares the reader for Wordsworth's generalized expression of anxiety about the future in the latter part of the stanza ("But how can he expect . . .").

The two moods are thoroughly illustrated and easily identifiable. "Gladness" and its equivalents ("mirth," "joy," "delight," "pleasant," "happy," "blissful") refer to the visionary joy that comes from a perception of the One Life, which is both a primary experience of the romantic poets and a primary theme of romantic poetry. All the lines devoted to the description of nature form a magnificent pageant of natural piety: the birds, the sky, the grass, the hare, are all presented as animated "blissful natures," and the poet is one of their crowd, the relationship being explicitly associated with childhood ("as happy as a boy," "happy Child of earth").

In *The Liberal Imagination*, Lionel Trilling suggested that *Resolution and Independence* is the "timely utterance" referred to in the *Ode: Intimations of Immortality*. This view was rejected by J. C. Ransom,[7] who reverts to Garrod's notion that the "timely utterance" is "My heart leaps up"—without, however, countering Trilling's argument that in *Resolution and Independence*, "and not in the rainbow poem, a sullen feeling occurs and is relieved."[8] According to Ransom, "the trouble which is healed by the meeting with the leech-gatherer can hardly be the trouble which is the burden of the *Ode*": in the *Ode*, "the poet's complaint is that he no longer

---

[7] J. C. Ransom, "William Wordsworth: Notes Toward an Understanding of Poetry," in *Wordsworth: Centenary Studies*, ed. G. T. Dunklin (Princeton, 1951), pp. 81–113.

[8] L. Trilling, *The Liberal Imagination* (London, 1955), p. 140.

obtains from natural objects the religious intimations which he ascribes to his youth; that is to say, the overwhelming sense of the presence of God," while *Resolution and Independence* deals with what Ransom calls "animal or economic discouragement."

Though Wordsworth's despondency in *Resolution and Independence* has economic features which are absent from the *Ode*, the poem also deals with the loss of a sense of nature identical with the natural piety of the rainbow poem. Moreover, this natural piety is linked, as we have seen, with mystical feelings reminiscent of *Tintern Abbey*. But whereas in *Tintern Abbey* this mood was a gift "more sublime," a possible revelation of ultimate truth, and an intimation of nature as the "soul of all my moral being," in *Resolution and Independence* the poet's enjoyment of his youthful vision is described as a mere "summer mood," with the obvious implication that life's business is something different. What, then, is life's business?

It appears, first, that life is to be lived among men, however "vain and melancholy" their "ways" may be, and not in the blissful solitude of imagination. In some sense, it is therefore wrong to "walk . . . far from the world . . . and from all care" (l. 33). For Wordsworth, at the time, such phrasing no doubt had a very concrete meaning. What Trilling calls his "reversal of feeling" occurred, we remember, when he was on his way to explain to Mary Hutchinson that he was leaving for France. This would postpone their marriage. The "care" of which he speaks is likely to be linked with his future responsibilities as a married man, and with the consequences of his affair with Annette Vallon. It is true that stanza vi deals wholly with the economic aspect of the problem. But the words "solitude, pain of heart, distress" of stanza v point to some deeper anxiety.

Trilling rightly says that "the second specific fear" (besides the economic fear) "is of mental distress." Unfortunately, he does not attempt to explain what exactly this mental distress may be. Perhaps a clue is to be found in *Stanzas Written in My Pocket-Copy of Thomson's "Castle of Indolence,"* which Wordsworth began on 9 May, the day *Resolution and Independence* was finished. The title is significant: Wordsworth found both Thomson's "indolence" and Thomson's stanza form most suitable for this portrait of himself and Coleridge, in which he fixed the blissful image of their life together—a life which is here described in terms of sheer spontaneous enjoyment of nature and utter social irresponsibility.[9] On the point of entering upon a new course of life, Wordsworth was casting a wistful glance on his past self—"For happier soul no living creature has / Than he had"—and on his and Coleridge's past way of living, "from earthly labour free / As happy spirits as were ever seen."

The stanzas, which in retrospect sound like a farewell song, contain two lines which may cast some light on the problem under discussion:

> Some thought he was a lover, and did woo:
> . . . .
> But verse was what he had been wedded to.

The wedding image is a telltale one, however conventional it may be. And one may suggest with due caution that Wordsworth had his own secret misgivings about the possibility of reconciling his devotion to his future wife and his dedication to poetry. This might be the mental distress which, together with the thought of economic cares, produced the mood of dejection.

In the first part, then, the visionary mood is presented as the highest joy of which man is capable. It is the privilege of the poet that this godlike bliss should be reserved for him: the poet is "deified" by his own spirit. But the communion with nature, which is childlike, is also childish: adult life is not to

[9] The components of this blissful mood have been listed by A. E. M. Conran, "The Dialectic of Experience: A Study of Wordsworth's *Resolution and Independence*," *PMLA*, LXXV (1960), 67.

be lived on the visionary plane of pure imagination. When the poet is brought face to face with the needs he had left unheeded, with the responsibilities he had previously escaped or evaded, his "genial spirits fail"[10] and the visionary mood vanishes. The greater the joy he had known, the more painful his disappointment. The reality of life and the reality of the vision seem to be mutually exclusive: this is the core of the problem and the substance of the author's "untoward thoughts," the agonizing dilemma, which is to be solved in the second part. As A. E. M. Conran observed, in his thoughtful study of the poem, it is also "the Romantic paradox, the main problem of Keats in his maturity: how to reconcile the world of the imagination with the dangerously humdrum world of everyday?"[11]

Wordsworth's characteristic interest in growth and continuity receives poetic expression in the skillfully managed coalescence of identity and diversity in the subject matter. As the reader comes to the second part of the poem, he is bound to notice that Wordsworth is at pains to present the old man as just another facet of the nature that was described in the first two stanzas: though the poet's attention was first attracted by "all *things* that love the sun," the old man seems to him "a *thing* endued with sense" (italics mine). Wordsworth himself has explained in the Preface of 1815 how, by using carefully

[10] Echoes of *Dejection: An Ode* are numerous in this poem. For a full account of the relation between both, see G. W. Meyer, *"Resolution and Independence:* Wordsworth's Answer to Coleridge's *Dejection: An Ode," Tulane Studies in English,* II (1950), 49–74.

[11] A. E. M. Conran, *op. cit.,* p. 71. However, Conran's refusal to take stanza VI seriously seems to me erroneous; he writes: "It is as though [Wordsworth] deliberately exaggerates his irresponsibility. I doubt whether he is really thinking of his own life in itself, so much as a stage in a cycle of Innocence and Experience which is eighteenth-century poetry." In fact, Wordsworth was, as usual, thinking of both his private experience and its general or symbolic significance. The *Stanzas* show that he was, at the time, genuinely convinced that his earlier life had been spent in the blissful irresponsibility of the imagination.

chosen similes, he reduced the old man to the nakedness of essential being. What remains of the first version of the poem gives us a clue to the impression he wanted to create. "What is brought forward?" he exclaims in a letter to Sara Hutchinson: " 'A lonely place, a pond' 'by which an old man *was*, far from all house or home'—not stood, not sat, but '*was*'—the figure presented in the most naked simplicity possible." [12] Whereas nature, in the first part, was presented under the most alluring aspects, overflowing with joy and vitality, here we have a vision of nature reduced to its bare essentials, without which there is no being. In his desolate setting ("pool bare to the eye of heaven," "on the bald top of an eminence"), in his immobility ("huge stone," "sea-beast crawled forth," "motionless as a cloud"), the old man embodies an aspect of nature which is utterly different from the colorful and animated picture given in the first part. He also embodies the opposite of the poet's "summer mood." He is indeed a most impressive image of "solitude" and "poverty." He is the main agent of the unity of the poem, being on a level with nature as well as with the poet. The continuity is also conspicuous in the poet's attitude: his deeply felt participation in the moral experience of the old man corresponds to his communion with nature in the first part.[13]

But the description in stanzas VIII to XII is only one stage in the development of the old man's figure. The important point is that he does not remain in absolute contrast to the joyful depiction of nature; he is not presented in an entirely negative way. As Wordsworth compares him to a sea beast that has

[12] *The Early Letters of William and Dorothy Wordsworth*, ed. E. de Sélincourt (Oxford, 1935), p. 306.
[13] Cf. M. Moorman, *William Wordsworth*, p. 542: "The Leech-Gatherer is of personal importance because it shows that he was still, in spite of the loss of his vision of the glory of Nature lamented in the *Ode*, capable of passing into the visionary state when deeply moved by human encounter." The process is summed up in the title of Book VIII of *The Prelude*: "Love of Nature leading to Love of Mankind," which was written in 1804.

crawled onto a shelf of rock or sand, "there to *sun* itself," we remember that the natural description at the beginning of the poem was of "all things that love the *sun*" (italics mine). Besides, only the objective features of his predicament—the "poverty" and the "solitude"—are emphasized. The subjective aspects, the "pain of heart" and the "distress," appear as much a thing of the past as does the delight of the poet in stanza IV. All this leads to the further development which is to take place and which shows that even the old man's extreme dereliction is imbued with high value, just as the slimy sea beasts in *The Ancient Mariner* are not deprived of beauty. As the poem goes on, the figure of the old man undergoes a gradual transformation; it is submitted to a process of enrichment and, one might say, of re-humanization.

In stanzas VIII to XI, the old man looks like a mere thing. Like the thorn-tree in the earlier poem, he is a figure of dereliction, a symbol of life at the lowest level, an emblem of humanity reduced by pain and poverty to "the most naked simplicity." From stanza XII onward, this figure becomes animated, as the old man, looking for leeches, stirs the "muddy water"—perhaps a reflection, in this new context, of the plashy earth from which the running hare was raising a glittering mist in stanza II. The full two-sidedness of the leech-gatherer is revealed in stanzas XIII and XIV when he begins to answer the poet's questions. Although he remains "feeble," it is now plain that there is more in him than met the eye at first. Not only are his eyes "yet-vivid," but his speech is not what one would expect from such a lowly being: it is "gentle" and "courteous," "solemn," "lofty," and "stately." It is also formal and fastidious ("choice word and measured phrase"). In brief, the description of the old man's manner of speaking is carefully designed to build up an impression of kindness, dignity, and even culture.

It has become customary to consider the leech-gatherer a representative of Wordsworth's solitaries, as R. D. Havens and Mary Moorman have done. But the most searching study of the Wordsworthian solitary so far is that of John Jones in *The Egotistical Sublime.* For Jones, the Old Cumberland Beggar, the Discharged Soldier of the *Prelude,* the Old Man Travelling, and the Leech-Gatherer "are in their different ways at peace with their environment": "The Leech-Gatherer," he writes, ". . . does not need to do or say anything—he is. Like all the great solitaries, he has a primordial quality, by virtue of which he stands anterior, in time and logic, to a divorce in human understanding." Although it is true, as Jones further observes, that "almost none of the Leech-Gatherer's conversation is reported in his own words," [14] the point, surely, is that the old man does speak and that Wordsworth takes pains to enlarge upon the articulateness of his speech, which, he says, is "above the reach of ordinary men." This makes him rather different from the Old Cumberland beggar of four years earlier, and suggests that the leech-gatherer has reached a wisdom which is not the same as the elemental and preconscious acceptance of life characteristic of other solitaries. In fact, if by "a divorce in human understanding," Jones means the awareness of the dilemma between the summer mood and the despondency formulated in the first part of the poem, it would seem that the old man's wisdom is not anterior, but posterior, to it; it is not a preconscious submission to life's ordeals, but a successful and conscious reconciliation of pain and happiness. The "pain of heart" and the "distress" that the poet now feels were experienced by the old man "in times long past," and then overcome to give way to the serenity of deliberate acceptance.

This, in fact, is why the leech-gatherer's predicament is relevant to the poet's problem. And it is this, too, which enables Wordsworth to identify himself with the old man in stanza xvi. Other elements intervene, of course, since there can be no identification where there are no points of similitude. Wordsworth describes himself as "a Traveller . . . upon

[14] J. Jones, *The Egotistical Sublime: A History of Wordsworth's Imagination* (London, 1954), pp. 61–63.

the moor"; the old man too is a traveler, roaming "from moor to moor." The element that stands uppermost in the poet's economic preoccupation with "life's business" is the very concrete problem of securing such "needful things" as housing and food; it is just to this problem that the leech-gatherer has found his own modest solution:

> Housing, with God's good help, by choice or chance;
> And in this way he gained an honest maintenance.
>
> (ll. 104-105)

Such particulars should not be mistaken for ultimates. Housing and food are only examples, though they may be particularly pressing ones, of the general duties and responsibilities a man assumes once he abandons the self-centered life of poetic isolation in nature. Robson is right in stating that the theme of the poem is "maturity; or rather, the recognition of a fact of moral experience without which there cannot be full maturity; that is, a successful emergence from the world of the child." Through his ecstatic identification with the leech-gatherer, Wordsworth raises himself from puzzled recognition to mature acceptance of the positive value of suffering. The cruel dilemma expressed in the first part of the poem now appears to be false; dereliction does not necessarily result in unhappiness; physical decrepitude can be reconciled with firmness of mind; life lived on the lowest level does not exclude cheerfulness.

The Stoic strain is unmistakable. "In the poem *Resolution and Independence*," Jane Worthington writes, "the Stoic precept that warns against anxious anticipation of misfortunes receives its first expression."[15] It is more important to note, however, as Mary Moorman has done, that "here we meet for the first time with a word new in Wordsworth's vocabulary—one which was to play an increasingly important

---

[15] Jane Worthington, *Wordsworth's Reading of Roman Prose* (New Haven, 1946), p. 61.

part in the poetry of the years to come. It is the word 'grace.' "[16] Elizabeth Geen has rightly recalled that the concept of grace necessarily excludes the metaphysics of immanence, to which all the romantic poets felt so strongly attracted in their early years; on the contrary, it implies a view of the world in which "God is conceived of as distinct from and unrelated to nature, with grace the means of a transcendent God's making known His favorable interest in man." But Elizabeth Geen's searching study is based on the assumption that Wordsworth's thought remained dominated by the notion of God's immanence from 1798 to 1807. In consequence, her discussion of *Resolution and Independence* tends to play down the implications of the word "grace" in that particular poem. She draws an obscure distinction between "a leading from above" and "a something given"; she states that "the original question whether a 'genial faith' is alone sufficient is implicitly answered in the affirmative"; and she suggests that the poem does not exhibit much "sense of dependence on other than human aid."[17]

The fact is that the formulation of the crucial lines in this respect is almost as tentative as is the phrasing of the pantheistic intuition in *Tintern Abbey*:

> Now, whether it were by some peculiar grace,
> A leading from above, a something given . . .
> (ll. 50–51)

But the cumulative effect of the three phrases used to account for the sudden appearance of the old man offsets to some extent the hypothetical note on which the sentence begins

---

[16] M. Moorman, *William Wordsworth*, p. 540. In fact, there are previous occurrences of the word "grace" in Wordsworth's poetry. They have been listed and analyzed by E. Geen. But this is indeed the first time it is endowed with anything approaching its full religious significance.

[17] Elizabeth Geen, "The Concept of Grace in Wordsworth's Poetry," *PMLA*, LVIII (1943), 689–715.

("whether"). Later in the poem, Wordsworth observes that the leech-gatherer "did seem" to him

> Like one whom I had met with in a dream;
> Or like a man from some far region sent,
> To give me human strength, by apt admonishment.
> (ll. 110–112)

One should never tire of stressing Wordsworth's caution and precision in his wording of such important statements: he does not assert that the old man "was," but that he "did seem"; and he is careful to present the two possibilities, the subjective one and the objective one. His determined refusal to pretend to certainty where there is none is equally conspicuous in a letter written to Sara Hutchinson on 14 June 1802, where he says: "I consider the manner in which I was rescued from my dejection and despair *almost* as an interposition of Providence." [18]

But after due attention has been paid to the exact meaning of the statements contained in the poem, it is also necessary to take its dramatic truth into account. It is an equally relevant fact that the old man is *not* a being that Wordsworth has met with in a dream, that he does provide "a leading," that he does give "apt admonishment," and that he does revive the poet's "human strength." Further, the leech-gatherer himself is described as one of those "Religious men, who give to God and man their dues" (l. 98), and the Scottish "grave Livers" with whom he is compared are most unlikely to be pantheistic visionaries. Finally, his humble and grateful acknowledgment of "God's good help" (l. 104) is emphatically echoed at the end of the poem when Wordsworth, speaking in his own name, exclaims: "God, . . . be my help and stay secure" (l. 139).

There can be little doubt that the poem intends to describe the workings of a transcendent power which Wordsworth was only beginning to recognize, somewhat obliquely and with

[18] *Early Letters*, p. 306; italics mine.

considerable caution, as the grace of God. Though he could not, as yet, be sure of its nature, he had no doubt of its effects, so that *Resolution and Independence,* in its strange mixture of certainty and diffidence, may be said to recreate, in a different key, the complex mood of *Tintern Abbey.* But the various pulsating movements which cause the poem to oscillate between the opposite poles of selfhood and otherness, of doubt and assurance, of joy and distress, operate within the upward spiral-like trend which provided the dynamics of Coleridge's conversation pieces. It is indeed difficult to agree with Robson's unexpected statement that "Wordsworth, in 'laughing himself to scorn,' laughs himself back to a happiness which is felt to be still there." Wordsworth's scorn is leveled both at his former delight (resulting from the undue self-deification mentioned in line 48) and at his former distress (resulting from undue fear of life, its trials and its responsibilities). The self to which he reverts is not the self that was his starting point. If he laughs himself back to happiness, it is not to the initial irresponsible bliss associated with youth and poetry, but to a happiness of a different quality, more serene, more complex, more mature: not the happiness of innocence and ignorance, but the happiness of experience, humility, and wisdom.

7 The Hopeless Quest:
SHELLEY'S *ALASTOR*

When Wordsworth achieved the balance of idealistic intuition and ethical insight embodied in *Resolution and Independence*, he was thirty-two. Neither Keats nor Shelley lived to reach that age. If they had, the kinship between the two romantic generations might stand out more clearly than it does. Although it would be idle to speculate too eagerly on this point, it is both legitimate and possible to argue that much of the younger writers' poetry derives from the same basic paradox and works out the same fundamental conflicts that inspired the Lake poets. By the time Shelley composed *Alastor* and Keats put the finishing touch to *Endymion*, both poets had seen their youthful aspirations and expectations overshadowed and thwarted by the experience of illness and moral suffering. The antinomy of the ideal and the real weighed upon them even more harshly than it did on the author of *Tintern Abbey*, and the perennial problem raised by the existence of pain and evil in a world that is supposed to be good and purposeful was therefore imbued with even greater urgency. But although their poetic expressions of it are marked by a more poignant, and, we may add, more ostentatious, form of pathos than were those of Wordsworth, the same problem preoccupied them.

Since the beginning of a close and systematic critical attention to romantic poetry in the mid-twentieth century, it has become apparent that the traditional view of Shelley as a blithe spirit, and little else beside, was in sore need of reappraisal. This view had been conveniently summarized in C. L. Finney's contention that "intentionally as well as instinctively, he fled from the world of human life into a world of ideal abstractions, to which his imagination gave ethereal voice and motion."[1] So far as "instinct," or rather innate sensitiveness, is concerned, a minute study of Shelley's imagery has since then enabled R. H. Fogle to show that "the ordinary critical generalization that Shelley's poetry lacks sensuous force and richness seems definitely to be baseless . . . One may speculate that [this] widespread misconception . . . has arisen partly from the thinness and tenuity of the material with which he works, his clouds, mists, dews, water-scenes, etc.; so that his critics have confused his subject matter with his ability to handle it." The new conception that emerged from Fogle's study is that there was in Shelley some sort of fruitful polarity between "a sensuous delight in forms, colors, and motions and a desire to transcend the realms of sense in search of the One."[2] Nobody would dream of denying Shelley's inclination toward an imageless truth. Yet, we must beware of taking too crude a view of the workings of a poet's mind. That this fruitful polarity was not arrived at without conflict is shown in *Alastor, or the Spirit of Solitude,* a poem which has challenged the sagacity of critics ever since it was printed for the first time. Most students, obediently following Mary Shelley's clue, have searched it for some single-minded *ex cathedra* statement about life and poetry, whereas it is a cathartic poem, in which Shelley embodies the dramatic wrestling of his saner self against the temptation of extreme idealism.

Written at the outset of Shelley's mature years, *Alastor*

[1] C. L. Finney, *The Evolution of Keats's Poetry* (Cambridge, Mass., 1936), I, 154.
[2] R. H. Fogle, *The Imagery of Keats and Shelley* (Chapel Hill, 1949), pp. 33, 36, and 55.

derives from two experiences which had been his in the year 1815. Mary Shelley tells us that in the spring an "eminent" physician had "pronounced that he was rapidly dying of a consumption." This, we may surmise, must have led him to meditate with a new sense of urgency upon the problem of death, on which he had expatiated in *Queen Mab* with such youthful assertiveness. His recovery provided a new climax, though in an opposite direction. His tour along the southern coast of Devonshire, his stay on the outskirts of Windsor Forest, his visit to the sources of the Thames, renewed his enjoyment of natural scenery and, we may presume, of life itself. The poem which ensued, *Alastor,* is an allegory in which Shelley tried to weigh the conflicting claims of dream and reality, of death and life, of spirit and matter; to push the idealistic attitude to the limit of its own logic; to work out the opposite aspirations of his own mind—and thus to settle the issue and lay the foundations of his own later attitude toward the great themes that ever swayed his thought and his poetry.

It has been argued that the Poet in *Alastor* is an impersonation of Wordsworth.[3] Though this is taking things too far, it seems that Shelley, while writing *Alastor,* was under the influence of the elder poet, whose *The Excursion* he had just been reading.[4] Not only does the poem contain unmistakable verbal echoes, which have often been mentioned, but in the invocation to the "Mother of this unfathomable world," in the youth's wanderings previous to his vision, and in some of his

[3] See P. Mueschke and E. L. Griggs, "Wordsworth as the Prototype of the Poet in Shelley's *Alastor,*" *PMLA,* XLIX (1934), 229–245, and the reply by M. Kessel, "The Poet in Shelley's *Alastor,*" *PMLA,* LI (1936), 302–310. Many other attempts have been made to identify Shelley's Poet. An interesting case was lately built up in favor of Coleridge by Joseph Raben, "Coleridge as the Prototype of the Poet in Shelley's *Alastor,*" *Review of English Studies,* n.s. XVII (1966), 278–292.
[4] L. H. Allen, "Plagiarism, Sources and Influences in Shelley's *Alastor,*" *Modern Language Review,* XVIII (1923), 133–151.

later experiences, we find a feeling akin to Wordsworth's piety toward the Spirit of Nature and its outward manifestations. In January 1812, Southey had shrewdly observed that Shelley was "not an Atheist but a Pantheist." [5] Though the poet of *The Thorn* might have looked down with disapproving brow upon Shelley's somewhat Childe-Haroldish taste for apocalyptic scenery, "secret caves," "awful ruins," and "bitumen lakes," the description of the hero's *Lehrjahre* in *Alastor* tackles nature in the right Wordsworthian spirit, as a "prime teacher" speaking to the inner sense with "inarticulate language."

Nevertheless, to judge by some of the companion pieces to *Alastor* in the volume of 1816, Shelley's attitude to nature was as much perplexed as was Wordsworth's in his early years, and much more confused. While the sonnet *To Wordsworth* bewails the elder poet's desertion of the cause of "truth and liberty" on social grounds which need not concern us here, the poem "Oh! there are spirits of the air" does grapple, however clumsily, with fundamentals. Whether it was, as stated by Mary Shelley, "addressed in idea to Coleridge," or, as some prefer to think, to Shelley's own spirit, it delineates a cluster of characteristic attitudes which can be identified, although the writer by no means succeeds in clarifying their mutual relationships.

The poem begins with a confident assertion of spiritual modes of being:

> Oh! there are spirits of the air,
>   And genii of the evening breeze,
>   And gentle ghosts, with eyes as fair
>   As star-beams among twilight trees.

The intuition of spiritual existence, which is of course the focal experience of romanticism, is gained through solitary communion with natural objects:

---

[5] *The Complete Works of Percy Bysshe Shelley*, ed. R. Ingpen and W. E. Peck (London. 1965), VIII, 232.

> Such lovely ministers to meet
> Oft hast thou turned from men thy lonely feet.
>
> With mountain winds, and babbling springs,
>   And moonlight seas, that are the voice
> Of these inexplicable things,
>   Thou didst hold commune, and rejoice
> When they did answer thee.

The confusion appears in the unresolved paradox that the beings and shapes of the sensuous world ("natural scenes or human smiles"), although they are "the voice" of the spiritual universe, are nevertheless described as inconstant, false, faithless, and ultimately contemptuous of the poet's love:

> but they
> Cast, like a worthless boon, thy love away.

It is rather awkward that the poet's failure, thus attributed to nature's betrayal, should later be ascribed to the shallowness of his own mind:

> Ah! wherefore didst thou build thine hope
>   On the false earth's inconstancy?
> Did thine own mind afford no scope
>   Of love, or moving thoughts to thee,
> That natural scenes or human smiles
> Could steal the power to wind thee in their wiles?

This is of course more consonant with Coleridge's interpretation of his own loss in *Dejection*. But the point is that Shelley expresses misgivings about the possibility of obtaining an assured insight into the spiritual world through the external forms of nature.

In the third stanza, therefore, he turns to the direct mystical approach. The phrasing shows that the "starry eyes" in which his poet has sought "beams" of revelation are identical with the "eyes" as fair as "star-beams" attributed to the "lovely ministers" of the first stanza. The poet is thus hankering after an unmediated contact with spiritual being, with the spirits, the genii, the gentle ghosts. And here we come upon a second unresolved paradox in this rather muddled poem, namely, the statement that this mystical union, which is the poet's highest endeavor, is also outside the reach of man:

> And thou hast sought in starry eyes
> Beams *that were never meant for thee* (italics mine).

This is a minor lyric. Yet, it deals with essentials. The impression of puzzlement and despair it conveys results from the realization that of the two ways apparently open to the poet in his search for the ideal, the indirect (or Wordsworthian) one is treacherous, while the direct (or mystical) one is impracticable for mortal man.

The same pathetic dilemma and the same time scheme control the inner design of the Poet's grim progress in *Alastor*. The first two sections of this poem (ll. 1–49) are spoken by Shelley in his own name; sections three to five (ll. 50–128) describe the early stages of his hero's career. The parts are parallel and even repetitive. Taken as a whole, this long introduction closely corresponds to the second stanza of the lyric. Shelley seeks to probe nature's "deep mysteries" (l. 23), to unveil her "inmost sanctuary" (l. 38) in the same way that his Poet pursues "Nature's most secret steps" (l. 81) in the hope of discovering "the thrilling secrets of the birth of time" (l. 128). For this revelation they both rely on the intermission of natural objects. And when Nature recompenses their piety, they both live "in joy and exultation" (l. 144), like the nameless character in the shorter poem, who "rejoices" in his communion with wind, spring, and sea.

This "Wordsworthian" approach recurs at a later stage in *Alastor*, under the form of a temptation. As the Poet looks at the yellow flowers on the banks of the river, he is distracted for a while from his inhuman quest for the immediate vision by a nostalgia for his former mood of loving familiarity with the beauteous forms of nature:

> The Poet longed
> To deck with their bright hues his withered hair,
> But on his heart its solitude returned,
> And he forebore.
>
> (ll. 412-415)

The same pattern of temptation and rejection is repeated in a later vision:

> A Spirit seemed
> To stand beside him—clothed in no bright robes
> Of shadowy silver or enshrining light,
> Borrowed from aught the visible world affords
> Of grace, or majesty, or mystery;—
> But, undulating woods, and silent well,
> And leaping rivulet, and evening gloom
> Now deepening the dark shades, for speech assuming,
> Held commune with him, as if he and it
> Were all that was, —only . . . when his regard
> Was raised by intense pensiveness, . . . two eyes,
> Two starry eyes, hung in the gloom of thought,
> And seemed with their serene and azure smiles
> To beckon him.
>
> (ll. 479-492)

This vision too is redolent of Wordsworth insofar as mystic communion is gained through the beauteous, though, after all, concrete and, in a way, commonplace forms of nature. Furthermore, there are definite verbal connections with the earlier poem: there too the poet "held commune" with natural objects which were "the voice" of the spirit of nature; and the image of the "starry eyes" is bound to recall two of its most significant lines:

> And thou hast sought in starry eyes
> Beams that were never meant for thine.

This short episode reflects the whole scheme of the poem: the Poet receives intimations of the spiritual world through the visible shapes of nature; but there is an inner urge that prompts him to seek more mystical ecstasies.

The reason for this reorientation is to be found in the introductory sections which, while they illustrate the Wordsworthian approach, contain revealing undertones of imperfection and dissatisfaction. Shelley merely *hopes* "to still these obstinate questionings" (l. 26); Nature has "ne'er yet . . . unveiled" her inmost sanctuary (l. 37); the world remains "unfathomable" (l. 18); the dream remains "incommunicable" (l. 39). Such phrases, together with the Poet's indifference to the earthly devotion of the Arab maiden (ll. 129-139), point to a *Sehnsucht* which goes beyond the reach of the senses. We are thrown back upon the familiar dilemma of the romantic poet, whose hankering after the purity of the immutable One keeps uneasy company with his happy sensitiveness to the kaleidoscopic and transient beauty of the external universe. We have seen Coleridge striving to overcome the apparent antinomy of a purely spiritual intuition obtained through sensory perception. Obviously this paradox is puzzling to Shelley as well. But his Poet never attempts to effect the symbolic compromise between the world of spirit and the world of matter. Only at a later stage will Shelley be able to express the abstract idea that it is possible to worship simultaneously both "the Spirit of Beauty" and "every form containing" it—and later still, to transmute this notion into the genuine poetic symbolism of the *Ode to the West Wind* and *To a Skylark*. Meanwhile, the protagonist of *Alastor* must have the thing itself, not the hieroglyph; he must have the white radiance of eternity unrefracted by life's dome of many-colored glass. In this, his kinship is rather with the German romantics, who also were unable to reconcile their perception of the actual and their visionary glimpses of the ideal.[6]

[6] F. Strich, *Deutsche Klassik und Romantik* (Bern, 1949), p. 62: "Der romantische Mensch erbaute sich seine Welt des Traumes, des Wahns, der Dichtung, und diese ging mit der 'gegenständlichen' Welt nicht zusammen. So entstand jene Kluft zwischen Kunst und Leben, der inneren und der äuszeren Welt, an der die Menschen litten, in der so manche versanken. Der unendliche Traum war das romantische Masz, dem keine Wirklichkeit entsprechen wollte."

It is misleading to equate the Poet's spiritual career with that of his author. That *Alastor* is partly autobiographical can legimately be inferred from the inside evidence of the parallels between sections I–II and III–V. But in the main, it is an imaginative artifact built up in order to work out the consequences of a definite attitude toward the existential problem which each romantic poet, at a crucial step in his development, had to face. Shelley's hero is imbued with the same yearning for the mystical experience of spiritual oneness which had been so eloquently delineated in the early poems of Coleridge and Wordsworth. The Lake poets, as we have seen, felt the need to reconcile this idealistic impulse both with Christian doctrine and with factual experience. Shelley's hero, on the contrary, abandons himself entirely and deliberately to his inner *Sehnsucht,* and his story as narrated by Shelley should be viewed as an experiment designed to find out what such single-minded solipsism can lead up to. The character of the Poet is a projection of one side of Shelley's mind: the proclivity to extreme idealism which is so powerful in all romantic writers.

The precocious subtlety and the genuine difficulty of the poem derive from this dual point of view: the author's and the hero's. The Poet embarks hopefully and courageously on a quest which the writer knows to be hopeless, however meritorious and admirable.

But while we must keep this ambiguity in mind, we must also realize that the hero's quest fails because it negates his own inner duality. His conception of self-fulfillment actually involves self-mutilation; his yearning for the absolute is contrary to the essence of his own contingent being. The obvious erotic overtones of the dream that launches him on his fateful voyage testify to this inescapable ambiguity of human nature.

Although the first vision in *Alastor* is an early prototype of a frequently recurring experience in Shelley's poetry, it has a peculiar character which can be defined by the fact that it develops through two stages, one abstract in content and mainly musical in the choice of images, the other more carnal in content, mingling visual with auditory imagery. As the "veilèd maid" whose "fair hands were bare alone" gradually comes to reveal

> Her glowing limbs beneath the sinuous veil
> Of woven wind, her outspread hands now bare,
> (ll. 176–177)

her message also shifts from ideal abstraction to sensual attraction. Whereas at the beginning

> Knowledge and truth and virtue were her theme,
> And lofty hopes of divine liberty,
> Thoughts the most dear to him, and poesy,
> Herself a poet. . . .
> (ll. 158–161)

at the end, she,

> yielding to the irresistible joy,
> With frantic gesture and short breathless cry
> Folded his frame in her dissolving arms.
> (ll. 185–187)

It will be readily perceived that the whole process runs directly counter to the Platonic scheme, which passes from admiration for physical beauty to appreciation of intellectual and ethical beauty, and ends with fulfillment in the mystic contemplation of the transcendent Idea of Beauty. In its rapid shifting from the ideal to the corporeal and thence to frustration, the *Alastor* vision sets a pattern which prefigures the entire course of the Poet's doom. It is as if the willful negation of the world of matter, combined with the body's embarrassing ability to reassert itself at the most unexpected moments, would cancel each other into nothingness.

Together with other elements, the erotic quality of the abortive embrace described in the vision has led a number of critics to treat *Alastor* as a poem about love. And Shelley's biographers have legitimately tried to provide a definite identity for this evanescent lady. But even if Shelley drew some inspiration from his intricate entanglements of the time, the temptation to see in the vision a glorified version of the boy-meets-girl motif, a mere allegory of a man's desire to find the woman of his dream, leads to a considerable measure of over-simplification. It has been argued above, in connection with Coleridge's alleged egotism, that the romantic writers, as writers, were not interested in themselves as individuals, but as representative human beings. Indeed, in discussing Wordsworth's poems, we constantly find that such elements from personal experience as are traceable in his works appeared to him to be valid material not because they were unique and singular but because they were symbolic, pointing to wider meanings. In *Alastor,* the hero is by no means presented in his sole capacity as a lover. As Shelley expressly states in the Preface, "the vision in which he embodies his own imagination unites all of wonderful, or wise, or beautiful, which the *poet,* the *philosopher,* or the *lover* could depicture" (italics mine). In the chronological structure of the vision, the philosopher comes first, with the lover following close upon his heels. But the fusion of the philosopher with the lover constitutes the poet, who combines the former's ethereal sense of ideal perfection with the latter's interest in sensuous shapeliness. This very human duality of Shelley's hero covers the conflicting, yet complementary, aspects of the romantic outlook. As a "philosopher," he is able to frame a conception of the ideal. As a "lover," he cannot exist without human sympathy. As a "philosopher," he is best satisfied with the figments of his imaginative mind, upon which he is liable to confer some higher sort of reality than on the external world. As a "lover," he is in need of the external world, which alone can gratify the emotional aspirations of his soul.

But whereas the Lake poets were ultimately content to find in the world of created matter a product and an emblem of the divine presence, to see a heaven in a wild flower, and so to

The Hopeless Quest

reconcile idealism and realism in a satisfactory synthesis, Shelley was to remain at all times fascinated by the attractive idea that the sensory world is a world of flimsy fleeting shadows, and it is to this temptation that his hero eventually succumbs—though Shelley himself did not. In fact, *Alastor* is symptomatic of Shelley's resistance to the allurements of extreme idealism. It is a demonstration *a contrario*, where the hero is made to follow the logic of idealism to the bitter end. His self-centeredness—mentioned in the Preface and illustrated in the Arab maiden episode—causes him to lose his psychological balance: he falls in love with the image of the ideal which has arisen in his own mind, and so allows his sensitiveness to life and the outside world to wither away. For the infinite cannot be enclosed in a finite form, the ideal cannot become an object for the senses and yet remain itself. It is highly significant that, already in the Poet's dream, "dissolution" should precede, and so prevent, consummation. His frustration is, therefore, complete: his eyes cannot catch beams that were never meant for them; on the other hand, compared with the absolute beauty of his dream, the sensuous beauty of the external universe is a painted veil, a phantom, and he feels bound to reject such beams as were truly meant for him.

Alastor, then, appears to be a dramatic comment on the central problem of romanticism. The romantics' basic intuition of spiritual being, fully described from the first in *The Eolian Harp* and in *Tintern Abbey*, was throwing into new perspective the old question of the relationship between matter and spirit. In an age of budding science, swayed by the aftermath of Enlightenment skepticism, the romantics were trying to rekindle the dying embers of spiritualism and to vindicate a view of life based on faith and imagination rather than on proof and reason. The trouble with faith is that it gives only a kind of certainty which is not communicable by argument. Its object remains beyond the grasp of scientific method or rational demonstration. To the faithful, faith is intensely objective: it does not leave room for doubt; it assures the believer of the actual existence of its object. To the skeptic, faith is intensely subjective; it is grounded in personal intuition, in feeling, in an emotional attitude to life and the universe; it is not to be accounted for in terms of scientific experiment or ratiocinative thought. The notorious philosophical instability of Coleridge, Wordsworth's perplexity, Keats's varying moods and anguished questionings ("Do I wake or sleep?"), as well as Shelley's confused notions about the bizarre kind of "atheism" he professed as a youth—all this tends to show that the romantics were anxious to enshrine their original intuition in some sort of philosophical system. They could not define its objectivity in terms of the petrified religious thinking of the traditional churches. On the other hand, though they were not unaware of the subjective element in it, they could hardly bring themselves to reduce it to a form of "pathetic fallacy."

One way out, of course, could conceivably be found in the assertion that subjectivity is the ultimate reality. Indeed, throughout the pattern of early romantic thought, there runs a thread of subjective idealism which is logically consistent with the romantic exaltation of man and with the romantic yearning for the absolute. In a Fenwick note to *Intimations of Immortality*, Wordsworth claims he was able to recall ecstatic experiences of his boyhood, when, he says, "I was often unable to think of external things as having external existence, and I communed with all that I saw as something not apart from, but inherent in, my own immaterial nature."[7] And he gives us a glimpse of the connection between this "abyss of idealism," as he called it, and the use of dream and *rêverie* in romantic poetry, in the following passage from *The Prelude* (1805):

[7] *Poetical Works of William Wordsworth*, ed. E. de Sélincourt and Helen Darbishire (Oxford, 1962), IV, 463.

The Hopeless Quest

> Oft in those moments such a holy calm
> Did overspread my soul, that I forgot
> That I had bodily eyes, and what I saw
> Appeared like something in myself, a dream,
> A prospect in my mind.
>
> (Bk. II, ll. 367-371)

In this comparison, of course, Wordsworth carefully maintains the distinction between subjective impression and reality, between *percipiens* and *perceptum*. He is simply concerned with transcribing faithfully some fleeting reminiscences from his childhood. The Berkeleyan mood is not systematized into concept. In a quite different psychological setting, Coleridge was much more assertive when he wrote, in *Religious Musings*:

> Believe thou, O my soul,
> Life is a vision shadowy of Truth;
> And vice and anguish, and the wormy grave,
> Shapes of a dream!
>
> (ll. 395-398)

adding in a footnote that "this paragraph is intelligible to those, who, like the Author, believe and feel the sublime system of Berkeley."

It should be remembered that Shelley, prompted by Southey, had studied the philosophy of Berkeley in 1812 and 1813. Its influence made itself felt in two essays written in the year of *Alastor*: *On Life* and *Speculations on Metaphysics*, where the ingredients of the immaterialistic trend in English romanticism are conveniently brought together. One does not want to decide whether Shelley had understood Berkeley rightly. The denial of matter on philosophical grounds could not but appeal to people like the young Coleridge and the young Shelley, who found there a welcome means of explaining away the misery inflicted upon them by the occurrences of their lives, and of accounting for the compelling vividness of their poetic and mystical intuitions. In the essay *On Life*, Shelley confesses, in somewhat unconventional English, "that

I am one of those who am unable to refuse my assent to the conclusions of those philosophers who assert that nothing exists but as it is perceived." And after stating that "the solid universe of external things is 'such stuff as dreams are made of,'" Shelley goes on to claim that "the difference is merely nominal between those two classes of thought, which are vulgarly distinguished by the name of ideas and of external objects." [8] By thus equating the internal and the external, the subjective and the objective, the ideal and the sensuous, Shelley was obviously trying to infuse new life into the notions of soul, poetry, and imagination. The "solid universe of external things" is endowed with existence only in proportion as it is perceived; "external objects" are "a class of thought," productions of the mind; and those mental images that have no reference to material objects are therefore as true, as important, as worthy of consideration as those that have—indeed, more so. The belief that nothing exists outside the human mind is one of the temptations to which romanticism is permanently exposed by the very nature of its *Sehnsucht*, and as late as 1818 Shelley was to write in *Julian and Maddalo*:

> Where is the love, beauty and truth we seek,
> But in our mind?
>
> (ll. 174-175)

This intellectual background helps to clarify the significance of the Poet's quest. His dream, we recall, has offered him an immediate vision of spirit, an intimation of oneness not unlike Wordsworth's "blessed mood" or the experience which Coleridge expressed in terms of the Eolian metaphor. But whereas Coleridge felt bound to repress a pantheistic bent which seemed to him unholy, and whereas Wordsworth, at the end of *Tintern Abbey*, fell back upon the certainties of experience, leaving all mystical conjectures aside, Shelley's Poet yields wholly to "the strong impulse" that "hung upon his life" (ll. 415-418). In so doing, he makes the wrong

---

[8] *The Complete Works of Shelley*, VI, 194 and 195.

The Hopeless Quest

choice between two alternatives which Coleridge was shortly to define in his essay *On Poesy or Art*:

Of all we see, hear, feel and touch the substance is and must be in ourselves; and therefore there is no alternative in reason between the dreary (and thank heaven! almost impossible) belief that everything around us is but a phantom, or that the life which is in us is in them likewise.[9]

It is just to that "dreary belief" that Shelley's Poet is now committed. After the fellowship with essence he so nearly enjoyed in his dream, the brazen world of men and things is to him but an "empty scene" on which his wan eyes gaze "vacantly" (l. 202). But between the writer and his hero there is a revealing discrepancy which points to the divided mood of Shelley at the time of writing, at the same time that it provides a key to the structure of the poem. In line after magnificent line filled with the magic of his awareness of beauty, Shelley describes the ever-shifting sights of nature—yet his hero remains blind to this dazzling display of colors and shapes. Such apparent lack of coherence confirms our belief that we should think twice before identifying Shelley with his Poet. The latter embodies only one facet of his creator's mind—an aspect on which the poem itself passes judgment. And the narrative is an imaginative experiment, in which Shelley explores the implications of the rejection of the world involved in the idealistic impulse.

The dream vision has prompted the Poet to make his choice between the two ways—the mediate and the immediate—adumbrated in "Oh! there are spirits of the air." The purpose of his quest is to find out whether the vision gives "authentic tidings of an invisible world," as Wordsworth said, whether it is "shadowy of truth," whether it has any sort of existence "beyond the realms of dream" (l. 206)—or whether (to use again the formulas of Shelley's elders) it is "but a vain belief," a concoction of "idle flitting phantasies."

[9] S. T. Coleridge, *Biographia Literaria*, ed. J. Shawcross (Oxford, 1907), II, 259.

From the Preface and from the poem itself, it appears that Shelley was perfectly conscious of the illusory character of his hero's endeavor. As he explains in the first part of the Preface, the Poet's vision is a product of his own mind: "He images to himself the Being whom he loves"; in this dream image, "he embodies his own imaginations." The "Power" which awakens him to "too exquisite a perception of its influences" is "the spirit of sweet *human* love" (l. 203; italics mine). At several points in the poem, the subjective inwardness of the vision is emphasized: it is described as "hung in the gloom of thought" (l. 492), as "the light that shone within his soul" (l. 512).

T. J. Spencer has summed up the usual interpretation of the Poet's quest in saying that he "searches for the prototype of his vision throughout the world, finally seeking union with her in death."[10] This conception, however, does not seem to be entirely consonant with the indications in the poem itself. What the Poet is looking for throughout the world is not a prototype of his vision; from the very beginning he senses that the world of external forms cannot contain the ideal he is pursuing. His quest is a quest for death, because he feels that death alone can effect the kind of communion which is the object of his *Sehnsucht*. This is clearly intimated by the fact that Sleep and Death become associated in his mind immediately after the dream vision has dissolved:

> Does the dark gate of death
> Conduct to thy mysterious paradise,
> O Sleep? Does the bright arch of rainbow clouds,
> And pendent mountains seen in the calm lake,
> Lead only to a black and watery depth,
> While death's blue vault, with loathliest vapours hung,
> Where every shade which the foul grave exhales
> Hides its dead eye from the detested day,
> Conducts, O Sleep, to thy delightful realms?
>
> (ll. 211–219)

---

[10] T. J. Spencer, "Shelley's 'Alastor' and Romantic Drama," *Transactions of the Wisconsin Academy of Sciences, Arts and Letters,* XLVIII (1959), 233–237.

These anguished questionings cannot fail to remind one of Hölderlin's short poem about "unser Retter, der Tod":

> Sanft kommt er,
> Leis' im Gewölke des Schlafs,
> Aber er bleibt fürchterlich und wir sehn nur
> Nieder ins Grab, ob er gleich uns zur Vollendung
> Führt aus Hüllen der Nacht hinüber
> In der Erkenntnisse Land.[11]

The exaltation of death is an almost necessary corollary of romantic spiritualism. After all, death is the only experiential way of ascertaining whether there is any reality beyond the limited world that the senses can encompass. In a well-known letter to Bailey, Keats advocates a "Life of Sensations" because it is "a Shadow of reality to come"; and he adds, as "another favorite Speculation" of his, "that we shall enjoy ourselves here after by having what we called happiness on Earth repeated in a finer tone." That this speculation is not irrelevant to our consideration of *Alastor* appears from the concrete example provided by Keats:

Have you never by being surprised with an old Melody—in a delicious place—by a delicious voice, felt over again your very speculations and surmises at the time it first operated on your soul—do you not remember forming to yourself the singer's face more beautiful that [*for* than] it was possible and yet with the elevation of the Moment you did not think so—even then you were mounted on the Wings of Imagination so high—*that the Prototype must be here after*—that delicious face you will see.[12]

And Keats was merely formulating a romantic commonplace when he wrote, in the sonnet beginning "Why did I laugh to-night?":

> Verse, Fame, and Beauty are intense indeed,
> But Death intenser—Death is Life's high meed.

[11] *Der Tod* (1804).
[12] *The Letters of John Keats*, ed. H. E. Rollins (Cambridge, Eng., 1959), I, 185 (italics mine).

Shelley too, in *Queen Mab*, had indulged in similar optimistic "speculations" about death, which he had confidently described as

> a gate of dreariness and gloom,
> That leads to azure isles and beaming skies
> And happy regions of eternal hopes.
> (IX, ll. 161–163)

Such a death-wish follows logically from the more extreme forms of idealism. Indeed, it figures so prominently in German romanticism that death has been called "der romantische Augenblick an sich." [13] And although it is far less common in the work of the English romantics, the motif is to be found in one of the best-known passages of *Adonais*:

> The One remains, the many change and pass;
> Heaven's light forever shines, Earth's shadows fly;
> Life, like a dome of many-coloured glass,
> Stains the white radiance of Eternity,
> Until Death tramples it to fragments.—Die,
> If thou wouldst be with that which thou dost seek!
> (ll. 460–465)

The last sentence is an accurate description of the *Alastor* situation, and testifies to Shelley's lasting preoccupation with the death-wish. But *Adonais* was composed on the occasion of Keats's death, and Shelley was almost bound to indulge in this sort of idealization. When, however, the abstract, philosophical death-wish becomes dramatized and internalized as it does in *Alastor*, the awesome paradox of death comes to the fore. The writer realizes that death combines the highest expectation with the most frightening uncertainty, and the thought of death becomes loaded with doubt and anguish.

This is the emotional state of Shelley's Poet as he proceeds, with increasing misgivings, toward an experiment, the outcome of which is unpredictable. Yielding to his "restless im-

---

[13] F. Strich, *Deutsche Klassik und Romantik*, p. 123.

The Hopeless Quest 155

pulse" to meet "lone Death" (ll. 304–305), he is assailed by growing doubts which cast their murky shadow on his expectancy.

In *Alastor,* as in *Tintern Abbey,* doubt is the fundamental and pathetic uncertainty of those who are suddenly struck by the dismaying thought that their intuition of the absolute may be illusory, that their fondest hopes may be mere chimeras. It accounts for the ambiguous mood of the Poet, a mood which is expressed in verbal paradoxes curiously reminiscent of metaphysical conceit:

> This *doubt* with sudden tide flowed on his heart,
> The insatiable *hope* which it awakened, stung
> His brain even like *despair.*
> (ll. 220–222; italics mine)

Or again:

> A *gloomy smile*
> Of *desperate hope* wrinkled his quivering lips.
> (ll. 289–290; italics mine)

Doubt corrodes the very foundation of his ultimate endeavor. It makes him painfully diffident about his sacrifice of the happiness he could have enjoyed in the contemplation of nature and in the sharing of human sympathy. It even undermines his eager prospects to find in death the way back to his vision:

> For sleep, he knew, kept most relentlessly
> Its precious charge, and silent death exposed,
> Faithless perhaps as sleep, as shadowy lure
> With doubtful smile mocking its own strange charms.
> (ll. 292–295)

Perhaps the most puzzling thing about *Alastor* is that its final part brings no solution to this pathetic mixture of hope and doubt. The description of the Poet's death, however rich in pictural details, contains no indication whatever about the fate of his soul. This, on the part of Shelley, is both odd and significant. Seldom did he show so much respect for the silent mystery of the grave. We cannot help remembering the corresponding passage of *Adonais*, where he hails the return of the poet's spirit:

> to the burning fountain whence it came,
> A portion of the Eternal.
>
> (ll. 339-340)

In *Alastor*, what the Poet finds at the end of his pilgrimage is not eternal life. He is not absorbed into the oneness of the cosmic spirit. He fades away into nothingness:

> when heaven remained
> Utterly black, the murky shades involved
> An image, *silent, cold, and motionless*
> As their own voiceless earth and vacant air.
> Even as a vapor fed with golden beams
> That ministered on sunlight, ere the west
> Eclipses it, was now that wondrous frame—
> *No sense, no motion, no divinity*—
> A fragile lute, on whose harmonious strings
> The breath of heaven did wander—a bright stream
> Once fed with many-voicèd waves—*a dream
> Of youth, which night and time have quenched forever—
> Still, dark, and dry, and unremembered now.*
>
> (ll. 659-672; italics mine)

The ending of *Alastor, or the Spirit of Solitude* is so frustrating to those who share the usual preconceptions about the starry-eyed simplicity of Shelley's idealism, that a number of critics have chosen to ignore it and to view the work as an unconditional encomium of the Poet's attitude. This type of interpretation involves a stark contradiction between the poem on the one hand, the title and the Preface on the other. O. W. Campbell finds it difficult to understand how Shelley can "condemn" his hero in the Preface, and yet "glorify" him in the poem.[14] N. I. White pretends that "no one who had not

[14] O. W. Campbell, *Shelley and the Unromantics* (London, 1924), p. 188.

The Hopeless Quest

read the Preface would suppose that the author intended the poem as a criticism" of its hero.[15] Carlos Baker suggests that, in adopting the title proposed by Peacock, Shelley did not notice that it "threw the emphasis away from his primary theme," which he rather vaguely describes as "the conflict in a sensitive individual between allegiance to a kind of materialism and allegiance to a kind of idealism." [16] It would seem, on the contrary, that the end of *Alastor* clarifies the poem's relation to its title and to the Preface, at the same time that it brings into relief its true theme, which is the idea that if the spiritual *Sehnsucht* and the visionary insight are allowed to develop into extreme idealism, the poet becomes a prey to solipsism, solitude, and sterility. This point has been cogently argued by H. L. Hoffman,[17] although his description of the Spirit of Solitude does not make it sufficiently clear that Shelley's purpose is not so much to apply ethical criteria as to explore and define the tragic limitations of human nature.

The crux of the matter and the key to a right understanding of the poem are to be found in the second paragraph of the Preface:

The Poet's self-centered seclusion was avenged by the furies of an irresistible passion pursuing him to speedy ruin. But that Power which strikes the luminaries of the world with sudden darkness and extinction by awakening them to too exquisite a perception of its influences, dooms to a slow and poisonous decay those meaner spirits that dare to abjure its dominion. Their destiny is more abject and inglorious as their delinquency is more contemptible and pernicious.

[15] N. I. White, *Portrait of Shelley* (New York, 1945), p. 192.
[16] C. Baker, *Shelley's Major Poetry: The Fabric of a Vision* (Princeton, 1948), p. 46. Other critics for whom the poem is marred by a fundamental inconsistency include R. D. Havens, "Shelley's *Alastor*," *PMLA*, XLV (1930), 1098–1115, and F. L. Jones, "The Inconsistency of Shelley's *Alastor*," *Journal of English Literary History*, XIII (1946), 291–298. For a different view, see E. K. Gibson, "Alastor, A Re-interpretation," *PMLA*, LXII (1947), 1022–1045.
[17] H. L. Hoffman, *An Odyssey of the Soul: Shelley's Alastor* (New York, 1933).

If some sort of *moral* indictment is here pronounced, it does not apply to the Poet, but to those "meaner spirits" whose self-centeredness is willful and egoistic, unredeemed by faith, those who—in Shelley's own words—are "deluded by no generous error, instigated by no sacred thirst of doubtful knowledge, duped by no illustrious superstition." "These," he adds, "and such as they, have their appointed curse." Those "unforeseeing multitudes," however, appear only in the Preface, and the particular curse motif with which they are associated is extraneous to the poem itself. It is an offspring of Shelley's taste for moralizing in and out of season, and we may well be thankful that it is confined to the Preface.

What, then, according to the Preface, is Shelley's view of the Poet's character and of his fate? His character is emphatically described as ambiguous: he is "generous" and attracted by things "illustrious"; he is animated by a "sacred thirst" for "knowledge"; yet, he lives in "error" and "superstition," and such knowledge as he hopes to attain is "doubtful." Correspondingly, though he is one of the "luminaries of the world," he is struck with "darkness and extinction." It should be obvious that Shelley hardly means to condemn his hero. The poem is rather a lament on the fate to which he is doomed because of the very sublimity of his mind. It thus receives the character of a warning. The Poet does not belong among the "selfish," the "blind," and the "torpid" who incur Shelley's scorn. He is not entirely responsible, either for his own "errors"—he is "duped" and "deluded"—or for the fate which befalls him. His guilt is not a sin. It is a tragic hubris, similar to that of the heroes of Greek drama. It is a violation of the natural order of things, to which the culprit is unwittingly induced.

The Poet's reluctance to remain satisfied with the indirect approach, his "restless impulse" to achieve direct contact with the absolute, is first made apparent in the Arab maiden episode (ll. 129-139). There is an explicit connection between his neglect of the girl's selfless devotion and the occurrence of the dream vision:

> The spirit of sweet human love has sent
> A vision to the sleep of him who spurned
> Her choicest gifts.
>
> (ll. 203–205)

It has been claimed that these lines "do not imply an act of retribution but an act of grace." [18] It seems to me, however, that the concepts of grace and retribution are equally irrelevant—or equally suitable. Because it is a perception of the absolute, the Poet's vision, while it lasts, does gratify his "strong impulse"; because it is "a fleeting shade" (l. 206), unobtainable in the actual conditions of human life, it deludes him into his hopeless quest. The vision can thus be construed both as a punishment and as a reward, which suggests that it is essentially non-ethical: it illustrates the tragic paradox of the extreme idealist, whose noble refusal of the compromises inherent in terrestrial existence can only drive him to annihilation. Another example of this ambiguous logic is the fact that the "furies" which appear in the title as "the spirit of solitude" are the instruments of a higher "Power" which both brings temptation and metes out punishment. By allowing himself, through the purity of his character and the sublimity of his aspiration, to be awakened to "too exquisite a perception" of the Supreme Power and its influences (and the operative word is of course "too"), the Poet cuts himself off from the proper nourishment of the *human* soul, and so paves the way for his own destruction.

Like *The Eolian Harp* and *Tintern Abbey*, *Alastor* is a dialectical poem, the purpose of which is exploration rather than statement. Of course, Shelley's vantage point was different from that of his predecessors because of the very fact that they were part of his background. Although each of the romantic poets had to have the romantic dilemma reenacted in his own mind, Keats's and Shelley's perception of the implied alternatives was necessarily sharpened by the experience and

---

[18] A. M. D. Hughes, " 'Alastor, or the Spirit of Solitude,' " *Modern Language Review*, XLIII (1948), 465–470.

the achievement of their elders. Whereas the Lake poets were innovators, the younger writers were already working within a tradition. One aspect of this subtle modulation is that Shelley was probably more susceptible to the attraction of philosophical monism than his predecessors. Apart from personal idiosyncrasies, the reason for this may be that the mechanistic and dualistic tradition had already been shattered by Wordsworth and Coleridge, while Shelley's bent toward idealism was not held back by any adherence to Christian dogma. Being more acutely subjected to the idealistic temptation, Shelley was even more vitally affected by the romantic dilemma than Coleridge and Wordsworth could have been, and *Alastor* must be considered a cathartic attempt to work out his own perplexity by exploring imaginatively the dark passages to which a poet is driven when he rejects the indirect perception of the infinite through the finite, and so commits himself to extreme idealism. That its hero should be led to doubt, despair, and destruction shows that the poem is to be considered primarily an implicit repudiation of this extreme idealism, similar to the explicit repudiation of pantheism in *The Eolian Harp*. Other poems of the same period make it clear that, in spite of his intense concern with the ideal, Shelley himself, unlike his Poet, was convinced that

> This world is the nurse of all we know,
> This world is the mother of all we feel.[19]

Alastor demonstrates *a contrario* that the business of the poet is not to deny the realities of matter and of life, of nature and of human nature, but rather—as Shelley was to put it much later in his *Defence of Poetry*—to transmute "every form moving within the radiance of its presence . . . to an incarnation of the spirit which it breathes." The function of poetry is syncretic. It consists in informing the chaos of sensuous life with the harmony of the ideal; conversely, it consists in infusing the warm immediacy of sensuous experience into the icy

[19] *On Death*.

purity of the spiritual insight. To quote again from the *Defence*, the task of the poet is not to overstep the boundaries of human nature, but to clarify "the interpenetration of a diviner nature through our own." [20]

This definition of the purpose of poetry helps us understand how Shelley at last came to terms with the dilemmas and the ambiguities of *Alastor*. It is true that echoes of his Poet's ill-advised attitudes can be caught in several of his later works. But for the central concept which embodies the essential balance and sanity of his outlook, we must turn to Asia's exclamation in *Prometheus Unbound*:

> How glorious art thou, Earth! And if thou be
> The shadow of some spirit lovelier still,
> Though evil stain its work, and it should be
> Like its creation, weak yet beautiful,
> I could fall down and worship that and thee.
> Even now my heart adoreth.
> (Act II, scene 3, lines 12–17)

Here indeed, the right distinction is maintained between the two planes of being and apprehension: the plane of fact and that of the ideal, the plane of evidence and that of hope, the plane of knowledge and that of faith. The glory of life and nature, even though it may be limited and tainted with evil, is a matter of certainty. The if-clause, reminiscent of so many similar turns of speech in the poetry of Wordsworth and Coleridge, signals that any inference about the absolute can only be a hypothesis, that is, a matter of faith, because the absolute, as Shelley was to write in *The Sensitive Plant*,

> Exceeds our organs, which endure
> No light, being themselves obscure.
> (ll. 136–137)

Shelley, of course, was not torn, as was Coleridge in *The Eolian Harp*, between the intuition of spiritual oneness and some loyalty to Christian dogma. His predicament was much

[20] *The Complete Works of Shelley*, VII, 136–137.

nearer that of Wordsworth in *Tintern Abbey*: the same "blessed mood," the same fear lest it be but a "vain belief," the same aching need to ascertain the objective validity of the mystic intuition. Unlike *Tintern Abbey*, however, *Alastor* is in a way a negative poem: it does not offer a solution to the ontological problem from which it arises. We might rather say that it clears the ground by thrusting aside an impracticable and deceptive solution. Though Shelley's skepticism [21] is perhaps of a more intellectual nature than Wordsworth's perplexity, it has the same emotional intensity. And the bare statement of man's tragic condition contained in *Alastor* was a necessary step toward acceptance and reconciliation.

[21] C. E. Pulos, *The Deep Truth: A Study of Shelley's Scepticism* (Lincoln, 1954).

8 The Unextinguished Hearth: SHELLEY'S ODE TO THE WEST WIND

Asia's cautiousness in *Prometheus Unbound* reflects Shelley's own considered attitude to the primary—and unanswerable—problem of romanticism. In *Mont Blanc* the poet had already given shape to his perplexity in ways reminiscent of the old man's manner of speech in *The Thorn*—

> Some *say* that gleams of a remoter world
> Visit the soul in sleep . . .
>
> (ll. 49–50)

—and of the ambivalent interpretation of ecstasy in Coleridge's *Eolian Harp* and in Wordsworth's *Tintern Abbey*:

> Has some unknown omnipotence unfurled
> The veil of life and death? *or* do I lie
> In dream . . . ?
>
> (ll. 53–55; italics mine)

These lines also anticipate the central alternative in Keats's *Ode to a Nightingale*: "Was it a vision, or a waking dream? / . . . do I wake or sleep?" The poet refrains from deciding whether the mystical mood has indeed revealed the invisible world to him, or whether his intuition of supreme power is but a product of his mind:

> *I seem* as in a trance sublime and strange
> To muse on my own separate fantasy,
> My own, my human mind . . .
>
> (ll. 35–37; italics mine)

It might even be argued that the principle of uncertainty works more comprehensively for Shelley than for the Lake poets: in the poetry of Wordsworth and Coleridge, the doubt is usually cast upon the more exalted, the objective, interpretation of ecstasy; in the lines just quoted, it is the more modest, the subjective, interpretation which is presented as a mere seeming, a hypothesis, an appearance which, for all the poet knows, may be deceptive. Throughout *Mont Blanc*, the obvious tone of assertiveness, which results from what we might call the quantitative predominance of the descriptive element, is subtly counteracted by suggestions of skepticism leading up to the alternative of the last lines, which, as in the *Ode to a Nightingale*, take the form of a question:

> The secret Strength of things
> Which governs thought, and to the infinite dome
> Of Heaven is as a law, inhabits thee!
> And what were thou, and earth, and stars, and sea,
> If to the human mind's imaginings
> Silence and solitude were vacancy?
>
> (ll. 139–144)

This dialectical pattern of mutually challenging assumptions and unresolved contradictions is by no means exceptional in Shelley's poems of this period. As Newell F. Ford pointed out, the *Hymn to Intellectual Beauty* also centers on an awareness of alternatives which seem to exclude each other: "Beauty may be . . . part of the vast unknowable, casting its 'awful shadow' as well as its radiance upon us. Or it may be a no-thing, not an Essence resident in the cosmos, but a wishful projection of the human mind."[1] The only ex-

---

[1] Newell F. Ford, "Paradox and Irony in Shelley's Poetry," *Studies in Philology*, LVII (1960), 649–662. As I have repeatedly tried to

periential way to reach certainty is death—from whose bourne, unfortunately, no traveler returns to convey reliable information. *Alastor* was the imaginative embodiment of this search and of this failure. Like the Lake poets, then, Shelley was thrown back on the original *Angst*—the sense of meaninglessness, injustice, and dereliction—still coupled with the stubborn impulse to overcome it, that is, to find beauty and value in a world of evil and sorrow, to find lastingness in a world of transience. But whereas Coleridge and Wordsworth sought to restore meaning to experience through a return to the traditional faith—revitalized, it is true, by their very failure to achieve mystic union with transcendence—Shelley refused all supernatural, suprarational guidance, and constantly endeavored to find the significance of life in life itself.

The realization—not abstract and intellectual but felt in the blood—of such a dilemma, and the compulsion to overcome it, usually occur in times of stress, when a man feels burdened by life beyond his resilience. Such was the situation

---

emphasize, this sense of ambiguity is central to romantic thought and poetry, both of which spring from the perplexing urge to decide whether the intuition of oneness, or of beauty, or of transcendental existence, is truly cognitive or a mere delusion. Of the poetic vision, Shelley wrote, in the *Defence of Poetry:* "And whether it spreads its own figured curtain, or withdraws life's dark veil from before the scene of things, it equally creates for us a being within our being" (*The Complete Works of Percy Bysshe Shelley*, ed. R. Ingpen and W. E. Peck [London, 1965], VII, 137). What we find here is not only what M. H. Abrams has rightly called "a combination of Platonism and psychological empiricism" (*The Mirror and the Lamp: Romantic Theory and the Critical Tradition* [New York, 1953], p. 130): it is a deeply felt awareness that, while Platonism and psychological empiricism may be mutually exclusive, the creative power of the poet cannot be doubted. As we shall see, the *Ode to the West Wind* testifies to Shelley's determination to bypass the dilemma of Platonism v. empiricism, and to find significance in the world as man perceives it, without relying on voices "from some sublimer world." For a full discussion of the meaning of *Mont Blanc* in this respect, the reader is referred to Earl R. Wasserman's wholly admirable chapter on that poem in *The Subtler Language: Critical Readings of Neoclassic and Romantic Poems* (Baltimore, 1959).

of Wordsworth when he wrote *Resolution and Independence*. Such was the situation of Shelley in the autumn of 1819. The year 1818 had been one of illness and dejection, reflected in such poems as *On a Faded Violet*, the *Invocation to Misery*, the *Stanzas Written in Dejection, near Naples*, and of course the well-known sonnet, "Lift not the painted veil." Bereft of Harriet's children by a ruling of the Lord Chancellor, Shelley had left England in March for his Italian exile. Significantly, it was in the autumn of 1818 that he started writing *Prometheus Unbound*, where he was to work out the value of suffering in terms of man's power to control his own fate. The poet's Roman spring of 1819 was one of great creative activity, chiefly marked by the composition of Acts II and III of *Prometheus Unbound* and the beginning of *The Cenci*. But Shelley was relentlessly pursued by contrarieties which were of a personal, a political, and a literary order. His health was failing, and on June 7 his son William, aged three and a half, died of an apparently benign trouble. In consequence, his exile was becoming almost unbearable: "I most devoutly wish I was living near London," he wrote to Thomas Love Peacock in August. "All that I see in Italy . . . is nothing; it dwindles into smoke in the mind, when I think of some familiar forms of scenery, little perhaps in themselves, over which old remembrances have thrown a delightful colour."[2] But England was not all attraction for a young radical in those days. In that month of August, the Peterloo Massacre prompted Shelley to write *The Mask of Anarchy*, and in November the mean trial of a mediocre publisher who had ventured to reprint Tom Paine's *Age of Reason* provided fresh evidence of religious intolerance and political tyranny. In mid-October, Shelley had come across an issue of the *Quarterly Review* containing John Taylor Coleridge's venomous attack on *The Revolt of Islam*. His own ailments, the death of his son, the hopelessness of his

---

[2] *The Letters of Percy Bysshe Shelley*, ed. R. Ingpen (London, 1909), II, 709.

progressive ideas, the public failure of his poetry—all this could only lead to dereliction and despair.

If any one poem of that period can be singled out as the "timely utterance," the successful catharsis, through which a writer of genius explores his most painful experiences and endows them with significance and value, the *Ode to the West Wind* is that poem. From Neville Rogers's account of its genesis, it appears that the *Ode* resulted from the confluence of two entirely different streams of inspiration.[3] In his own footnote, Shelley asserts that

This poem was conceived and chiefly written in a wood that skirts the Arno, near Florence, and on a day when that tempestuous wind, whose temperature is at once mild and animating, was collecting the vapours which pour down the autumnal rains. They began, as I foresaw, at sunset with a violent tempest of hail and rain, attended by that magnificent thunder and lightning peculiar to the Cisalpine regions.

The Notebooks specify that this occurred on October 20. Strangely enough, when we keep in mind the destructive wind depicted in the poem, Shelley's first jottings, like his note, are chiefly concerned with the awesome beauty of the sight. Simultaneously—but, it would seem, quite independently—Shelley was preoccupied with his own fate and fame. He breathlessly composed a fairly long fragment in terza rima, the germ which was to flower into the last two stanzas of the poem. The first part of the *Ode* developed in isolation, except that Shelley adopted the terza rima for the description of nature, which was finished by October 25. It was not until an undetermined but slightly later date that he came across the idea of linking the two themes of nature and self, and drafted stanza IV, thus beginning to clarify the symbolism of stanzas I–III.

The whole process illustrates once more the workings of the

---

[3] Neville Rogers, *Shelley at Work: A Critical Inquiry* (Oxford, 1956), pp. 221–229.

symbolic imagination. Like the Eolian harp for Coleridge, like the Tintern landscape or the thorn in a storm for Wordsworth, the tempest in the wood presented Shelley with a natural phenomenon pregnant with a wider significance which the poem endeavors to elucidate and communicate. Whether it does so successfully has been seriously doubted by the antiromantic school of criticism. In *Revaluation*, F. R. Leavis concluded his pungent attack on Shelley's poetry with an indictment of the imagery of the *Ode*:

> In the growth of those "tangled boughs" out of the leaves, exemplifying as it does a general tendency of the images to forget the status of the metaphor or simile that introduced them and to assume an autonomy and a right to propagate, so that we lose in confused generations and perspectives the perception or thought that was the ostensible *raison d'être* of imagery, we have a recognized essential trait of Shelley's: his weak grasp upon the actual.[4]

Several years later, F. W. Bateson criticized the structure of the poem in no less devastating terms:

> Shelley's structural *intentions* are clear enough. . . . Shelley wants his reader to see the West Wind as a symbol of the forces of progress. That is what the poem *ought* to be about.
> But is it? Is not the real subject of the poem (i) Shelley's delight in natural violence, (ii) Shelley's self-pity, (iii) Shelley's consciousness of failing inspiration? . . . Like Wordsworth in his Ode, Shelley is *primarily* cheering himself up![5]

In those passages, we can recognize three of the major strictures raised by the antiromantic critics against romantic po-

[4] F. R. Leavis, *Revaluation: Tradition and Development in English Poetry* (London, 1936), p. 206. One commentator at least has since made a valiant but none too successful attempt to visualize the image in terms of acceptable meteorology: "The tangled boughs of Heaven and Ocean are the higher, more stationary clouds; the loose clouds beneath them are driven by the wind, just as the dead leaves are driven below" (Harold Bloom, *The Visionary Company: A Reading of English Romantic Poetry* [Garden City, N.Y., 1963], p. 314).

[5] F. W. Bateson, *English Poetry: A Critical Introduction* (London, 1950), pp. 215–216.

The Unextinguished Hearth 169

etry: its weak grasp upon reality, its querulous self-centeredness, and its lack of a coherent intellectual texture. Leavis and Bateson have thus made it inevitable that any discussion of the *Ode* must concern itself with the three main motifs of this book: the communication of meaning through structure, the function of symbolic imagery, and the quality of the poem's generalized significance in so far as this is conveyed through personal experience and emotion.

For a romantic poem, the *Ode to the West Wind* has an exceptionally strong tectonic character. Compared with the works of Coleridge and Wordsworth that have been analyzed so far and with the odes of Keats to which we shall turn later, its composition is of pellucid clarity. It falls very obviously into two unequal parts: stanzas I to III deal with nature, stanzas IV and V with the poet. The overall structure, therefore, raises the problem of the relevance of natural processes to man's predicament. Each of those two parts is constructed with equal care: the first three stanzas deal in succession with the wind's action on land, in the air, and on the water; each has a well-defined nucleus of imagery: the leaves and seeds, the clouds, the sea. The subject matter of the last two stanzas also comes out in sharp outline: stanza IV is an utterance of despair, while stanza V conveys the new awareness of value and purpose the poem has been leading up to.

All this is obvious and commonplace enough. But we tread on less familiar ground when we come to deal with the inner arrangement of each stanza and with the relation of the stanzas to each other on the plane of imaginative thought. After more than a century of exposure of the *Ode* in schools, it is not surprising that our perception of the poem should be blurred and prejudiced. The fact that the critic knows the last line by heart—so memorably simple, and carrying a message so comfortably suited to the requirements of Sunday-school stoicism—tends to make him feel that everything in the poem is or ought to be visibly directed toward that final statement.

Hence two misconceptions. Many critics have failed to see that stanzas II and III deal only with the destructive aspect of the wind's activity.[6] Bateson, on the other hand, assuming that Shelley "wants the reader to see the West Wind as a symbol of the forces of progress," considers those two stanzas defective because they stand aside from the straightforward line of such symbolism. It is therefore not superfluous to reexamine the structure of the poem as it stands, in order to clarify the purpose of the writer.

The first stanza has a very complex design, the principle of which is the same wavelike overlapping of several points of view that we observed in *Resolution and Independence*. Grammatically, it is divided into three parts, each of which begins with an apostrophe: "O Wild West Wind, . . . O thou, . . . Wild Spirit, . . ." Prosodically, run-on lines link the four tercets to each other and bolster the terzina rhyme scheme to produce a continuous flow which carries the reader irresistibly forward until the pause before the final couplet. From the point of view of subject matter, the stanza resembles a sonnet: as in a classical sonnet, there is a shift after the eighth line, when the poet's attention passes from the West Wind to its "azure sister of the Spring"; as in a Shakespearean sonnet, the heroic couplet at the end forms a self-contained unit. This intricate construction can be summed up graphically as follows:

---

[6] A recent instance appears in Irene H. Chayes's article "Rhetoric as Drama: An Approach to the Romantic Ode," *PMLA*, LXXIX (1964), 67–79, where she writes: "The first three stanzas are devoted to a formal invocation, in which the wind is characterized, and *praised*, in its role of destroyer *and preserver* in nature by its effect on the land vegetation, *the sky, and the sea*" (italics mine). In "Imagery, Ideas and Design in Shelley's 'Ode to the West Wind,'" *Studies in Philology*, XLVII (1950), 634–649, S. C. Wilcox strangely speaks of the wind's "gentler ministrations in stanza III," presumably forgetting that these gentle ministrations make the foliage turn gray with fear. Still earlier, G. Wilson Knight had asserted that "the wind is *throughout* destructive *as well as creative*" (*The Starlit Dome* [London, 1943], p. 200; italics mine).

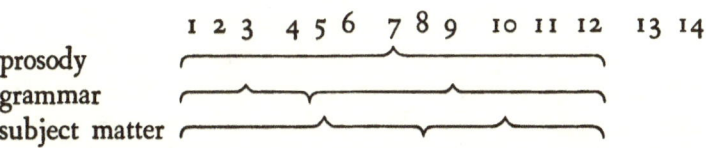

It will be perceived that everything is calculated to place the strongest possible emphasis on the final couplet, which indeed appears as the concluding stage in an almost scholastic—or Hegelian—ternary pattern. The four tercets illustrate two apparently antagonistic aspects of the Wind's action. After line 8, the zephyr's "clarion" takes the place of the West Wind, "breath of Autumn's being"; the dead leaves driven like ghosts are replaced by sweet buds driven like flocks; the death images ("leaves dead," "ghosts," "corpse," "grave") vanish to make room for the *"living* hues and odours" (italics mine) which at the same time contrast with the unpleasant olfactive connotations of the "pestilence-stricken multitudes." That this shift in mood, motif, and imagery occurs within the unbroken course which characterizes the prosodic oneness of the stanza is of the utmost importance: it is the structural correlative of the central intuition which is the theme of the poem and which the poet formulates in the couplet: the sense that one wind is both destroyer and preserver,[7] that destruction and regeneration are polar aspects of one process.

The couplet thus anticipates in unequivocal terms the meaning of the poem: a paradox, each of whose antithetical components (decay and horror versus beauty and fertility) has been imaginatively defined in the tercets. And the structure of the first stanza provides a miniature model which the poem itself will amplify and modulate in various ways: lines 1–8 are devoted to the wind as destroyer and lines 9–12 to the wind as preserver; a roughly similar proportion is maintained

[7] R. H. Fogle has insisted that the West Wind is destroyer and preserver, but that the agent of regeneration is the Spring wind. In reply to this, W. Clemen pointed out that in stanza v it is the West Wind which appears as the principle of rebirth. This apparent discrepancy will be discussed later.

throughout the *Ode*: stanzas II to IV deal with destruction and are permeated with a sense of horror, while stanza V strikes a new note of hope. Furthermore, the couplet describes the wind as "moving everywhere": this announces the systolic rhythm of the poem, in which the prospect is first widened to include the elemental worlds of air and water, and then narrowed down and internalized to concentrate on the mind of the poet, finally to expand again and embrace the future of human society.

A clear perception of this structure ought to dissipate current misconceptions about Shelley's intentions in stanzas II and III and about their proper role in the economy of the poem: they reflect the despondency of the author in the autumn of 1818; they illustrate the destructive power of the wind as defined in the first two tercets of stanza I; and they prepare the description of human misery in stanza IV. But there are subtler suggestions running through those two stanzas. For all their homogeneity in subject matter, each is divided into two antithetic and complementary parts like the tercets in stanza I, with the difference that the shifts in syntax and imagery coincide and occur in the third tercet. The result is that the dominant theme of destruction is strangely relieved with undertones of beauty.

In stanza I, the images of death and sickness made way for the depiction of the living sweetness of spring. This trend is reversed in stanza II, which thus appears as a kind of mirror reflection of the previous one. In the first part, the destructive fierceness of the wind is conveyed in terms ("tangled boughs," "angel," "blue surface," "aëry surge," "locks") which permeate it with a beauty of its own: the dynamic beauty of sheer energy in its free and wild display. The second part of the stanza, however, is filled with a renewed sense of choking horror kindled both by the claustrophobic imagery ("closing night," "dome," "sepulchre," "vault," "solid atmosphere") and by the final picture of destruction breaking loose in the shape of "black rain, and fire, and hail." Likewise, the tomb imagery echoes and amplifies elements already present in the first stanza: the "wintry" earth was merely the "grave" of the seeds; the vault of clouds in stanza II is the "sepulchre" of the "dying year," so that in retrospect the fate of the seeds is seen to be a micro-analogue of the fate of the year, that is, part of the wider cosmic pattern of mortality.

The first part of stanza II, then, introduces a new quality into the total concept of the wind, suggesting as it does that its destructiveness is in itself beautiful. This in turn strengthens the ambiguous, oxymoronic character of the wind. In stanza I, it was stated to be both destroyer and preserver. In stanza II, the wind's nature ramifies into another paradox: our perception of its destructive power is modified by an oblique intimation that its action is in itself beautiful, irrespective of its effects; the "black rain, and fire" which burst out at the end and signal the death of the year, break forth from the clouds, previously described as "Angels of rain and lightning"; the clouds may be angels of destruction, yet they are angels, and this strange association dissolves, as it were, the connotations of evil which might otherwise be implied in the death-bringing fury of the wind. Indeed, it locates the whole poem outside the sphere of good and evil, beyond the grasp of ethical judgment, on a plane which could with equal cogency be labeled spiritual or biological.

Stanza III, too, although homogeneous in subject matter, is divided into two parts with regard to both motif and syntax. The invocation in the third tercet ("Thou / For whose path . . .") launches the poem in a new direction: from the Mediterranean to the Atlantic, thus providing yet another spatial illustration of the Wind's omnipresence. This stanza, like the previous one, is wholly occupied with the theme of destruction, yet contains suggestions of a close relation between horror and beauty. Within this repetitive pattern, however, Shelley introduces a new variation as he now applies his well-known technique of viewing reality at second remove: what the Wind destroys is the dream-vision, by the Mediterranean, of the immersed "palaces and towers . . . All overgrown with azure moss and flowers," that is, of objects which—insofar as they were built for human usage—have already been destroyed, by the sea itself.

This passage, as is well known, is a reminiscence of an actual sea trip which Shelley had described in December 1818 in a letter to Thomas Peacock:

After passing the bay of Baiae, and observing the ruins of its antique grandeur standing like rocks in the transparent sea under our boat, we landed to visit lake Avernus.[8]

The point is, of course, that the beautiful buildings, though ruined, are still beautiful as ruins. So the paradox of decay becomes more and more intricate as the poem goes on. In the first stanza, death is shown to be a preparation for rebirth; in the second, the very process of destruction is imbued with the intrinsic beauty of boundless energy; in the third stanza, the result of destruction, too, appears to be a thing of beauty. A poetic link brings together the three branches of this connection between destruction and beauty: the phrase "*azure* moss and flowers" recalls the Wind's "*azure* sister of the Spring" in stanza I and echoes the "*blue* surface" of the Wind's aëry surge in stanza II (italics mine); at the same time, the architectural imagery of the "palaces and towers" enlarges on the "dome" and "sepulchre" of stanza II and on the "graves" of stanza I. This complex network, which is the equivalent in imagery of alliteration in prosody and patterning in structure, defines the microcosmic unity of the poem and turns the poetic artifact itself into an objective correlative of the macrocosm in which all things are linked together—not only, as is

[8] *Letters*, II, 656. Shelley also tells Peacock that the sea "was so translucent that you could see the hollow caverns clothed with the glaucous sea-moss, and the leaves and branches of those delicate weeds that pave the unequal bottom of the water." That he chose to move those vegetables from the Mediterranean, where he actually saw them, to the Atlantic, is evidence of his conscious intention to amplify the spatial framework so as to emphasize the omnipresence of the wind.

explicitly stated, Heaven and Ocean, but also, as is implicitly conveyed, life and death, beauty and horror.

The shift from nature to man which occurs after stanza III is prepared in two ways. The last item in the description of the Atlantic was the "sapless foliage," which leads to the poet's wishing that he were "a dead leaf." At a deeper level of imaginative perception, it should be noticed that the ruins in Baiae's bay, unlike the leaves and the clouds, were the work of man, works of art, so that a smooth transition is effected to the consideration of the poet's fate and of the use of poetry which will occupy the last two stanzas.

As a group, stanzas IV and V reproduce the same design of destruction and rebirth that underlay the structure of stanza I. And each is divided into two distinguishable parts, separated by a "prayer."

Though the central theme of stanza IV is human sorrow and anguish, it begins with evocations of harmony and happiness in the form of two unrealizable hypotheses ("If I were . . ."). There is unconscious harmony and happiness in the mindless world of things. There was illusory harmony and happiness in the world of fantasy where the poet moved as a boy. The prayer in line 12 is a nostalgic, futile bid to revert to such preconscious organic harmony with life. It is of course not capable of fulfillment. No miracle can enable the mature man to evade, or even to forget, his existential predicament, and the stanza ends on a note of sorely felt ambiguity: the poet is "chained and bowed" although he is "tameless, and swift, and proud."

This is the tragic awareness of an experiential antinomy, with which the poet, in the last stanza, comes to terms through two stages which reflect in succession the two positive approaches intimated throughout the poem: the aesthetic and the vitalistic. In the first part, he accepts the redeeming though melancholy paradox of beauty in destruction. Reverting to the images of the first stanza, he compares himself to the forest which, while it is shorn of its leaves, is the "lyre" of the Wind: his own song will tinge with sweetness the "tumult" of the Wind's "mighty harmonies." The tone of these lines is autumnal: they are related to the inherent beauty with which energy, however deadly, was endowed in stanza II. But after the new invocation—which is structurally parallel to that of the preceding stanza—the poet rises to a different plane of apprehension. Whereas stanza IV descended from preconscious integration to tragic clear-sightedness, stanza V has a continuous upward movement from aesthetic acceptance to vitalistic revaluation. The sweet sadness of the lyre now makes room for "the trumpet of a prophecy," which echoes the zephyr's "clarion" in stanza I. The poet identifies himself with the Wind, not in illusory bliss, or in elegiac resignation, but in a positive realization that his personal sacrifice, if he wills it, can help mankind on its way to rebirth.

At the end of the first stanza, the very naturalistic West Wind is apostrophized as "Wild Spirit." In a neoclassical ode, "Spirit" would be a metaphor for the wind, designed to enhance our imaginative perception of the wind's nonsensory nature. In Shelley's poem, on the contrary, it is the Wind which is a metaphor for the Spirit, a device intended to endow with sensuous quality our insight into the all-embracing, nonmaterial forces which sway over the universe. The figurative use of the wind, however, does not become unequivocally clear until stanza IV, where man too is seen to be a victim of a destroying power, which the poet chooses to describe in terms of the wind; at the same time, the conjunction of the material and the psychological, the inorganic and the human, raises the poem to a third level, the level of universal, "spiritual" apprehension. This equating of natural processes with human experience is made acceptable through Shelley's peculiar handling of imagery.

It is obvious enough that what Shelley describes in the three nature-centered stanzas is what actually happens in nature: the falling of leaves and the burying of seeds, the renewal of vegetable life in spring, the tumultuous conglomeration of drifting clouds into the murky sky of the tempest, the disturbance of sea waters—all this is accurately observed and accurately rendered. But those realistic physical processes are described by means of images, similes, and metaphors which all tend to suggest nonphysical afterthoughts.

It should first be noted that the natural objects are discreetly personified: the leaves are "like ghosts," the Wind is a "Spirit," the clouds are "Angels," the Mediterranean "dreams . . . in sleep," the sea-blooms "grow gray with fear." These images have one thing in common: they attribute to physical objects qualities and feelings which are not theirs by right. But each of them has its own definable function. The purpose of "ghosts" and "Spirit" is to provide what we may perhaps venture to call, in the etymological sense, a meta-physical background, and to suggest that the endless and seemingly senseless process of destruction and regeneration is the work of some purposive force, represented by the Wind, and by the leaves as instruments of the Wind. On the contrary, "dream" and "fear" refer in human terms to the sea and to the oceanic foliage as victims of the wind: located in stanza III, they prepare the sudden turning of the poet to his own, all too human predicament in stanza IV. Finally, the comparison of the dead leaves to "ghosts from an enchanter fleeing" establishes from the very beginning an implicit connection between the three planes of being: the leaves are natural objects; ghosts are supernatural entities; but they are also emblems of human mortality and they are endowed with the human emotion of fear. All this, we need hardly add, does not result from intentional application, but illustrates the subconscious workings of true poetic genius. Each image plays its own minute but necessary role in conveying the total impression of an interlocking, cosmic unity.

Another important aspect of Shelley's imagery is its nonvisual quality, which has provoked so much controversy in the past thirty years. It can be said that most of the imagery of the

Ode is visual in nature and nonvisual in effect. We have no difficulty in visualizing "tangled boughs," but it is clearly impossible, as Leavis pointed out, to visualize "the tangled boughs of Heaven and Ocean." The problem is whether this is, as Leavis contended, a flaw in Shelley's artistry, or whether the effect ought to be considered a function, that is, whether it was part of Shelley's intention to deflect visual imagery from its normal purpose, to confuse the reader's eye, and thus to prevent any clear sensory representation of the object, much as Turner used melting colors and blurred shapes in order the better to create an impression of pure light.

The clue to Shelley's intention in this respect is to be found in the description of the wind as an "unseen presence" (l. 2). This, we may remark, is a realistic observation. The wind cannot be seen. Only its effects are visible, and it is solely through a kind of immediate induction that we make inferences about the existence and the nature of the wind from our visual perception of its effects. It is precisely this quality of the wind which provides it, in Shelley's eyes, with its symbolic potentiality. The poet had long been experimenting with verbal ways of conveying a sense of the invisible. The first two lines of the *Hymn to Intellectual Beauty* are characterisic:

> The awful *shadow* of some *unseen* Power
> Floats though *unseen* among us (italics mine).

What could be more invisible than the unseen shadow of an unseen power? In the *Ode*, too, Shelley endeavors to convey simultaneously the presence and the invisibility of the wind, a combination which turns it into an apt symbol of the vital force that is Shelley's true subject. His manipulation of imagery is not an indication of his weak grasp upon the actual. Nor is it a lapse in poetic technique, a departure from imaginative coherence. It is a method with a purpose of its own.

Time and again, the poet uses images, similes, and metaphors, not in order to intensify the eidetic accuracy of his description, but, on the contrary, in order to distract the reader's attention from the concrete and individual, to blur all outlines that might isolate the objects in their self-contained shapes, to dematerialize what is of itself sensory, and thus to bring the physical and the particular nearer to the spiritual and the universal of which it is part and to which it is subordinated. The central image of stanza II is the cloud, which is shapeless enough; the comparison of clouds with leaves—necessary as a link between the first two stanzas—creates a definite eidetic effect which is immediately counteracted by the unvisualizable image of "the tangled boughs of Heaven and Ocean"; the clouds are thus removed from the sphere of the concrete and the sensory; they can be described as "Angels" in the same way that the leaves were equated with ghosts and that the Wind had become a Spirit in stanza I. Likewise, the clouds appear as "bright hair" and "locks"—but they are the hair and locks of a mythical being.

A similar dematerializing treatment applies to the architectural images. The dome of the night's sepulchre is vaulted with the "congregated might" (abstract) "of vapours" (visual but indistinct and unsubstantial), leading to the oxymoron of a "solid atmosphere." In stanza III, the "old palaces and towers" are, in themselves, solid shapes, but they are seen in a dream and their outlines are blurred in two ways: they are "quivering within the wave's intenser day," and they are "all overgrown with azure moss and flowers."

The imagery of the first three stanzas operates at two different levels. Thus far we have dealt with what might be called the secondary imagery, that is, the kaleidoscope of similes ("like ghosts," "like earth's decaying leaves," "Like the bright hair"), of metaphors ("graves," "tangled boughs," "Angels," "sepulchre"), and of vignettes ("old palaces and towers," "sea-blooms," "oozy woods"), which Shelley uses in order to dematerialize the leaves, the cloud, and the sea, and so to expand the programmatic equation Wind-Spirit which, at the outset, fixed the main trend of the poem. But this dazzling pageant of images should not blind us to the primary, realistic imagery of the leaves and seeds, the clouds and the sea, taken in themselves. The function of the secondary imagery, especially in stanzas II and III, is to bring out the general ambiguity of the forces of nature by introducing a strain of beauty into the horror of decay, destruction, and death. But the primary images have their own inherent ambivalence, which bears directly upon their symbolic meaning in terms of human experience. The clouds and the waves are both victims and auxiliaries of the wind: the clouds, shaken from the sky, in their turn burst into "black rain, and fire, and hail"; the Mediterranean, awakened from its dream, had previously engulfed the "old palaces and towers." The relevance of this duality becomes clear in stanza IV: the complaint of the poet is not so much that he is a victim of overwhelming forces, as that he is a victim without being an auxiliary as well; he would not moan, he says in effect, if, while panting beneath the wind's power, he could also share the impulse of its strength—whether his participation was vital and unconscious (ll. 43–47) or visionary and imaginary (ll. 47–50).

The vegetal imagery is ambiguous, too, but with a difference which accounts for its privileged position in the total symbolism of the poem. The leaves and seeds are victims of the wind. They are auxiliaries as well, but not of its destructive power. The seeds are the germs of rebirth; as for the leaves, in their association with the seeds, which they protect and feed with their own decay, they share the wind's preserving and regenerative power. The symbolic potentialities of the vegetal imagery are gradually realized as it becomes restored to the prominent place it had occupied at the beginning of the *Ode*. In stanza IV, we remember, Shelley envisions himself as a human victim, falling, chained and bowed under the burden of life; accordingly, the leaves are lumped together with the cloud and the wave into a composite image of organic, nonconscious integration: they are borne and lifted by the wind, and they participate passively in its power. The transition of man to poet is adumbrated in the first two tercets of stanza V.

Shelley identifies himself, not with the leaves, but with the forest shorn of its leaves. That the poet's "falling leaves" may stand for the public rejection of his poetry is only implicit at this stage; the poet accepts destruction in the name of its intrinsic, elegiac beauty; there is as yet no intimation of fertility and rebirth; the solace is purely aesthetic. While the forest image refers us back to the first stanza, the musical image of the poet as lyre, the "autumnal tone," and the "sweet sadness" of its melody, recall the "dirge" in stanza II.

The *Ode* finally reaches its climax as the poet passes from futile nostalgia and elegiac acceptance to positive integration. This is conveyed through the fusion of the various trends of imagery which had been running through the poem. So far, Shelley had concentrated on his own self as man and (in a vaguely suggestive way) as poet, on his sorrows and on his failures. But now, his attention focuses on the theme of poetry which occupies lines 61–67. The leaves motif and the seeds motif melt into each other. The reference of "withered leaves" is obvious; but the phrase "dead thoughts" simultaneously recalls the "leaves dead" and the entombed seeds of the first stanza, as well as the funereal architecture in stanza II, while "to quicken a new birth" is a reminiscence of the germinative power of the seeds; furthermore, the poet's "words" are described as "Ashes and sparks," a metaphor which combines suggestions of rebirth ("sparks") with suggestions of death ("ashes") and thus adds a new, constructive dimension to the destructive fire image of the second stanza.

But the treatment of the "verse" theme is enframed by two emphatic references to the poet: the *Ode* deals simultaneously with the function of poetry in human society and with the value of the poet's life and sufferings and failures. And after examining the secondary imagery, and the primary images of the leaves and seeds, the cloud and the sea, we are thus brought back to the central symbol of the poem: the wind. The two active verbs ("Drive" . . . , "Scatter" . . .) which signal poetry as an agent of the wind, are preceded and followed by the copula ("Be thou, Spirit fierce, / My Spirit! Be thou me, impetuous one" and "Be through my lips to unawakened earth / The trumpet of a prophecy") which signals the identification of the poet with the creative power of the wind. Here too we observe a fusing of images which had originally been kept apart. In the first stanza, two winds had been mentioned: the West Wind and its "azure sister of the Spring." In the last stanza, the two are unobtrusively intimated to be different aspects of a single force. It is at first with the West Wind that the poet identifies himself, as appears from the words "Spirit" and "impetuous" in lines 61–62. But after he has recognized the function of poetry, he also becomes triumphantly aware of the function of his own being. Though his task of "awakening" the earth sounds at first similar to the West Wind's action in "wakening" the Mediterranean, the difference is of paramount importance: the wind awakens the sea from its summer dream of beauty; the poet will awaken mankind from its deathlike winter slumber. In this, his identification is with the zephyr which, in the first stanza, awakened "the *dreaming* earth" to the intenser reality of "*living* hues and odours" (italics mine); and the shift is clarified as the elegiac lyre of the first line becomes superseded by the "trumpet of a prophecy" which of course echoes the zephyr's "clarion" in the first stanza.

This double fusion (of the leaves and the seeds, of the autumn wind and the spring wind) is definitely not a token of inconsistent thinking and confused inspiration. It is deliberate and purposive. It conveys the inextricable correlation of death and birth at the same time that it subsumes the two winds as polar manifestations of a single overwhelming power in which the poet participates.

Wind and leaves are recurrent images in Shelley's poetry, and in order to realize how their symbolic power grew in depth and complexity, it seems profitable to quote their first appearance in *Queen Mab*:

> They rise, they fall; one generation comes
> Yielding its harvest to destruction's scythe.
> It fades, another blossoms . . .
> (IV, ll. 227-229)

> Thus do the generations of the earth
> Go to the grave, and issue from the womb,
> Surviving still the imperishable change
> That renovates the world; *even as the leaves*
> Which the keen *frost-wind of the waning year*
> Has scattered on the forest soil, and heaped
> For many reasons there—though long they choke
> Loading with loathsome rottenness the land,
> All *germs* of promise, yet when the tall trees
> From which they fell, shorn of their lovely shapes,
> Lie level with the earth to moulder there,
> *They fertilize the land* they long deformed,
> Till from the breathing lawn a forest springs
> Of youth, integrity, and loveliness,
> Like that which gave it life, to spring and die . . .
> (V, ll. 1-15; italics mine)

Here, indeed, are many of the basic ingredients that will go to the making of the later poem. But the lines that follow show that the kind of cyclic return which Shelley had in mind in *Queen Mab* was a far cry from the complex intuition of the *Ode*. It was a common topos referring to the historical process of action and reaction as generation succeeds generation:

> Thus suicidal selfishness, that blights
> The fairest feelings of the opening heart,
> Is destined to decay, whilst from the soil
> Shall spring all virtue, all delight, all love,
> And judgment cease to wage unnatural war
> With passion's unsubduable array.
> (V, ll. 16-21)

In *Queen Mab*, the dead leaves are not the poet's thoughts, but the "loathsome rottenness" of smoldering tyranny, which is bound to make room—so the youthful poet chooses to hope—for the growing seeds of love, virtue, and happiness. Accordingly, there is no touch of awe or sympathy in the writer's emotional response to the leaves, but only contempt. The generating idea of the *Ode* springs from deeper strata of experience and speculation than Shelley could have reached and exploited at the time of *Queen Mab*. In the later poem, the image of nature's death and rebirth is not an allegory which applies mechanically to historical processes; in abiding itself "as a living part in that unity, of which it is the representative," it aptly illustrates Coleridge's definition of the symbol.

After examining the structure and the imagery of the poem, we are thus led to a question which is by no means as supererogatory as it may sound: What is the symbolism about?

Like most major romantic poems, the *Ode to the West Wind* deals with the nature of reality. *Alastor* was a dramatic allegory, in which Shelley embodied both the quest for ultimate truth and its inevitable failure; his hero was destroyed by the sheer impossibility—built into man's condition—of reaching mystical union with, that is, of experiencing and demonstrating the existence of, the transcendent essence which alone (he thought) could endow human life with meaning and value. As we have seen, the Lake poets in their maturity found peace and solace in a return to the traditional conception of faith and divine grace. Whether Shelley would have reached that stage, had he lived, can only be a matter for vain speculation. What we can say, however, is that any evidence found in his poetry points to a different direction, although this is often obscured by his resorting to the idealistic vocabulary of his time.

Alastor started in blissful illusion, only to end in frustration and annihilation. The *Ode* progresses in the opposite direction. Like so many romantic lyrical poems, it defines not a mood but a movement; it follows what Earl R. Wasserman has aptly described as "a dynamic and consistently evolving course of discovery"⁹ leading to revelation. Its basic tone is less assertive than exploratory inasmuch as successive assertions are merely stages in a process of exploration which aims at an ever more refined and explicit insight into the paradox of life and beauty. Its spiral structure, therefore, expresses a change in the mind, a dialectical growth in understanding and wisdom. Its dynamic principle begins where *Alastor* ended. It goes from horror to hope, from negative to positive, from a perception of *vanitas* to an assertion of purpose. Its surface meaning was aptly summarized many years ago by I. J. Kapstein:

The Wind, as the destroyer of the old order and the preserver of the new, for Shelley, symbolized Change or Mutability, which destroys yet re-creates all things; while the leaves signified for him all things, material and spiritual, ruled by Change. The poem epitomizes Shelley's conception of the eternal cycle of life and death and resurrection in the universe.¹⁰

But these words could equally apply to Shelley's use of eolian and vegetal imagery in *Queen Mab*, whereas the *Ode* explores the network of relations linking destruction and rebirth, forces and things, with far greater penetration and subtlety.

In the first stanza, there was a clear distinction between the West Wind, "destroyer and preserver," and the zephyr, which was the true agent of restoration; in the last stanza, this distinction is obliterated, and the wind appears as a generalized image of a single force which commands the whole cycle of natural decay and rebirth. In the first three stanzas, the wind was naturalistically described in its actual action on natural objects; in the last two stanzas, it appears figuratively, as a trope for a force which acts in a similar way in the world of man. Obviously, Shelley thought of the wind as a really existing part, as well as the metaphorical representative, of a single cosmic power or law, to which both the world of nature

⁹ Earl R. Wasserman, *The Subtler Language*, p. 208.
¹⁰ I. J. Kapstein, "The Symbolism of the Wind and the Leaves in Shelley's 'Ode to the West Wind,'" *PMLA*, LI (1936), 1070.

and the world of man are subordinated. It is this intuition of an all-embracing reality which entitles him to describe the wind as "Spirit." But what does "Spirit" mean?

In what is probably the fullest extant explication of the poem, Wolfgang Clemen perceptively observes that Shelley spiritualizes the wind, but does not deify it: however powerful, the wind remains a spirit of this world.[11] This is true not only of the wind as a natural power, but also of the other, unnamed force, which sways over the fate of man. But Shelley had not always been quite so cautious; in the *Essay on Christianity*, he had written that even "our most imperial and stupendous qualities" are "the passive slaves of some higher and more omnipresent Power. This Power is God."[12] The word "Spirit" in the *Ode* undoubtedly radiates suggestions of transcendence and otherworldliness, but the poem itself forces us to discard those connotations. Insofar as the West Wind is a distinct entity acting upon leaves, clouds, and waves, it could be conceived as transcendent, but the structure and the imagery of the poem are expressly designed to counteract any such impression: in their various ways, the leaves and seeds, the clouds, the waves, are shown—and, in stanza IV, it is so stated—to participate in the wind's strength, either in its destructive or in its regenerative aspect. And so, even within the limited framework of the nature-centered stanzas, the wind appears as a symbol for an immanent, universal force, which is also present in all natural objects.

If we manage to clear our minds of the usual connotations of the word "Spirit," we can hope to achieve a more accurate definition of what Shelley was trying to express. He was not thinking of ultimate reality in terms of a supernatural, personal being, as were Wordsworth and Coleridge. His attitude

[11] Wolfgang Clemen, "Shelleys Ode to the West Wind: eine Interpretation," *Anglia*, LXIX (1950), 369: "Er vergeistigt seine Naturkräfte, aber er vergöttlicht sie nicht. Der Geist, der im Westwind als ein so machtvolles Wesen sich zeigt, bleibt Geist der Erde, aber er ist nicht, wie bei Hölderlin, Geist aus einer jenseitigen Welt, der sich als ein Göttliches offenbart."

[12] *The Complete Works of Shelley*, VI, 231.

in this respect was one of cautious agnosticism. He did not expressly deny the possible existence of an absolute and transcendent deity; rather, like Kierkegaard and like Melville at the time of *Pierre*, his mind was chiefly impressed by the absence of any channels of communication between Creator and creature; if there was a God, he was the unknowable. The ultimate reality, *for man*, was the reality of the world. The cosmos in which the *Ode* moves and develops is the world that man can apprehend, the world of outside nature and of personal experience.

To the myopic eye, it is a world of decay and death, of horror and despondency, of failure and frustration—a by no means unworthy vision, which permeates much of Shelley's poetry. It was one of his earliest intuitions that, in the world as experienced by man, "Nought may endure but Mutability." But this perception, which may lead to a nihilistic sense of *vanitas* and universal transitoriness, can also prompt the poet to outgrow the myopic view and find the ultimate significance of life in change itself. This is Shelley's attitude in the *Ode*. In the first three stanzas, the poet emphasizes the positive aspects of mutability through both direct statement and oblique intimation: this immanent, impersonal force which is active through nature has a fine intensity in the free display of its energy (stanza II); it dislocates beauty only in order to transmute its elements into other beautiful shapes (stanza III); while it destroys, it also preserves and re-creates (stanza I), thus perennially ensuring the everlasting continuity of being. Shelley, it will be seen, is very near to Friedrich Schlegel, according to whom the highest reality that philosophy can reach is not an everlasting, unchanging substance, but the continuous becoming (*Werden*) of an infinite activity.[13] But

[13] F. Schlegel, *Philosophische Vorlesungen aus den Jahren 1804 bis 1806*, ed. C. J. H. Windischmann (Bonn, 1837), I, 112: "Die wahre Philosophie kann nirgends eine beharrliche Substanz, ein Ruhendes, Unveränderliches statuieren, sie findet die höchste Realität nur in einem ewigen Werden, einer ewig lebendig beweglichen Tätigkeit, die unter stets wechselnden Formen und Gestalten eine unendliche Fülle und Mannigfaltigkeit aus sich erzeugt."

whereas to Schlegel this unending process constitutes the essence of the godhead,[14] Shelley's outlook is determinedly man-centered. The *Ode* contains no suggestion of metaphysical existence. Everything in it takes place within the sphere of human perception. And the last two stanzas contain Shelley's attempt to transfer to human experience the intuition of purpose and meaning that he had obtained in his apprehension of nature.

Many years ago, Sir Herbert Read pointed out that "writing before Kierkegaard was born, Coleridge had already formulated the terms of an existentialist philosophy."[15] This is probably even truer of Shelley. He shared with Coleridge—and, for that matter, with Wordsworth and Keats—the fundamental *Angst* that arises when man realizes his estrangement, the limitations built into his condition, and the unresolvable contradiction between the ideal and the actual. But that is not all, and I would venture to suggest that the existentialist distinction between *Ding an sich* and *Ding für sich*—which is perhaps little more than the familiar duality of object and subject in new guise—is not irrelevant to the significance of the *Ode*.

That this distinction is somehow present in the poem appears from the difference in tone and meaning between the prayers addressed to the wind in stanzas IV and V. The conjuration in stanza IV—"Oh, lift me as a wave, a leaf, a cloud!"—is querulous in tone and escapist in intent. The poet would like to divest himself of his all too human consciousness and sensitiveness, the sources of his suffering, in order to become a sheer object, a *Ding an sich,* mindlessly and organically subjected to and integrated in the everchanging flow that is the ultimate ground of all being. This supplication cannot be fulfilled because man cannot be reduced to a sheer object. He is at the same time a *Ding an sich* and a *Ding für sich,* an

[14] *Ibid.,* II, 190, where the world is conceived as "ein unendliches Ich im Werden—gleichsam eine werdende Gottheit."
[15] Herbert Read, *Coleridge as Critic* (London, 1949), p. 30.

object and a subject, a fragment of reality, but a fragment which is irretrievably endowed with sensitiveness, consciousness, and will.[16] Stanza IV leads up to that recognition of man's dual status. It is Shelley's very suffering which forces upon his mind the awareness that, unlike leaf, cloud, or wave, he has a freedom and a pride which make him share, not simply in the strength, but in the very being of the wind, that is, which make him—so far, potentially—not a mere victim, nor even an instrument, but a living part, of the universal energy of life.[17]

The poet's self-description as "tameless, and swift, and proud" should invite us to question the common assumption that the *Ode* is a prayer. In fact, the development of the last two stanzas is controlled by a gradual reversal in the poet's relation to the West Wind, which is a metaphor for the poet's relation to life itself. It is true that the first part of stanza V has a humility not unlike that of the prayer in the preceding stanza; but the poet no longer sees himself as a passive object driven by the wind's power: he becomes a creative auxiliary in the sense that his melancholy strain contributes to the total harmony of life. It was always Shelley's idea that part, at least, of the function and value of poetry lay in its power to transmute truth into beauty, to give melodious shape to man's anguish and nostalgia—a notion that is also basic to Keats's

[16] This should be compared with Camus' description of the origin of the existentialist dilemma: "Si j'étais arbre parmi les arbres, chat parmi les animaux, cette vie aurait un sens ou plutôt ce problème n'en aurait point car je ferais partie de ce monde. Je *serais* ce monde auquel je m'oppose maintenant par toute ma conscience et par toute mon exigence de familiarité. Cette raison si dérisoire, c'est elle qui m'oppose à toute la création. . . . Et qu'est-ce qui fait le fond de ce conflit, de cette fracture entre le monde et mon esprit, sinon la conscience que j'en ai?" *Le Mythe de Sisyphe* (Paris, 1943), p. 74.

[17] The same internalization of universal energy is applied in the *Defence of Poetry* by means of the same cluster of wind-and-fire images: "The mind in creation is as a fading coal, which some invisible influence, like an inconstant wind, awakens to transitory brightness; *this power arises from within* . . ." (*The Complete Works of Shelley*, VII, 135; italics mine).

conception of art. A year later, in the ode *To a Skylark*, Shelley was to state, in words reminiscent of the *Ode to the West Wind:* "Our *sweetest* songs are those that tell of *saddest* thought" (italics mine). And in the *Defence of Poetry*, he was to assert that "a Poet is a nightingale, who sits in darkness and sings to cheer its own solitude with sweet sounds." [18] But in our poem, he does not remain satisfied with that notion of poetry as the beautiful expression of the pathos and tragedy of human experience. The explosive force of the copula in his second invocation ("Be thou, Spirit fierce . . .") and the pounding, hammering syntax, indicate that a new man is speaking: not the humble, querulous, and resigned sufferer that had been praying so far, but truly a "tameless, and swift, and proud" being, who boldly asserts his indomitable will. This second invocation is not a prayer, but an order. From now on, the imperatives will indeed be imperative: Be, Drive, Scatter, Be . . . ! Through the discovery of his freedom, man discovers his power. And it is this revelation which makes sense of the poet's commitment.

If there is no transcendent deity supplying from on high a programmatic ideal to which it would be man's duty to conform, life can have no meaning except the meaning the human mind decides to impose upon it. And it is when man has acknowledged this that he is faced with the existential option. He is free to drift aimlessly along the stream of history; but he may also try to channel the immanent energy of life and provide it with direction and purpose. Shelley's choice anticipates that of the hero of Camus' *La Peste:* it is to use his own share of life's energy to help mankind on its way to freedom and happiness. This is the point where egotism melts into social involvement. Apart from the fact that the poet is, as it were, a synecdoche for mankind, his self-centered meditation on his own nature, his own condition, his own fate, leads to the recognition that fulfillment of the self involves service to others. In January 1819, Shelley had gone so far as to write to Peacock: "I consider poetry very subordinate to moral and

[18] *Ibid.*, VII, 116.

political science, and if I were well, certainly I would aspire to the latter." [19] A considerable part of his activity in 1818 and 1819 was indeed directed toward subordinating poetry to moral and political ends. And the *Ode* formulates in dazzling images his triumphant consciousness of being able to shape the blind, impersonal processes of historical evolution to purposes of his own.

It is this exhilarating sense of complete mastery which transpires in the last invocation to the wind:

> Be through my lips, to unawakened earth
> The trumpet of a prophecy.

The figurative relation between wind and poet is now completely reversed. It is only through the poet's lips and through the incantation of his verse that the wind can become the trumpet of a prophecy. It is only through the power of man's mind that "the secret Strength of things"—as Shelley termed it in *Mont Blanc*—can be discovered and invested with purpose. Indeed, this third invocation answers the question at the end of the earlier poem and solves, or rather abolishes, the dilemma which led to it.

In his discussion of *Mont Blanc* already referred to, Earl Wasserman makes the point that Shelley's "ultimate doctrine of the Intellectual Philosophy is that reality is an undifferentiated unity, neither thought nor thing, and yet both." Much of the poet's later work is an obstinate attempt to elucidate the nature of this elusive unity in a more concrete way. By the very nature of the problem, it is hard for us to define exactly what he meant. For one thing, we have no objective frame of reference, since we do not know for sure what ultimate reality is, any more than he knew. And there is the superadded semantic difficulty that the poet was constrained to use such words as "thought" and "thing," "spirit" and "matter," "God" and "nature," "internal" and "external," to represent concepts which were totally irrelevant to the definition of ultimate reality as he envisioned it, since they refer not to the substance

[19] *Letters*, II, 660.

of reality but to its modes, or even merely to human fantasies about reality. Had he lived in the days of Einstein, Shelley might conceivably have availed himself of words and concepts better suited to express his insight. For the *Ode to the West Wind* shows that the way out of the dilemma in *Mont Blanc* lies in the notion that the substance of reality is energy, ever producing, and acting upon its own products, in a continuous process of change which inevitably involves both destruction and rebirth.

The *Ode* is suffused with this view of energy (or "Strength," or "Power") as the single undifferentiated ground of all differentiated forms and forces, whether material or mental. But its structure establishes a hierarchized evaluation of the workings of energy, and so makes it possible to locate the poem in the development of Shelley's doctrine of necessity and free will.[20] If energy is the ultimate ground of reality, change (or "Mutability") is the universal law to which all

[20] In *Shelley's Major Poetry: The Fabric of a Vision* (Princeton, 1948), Carlos Baker has provided the following summary of Shelley's evolution in this respect: "Up to 1818 Shelley explored and exemplified four views of the mind's relationship to outer and inner forces. The first was a materialistic necessitarianism, a conception of the inevitability of progress which Shelley inherited directly from the Enlightenment. The second was a form of psychological determinism, concerned with the idea of the inevitability of aspiration, the striving of the imperfect man towards self-realization. The third retained the deterministic bias to the extent that Shelley's myth was projected upon the broad screen of a cyclic theory of history; yet the stress fell upon the necessity for idealistic human leadership which despite, or perhaps because of, the inevitability of martyrdom for the principals, could point the way towards the moral conditions which ought to obtain in human society. The fourth returned to the psychological aspects of the problem, reaching the conclusion that the real key-concept was self-determinism: what is necessary to the clear vision, the discovery of law, and the assumption of moral leadership is the realization of the need for spiritual katharsis, followed at length by a willed rejection of all such dismal hatreds and fears as inhibit and corrupt the soul's receptivity" (pp. 273–274). In a way, the *Ode to the West Wind* can be considered a description of how the poet reaches this last phase and arrives at the key concept which Carlos Baker calls "self-determinism," a somewhat unexpected synonym for free will.

objects are submitted. But as far as man is concerned, determinism (or "Necessity") is—or at any rate, can be—confined to this very general law of change and need not apply to its orientations. Man may seek to identify himself with the impersonal energy of the universe through passive submission: indeed, this is just what the poet vainly yearns to do in stanza IV. But he can also seek to control and direct it through heightened awareness and the purposive use of his free will.

As the *Ode* draws to a close, the poet, as we have observed, reverts to the imagery of its beginning. But this "return" is accompanied by a shift upward to a higher level of inspiration, and after contracting to self-searching and self-discovery, the focus again widens to embrace the world of man. The subject matter is no longer limited to biological processes in nature, but concerns the historical evolution of human society; the "dreaming earth" of trees and leaves and buds has become the "unawakened earth" of men; the zephyr's "clarion" has become the poet's "trumpet," and the Wild Spirit that is at work in the last stanza is no longer the wind but the prophetic imagination of the poet. The ultimate reality, which had hitherto been metaphorically identified with the wind's energy, that is, with change, is now seen to reside also in the power of the human mind to transmute change into growth. The wind itself has become subservient to the poet's will. This does not mean that man himself is the ultimate ground, the sole principle of universal power. It means that the cosmic energy as it is present in man can govern the forms it takes in nature and in human society. Consciousness and free will are uniquely human manifestations of the secret strength of things. They are power become aware of itself, aware that underneath the mutability, the transience and the frustrations of life there is the everlasting, ever-changing continuity of being. And they are power controlling its own workings, making full use of man's redeeming privilege to impress shape and significance and purpose on all forms of being.

9 Greeting Uneasiness:
KEATS'S *ENDYMION*, BOOK IV

Between *Alastor* and parts of *Endymion* there are so many similarities that Keats certainly owed a debt to Shelley in the composition of this, his first ambitious work.[1] The later poem, however, deals with some issues which are far more concrete, more strongly rooted in the author's experience than anything that can be found in *Alastor*. Keats, of course, was considerably preoccupied with the ontological problem of the nature of being, which is central to so much of romantic poetry. Endymion's love for Cynthia offers a clear parallel to the Poet's vision in Shelley as well as to the hankering after spiritual oneness in Coleridge. Keats too was prompted by the mystical yearning for "fellowship with essence." But the most interesting feature of *Endymion* is the young writer's concern with the ethical problem of loss and suffering, for which Wordsworth had worked out his own solution in *Resolution and Independence*. This problem comes to the fore in the last book, and is treated allegorically, but with considerable subtlety, in the episode known as the "Cave of Quietude." The

---

[1] Many of these similarities have been pointed out in A. C. Bradley, *Oxford Lectures on Poetry* (London, 1904), pp. 140–144; L. Brown, "The Genesis, Growth and Meaning of *Endymion*," *Studies in Philology*, XXX (1933), 618–653; and J. D. Wigod, "The Meaning of *Endymion*," PMLA, LXVIII (1953), 779–790.

fourth book of *Endymion* was begun in the early days of October 1817. Keats had finished Book III by 28 September. On 22 November, he informed Bailey that he had written about five hundred lines of Book IV. He was thus probably about to start work on the Cave of Quietude, which occupies lines 511–562.

During those two months, Keats seems to have had the darker side of human nature very much on his mind. There had been some quibbling and bickering going on in the little literary world to which he belonged together with Hunt, Haydon, and Horace Smith. On 8 October, he wrote to Bailey: "every Body seems at Loggerheads," and he added: "I am quite disgusted with literary Men."[2] He had some reason to believe that Hunt had been unfair to him, and he was very bitter at Hunt or anybody else claiming to have had a hand in *Endymion*:

You see Bailey how independant my writing has been—Hunts dissuasion was of no avail—I refused to visit Shelley, that I might have my own unfetterd scope—and after all I shall have the Reputation of Hunt's elevé—His corrections and amputations will by the knowing ones be trased in the Poem—This is to be sure the vexation of a day—nor would I say so many Words about it to any but those whom I know to have my wellfare and Reputation at Heart (I, 170).

It is difficult to take this last disclaimer at its face value. Keats was wounded in his pride as a poet and in his friendship for Hunt.

Illness was another source of dejection. James Rice was ill (I, 169), John Martin was ill (I, 172), and Keats himself was just recovering from some unspecified ailment: "The little Mercury I have taken has corrected the Poison and improved my Health," he wrote on 8 October, "though I feel from my

[2] *The Letters of John Keats,* ed. H. E. Rollins (Cambridge, Eng., 1958), I, 169. Further quotations from the *Letters* in this chapter are from this edition and are identified by volume and page in parentheses.

employment that I shall never be again secure in Robustness" (I, 171). And a little later: "For this fortnight I have been confined at Hampstead—Saturday evening was my first day in town" (I, 172). Reynolds, too, had his share of troubles: on 22 November, Keats wrote that he was not going to "talk any sorrow" to him, as he must have "enough vexations" (I, 188). But the poet was chiefly concerned with the health of his brother, which led him to some angry generalizing: "In this World there is no quiet nothing but teasing and snubbing and vexation—my Brother Tom look'd very unwell yesterday and I am for shipping him off to Lisbon. perhaps I ship there with him" (I, 172).

On 3 November, Keats heard of the trouble Bailey was having in connection with his ordination, and he worked himself into an unexpected frenzy of indignation, writing to Bailey in what M. B. Forman does not hesitate to call "terms of almost incoherent abuse about the Bishop of Lincoln." [3] His preoccupation with pain and corruption was not on an altogether personal level. On 22 November, he wrote to Bailey: "The world is full of troubles and I have not much reason to think myself pesterd with many" (I, 186). But his own illness, the poor state of his brother's health, the ailments of his best friends, Hunt's tasteless boasting, and Bailey's disappointment must have had a cumulative effect, namely, to make him ponder with unaccustomed intensity on human suffering in general and on the imperfection of human nature. Disabused or angry references to "this world" abound in the letters of October and November. Nor are these the facile generalizations of the tearoom pessimist: they express a genuinely philosophical concern, which was rapidly taking root in Keats's heart and mind as a result of his growing experience and awareness of life.

In the course of those October and November weeks, which are so crucial for our understanding of Keats's swift

[3] *The Letters of John Keats*, ed. M. B. Forman (London, 1948), p. 59.

Greeting Uneasiness   197

evolution, this concern with the ills of the world gave rise to various attitudes which can be disentangled and defined through the relevant letters. At the end of October, Keats wrote to Bailey:

I have received a proof of your utmost kindness which at this present I feel very much—and I wish I had a heart always open to such sensations—but there is no altering a Man's nature and mine must be radically wrong for it will lie dormant a whole Month— This leads me to suppose that there are no Men thouroughly wicked—so as never to be self spiritualized into a kind of sublime Misery—but alas! 'tis but for an Hour—he is the only Man "who has kept watch on Man's Mortality" who has philanthropy enough to overcome the disposition [to] an indolent enjoyment of intellect—who is brave enough to volunteer for uncomfortable hours (I, 173).

And he added in a postscript:

You ask after my health and spirits—This Question ratifies in my Mind what I have said above—Health and Spirits can only belong unalloyed to the selfish Man—the Man who thinks much of his fellows can never be in Spirits—when I am not suffering for vicious beastliness I am the greater part of the week in spirits (I, 175).

All this is admittedly rather obscure. It seems, however, that Keats is drawing a contrast between two moods or attitudes, both of which are fairly ambiguous. First, there is a state of "health and spirits," "open to sensations" of pleasure and gratefulness, and inclined to "an indolent enjoyment of intellect"; although apparently desirable, this state can "only belong unalloyed to the selfish Man," and it is described as "thouroughly wicked" insofar as it prevents a man from ever suffering on behalf of his "fellows." Second, there is a state of "self spiritualization," which results from the "philanthropy" and the "bravery" of the man "who has kept watch on Man's Mortality," "who thinks much of his fellows," and who is aware of life's "vicious beastliness"; it is an "uncomfortable" condition, which entails "suffering," and blunts the soul to all pleasant feelings, making it "dormant." In this respect, it can be described as "wrong" (though not "wicked"), but on the other hand, it is also "sublime."

John Keats, aged twenty-two, was about to leave the Chamber of Maiden Thought and—to use his own terms of 3 May 1818—there was taking place a "sharpening" of his "vision into the heart and nature of Man," a "convincing" of his "nerves" that the world is full of "Misery and Heartbreak, Pain, Sickness and oppression" (I, 281). The inventor of the pleasure thermometer was discovering the vanity, nay, the utter impossibility, of pure enjoyment and, what is more, its worthlessness on the moral level. And the ambiguity of the phrasing gives a measure of his anxiety and puzzlement, while his description of the numbness of his mind as a result of this new awareness reveals the intensity of his sympathy with human suffering.

The second stage in his evolution is apparent from the frantic letter of 3 November to Bailey:

Such is this World—and we live—you have surely [been] in a continual struggle against the suffocation of accidents—we must bear (and my Spleen is mad at the thought thereof) the Proud Mans Contumely—O for a recourse somewhat human independant of the great Consolations of Religion and undepraved Sensations. of the Beautiful. the poetical in all things—O for a Remedy against such wrongs within the pale of the World! Should not those things be pure enjoyment should they stand the chance of being contaminated by being called in as antagonists to Bishops? Would not earthly thing do? (I, 179)

From a sympathy that was somewhat querulous, Keats has moved on to indignation, contempt, and rebellion. He shows himself more and more disturbed by "the weariness, the fever, and the fret" which were to become a lasting and major theme in his mature writing. But he seems to have given up for the time being the mood of "dormant" apathy (an attitude, how-

Greeting Uneasiness 199

ever, which will recur more than once) in a desire that something shall be done, that a "recourse" and a "remedy" shall be found against the wrongs of this world. But Keats does not advise escapism. "Religion and undepraved Sensations. of the Beautiful. the poetical in all things" should be "pure enjoyment"; they should not become "contaminated" in a struggle against worldly evil. What he wants is a recourse "within the pale of the World."

This shrill note of ineffectual revolt was something new, and apparently it did not attract Keats for long. He does not seem to have believed that institutional measures, though most certainly "within the pale of the World," might prove an adequate "remedy" to the world's evils. Hence a third, purely ethical, approach, on which much light is shed by the two letters which Keats wrote to Reynolds and to Bailey on 22 November as well as by the Cave of Quietude episode in *Endymion*. His new attitude toward evil and suffering is hinted at in a question he asks Reynolds: "Why dont you, as I do, look unconcerned at what may be called more particularly Heart-vexations? They never surprize me—lord! a man should have the fine point of his soul taken off to become fit for this world" (I, 188). The crux of this passage is of course the precise meaning of the word "unconcerned." Does it imply a deliberate withdrawal from the attitude of sympathy which Keats had extolled in October, and a return to the "indolent enjoyment of intellect" which he had been indicting in no equivocal terms? This does not sound likely, and indeed, the letter he wrote to Bailey on that same day shows that the "unconcernedness" he now advocates is not to be equated with selfish disregard of others:

The first thing that strikes me on hea[r]ing a Misfortune having befallen another is this. "Well it cannot be helped.—he will have the pleasure of trying the resourses of his spirit, and I beg now my dear Bailey that hereafter should you observe any thing cold in me not to but [*for* put] it to the account of heartlessness but abstraction—for I assure you I sometimes feel not the influence of a Passion or Affection during a whole week—and so long this sometimes continues I begin to suspect myself and the genui[ne]ness of my feelings at other times—thinking them a few barren Tragedy-tears (I, 186).

In October, Keats had begun to see the futility of any hope for easy happiness; his mood had been one of sentimental participation, which quickly changed to indignant sympathy at the beginning of November. By 22 November, he had passed to a form of stoicism which combined both acceptance of, and detachment from, pain: an attitude toward suffering which he was to elaborate in greater detail in the future. The view of man's fate implied in the November letters to Bailey and Reynolds could be summarized as follows: there is a definite contradiction between the ideal and the real; the dream of perfection is only a dream; man should not expect pure unadulterated bliss—"I scarcely remember counting upon any Happiness," Keats writes (I, 186). But it does not follow that man should give up in despair all attempt to come to terms with life. On the contrary, he must be prepared to meet life on its own terms. He should expect and accept the corruption and the grief: the readiness is all. But he should not allow himself to be destroyed by them or to indulge in sentimental orgies of pity or self-pity. He should "abstract" himself, make himself "unconcerned," and then try to find out the good that may come out of evil, try to understand the creative value of suffering, to see it as a means of "trying the resources of his spirit." The way lies from suffering, through positive acceptance and detachment, to awareness and manly wisdom.

It was in those late months of 1817 that Keats became aware of the dilemma with which Coleridge, Wordsworth, and Shelley had already come to grips. The youthful dream of happiness, the enthusiastic rejection of the limitations of human nature, the eager expectation of mystical bliss, were now contradicted by the harsh inescapable facts of life, by the evidence of evil, pain, and loss. The cruder alternatives were either to follow the *Sehnsucht* and negate reality—which is the way of the Poet in *Alastor*—or to desert the ideal and fall back into complacent conformity—which is the way Shelley thought Wordsworth had ultimately chosen. In fact, however, it was precisely in order to find a way out of this dilemma that all English romantics were driven to probe deeper into the intricate relationship of the ideal and the actual, so as to discover whatever spiritual meaning might lie hidden underneath both the corporeal beauty of nature and the evils and griefs of life.

The most significant difference between *Alastor* and *Endymion* lies in the fact that Keats's hero is not blinded by his idealism. While Shelley's Poet discards the indirect approach through natural beauty and human love for a quest that will lead him to nothingness, Endymion embodies in allegorical and symbolical terms an attempt to have it both ways, to pursue simultaneously the ideal represented by Diana and the earthly represented by the Indian maiden.[4] But by 22 November, Keats had reached the stage—both in his own experience and in the writing of *Endymion*—when it becomes clear that any such attempt is bound to end in failure. The "grievous feud" of allegiances which was to lead Endymion to the Cave of Quietude has wrought in his soul a division of which he is acutely aware: "Would I were whole in love!" he exclaims.[5]

[4] In recent years, there have been several attempts to deny any interpretation of *Endymion* as spiritualistic allegory, most notably those of N. F. Ford in "The Meaning of 'Fellowship with Essence' in *Endymion*," PMLA, LXV (1947), 1061–1076, and of E. C. Pettet in *On the Poetry of Keats* (Cambridge, Eng., 1957), ch. 4. It is argued that the predominant element is of a sensuous nature, and that what Keats calls "essence" is no more than a substitute for "thing." Referring to what I have said about the coalescence of naturalistic perception and symbolic meaning, it seems to me that the ambivalence of *Endymion*, as demonstrated by such antinomic interpretations, is one more manifestation of the syncretic need to overcome experiential dualities.

[5] *Endymion*, Bk. IV, l. 472. All line references are to Book IV.

At the same time, two frightening occurrences have shown him that this dichotomy will forever prevent him from gratifying either of his two contradictory passions: as he is alternately attracted to Diana and to the Indian maiden, both the goddess and the girl "melt away," and Endymion is thunderstruck by the realization that wholeness is not to be achieved, that ideal beauty and sensuous love are not to be reconciled, that full happiness is an aim beyond the scope of man's endeavor. There is a parallel between the fate of Endymion and what was going on in the mind of Keats while he was writing this passage: in each case, we can witness the disappointment resulting from the destructive impact of experience upon the limitless expectations of innocence.

According to conventional views of romantic idealism, Endymion should have died on the spot, or at least committed suicide, following the example set by Hölderlin's Empedocles. Like the hero of *Alastor*, he should have been destroyed by his hopeless quest for the ideal. His attempt to grasp a plenitude which is beyond the reach of human nature is *hubris*, the proper reward of which is death. Indeed, Keats hints as much. Just at the beginning of the passage when Cynthia appears to Endymion, there is a revealing reference to Icarus:

> He who died
> For soaring too audacious in the sun,
> When that same treacherous wax began to run,
> Felt not more tongue-tied than Endymion.
> (ll. 441–444)

And after his stay in the Cave of Quietude, Endymion has the following significant remark:

> There never liv'd a mortal man, who bent
> His appetite beyond his natural sphere,
> But starv'd and died.
> (ll. 646–648)

What has Endymion been doing except "soaring too audacious" and bending "his appetite beyond his natural sphere"?

Why is it, then, that—untrue to the *Alastor* pattern—he does not die? The answer, obviously, must be sought somewhere between the experience of the failure and the recognition of its cause, that is, in the Cave of Quietude episode.

In order to grasp the meaning of this section,[6] we should have a clear picture of its topography, which Keats mapped out with sufficient accuracy for us to find interesting similarities to the geography of his own mind as revealed in the letters. First of all, we should note the distinction between the cave itself and its setting. The cave lies in the middle of "dark regions" which are "the proper home of every ill" (ll. 521–522). The word "every" explains why

> the man is yet to come
> Who hath not journeyed in this native hell.
> (ll. 522–523)

While those dark regions stand for terrestrial life and common human experience, the den itself is a different place. It lies

> Beyond the seeming confines of the space
> Made for the soul to wander in and trace
> Its own existence.
> (ll. 513–515)

This location, in its turn, accounts for the fact that

> But few have ever felt how calm and well
> Sleep may be had in that deep den of all.
> (ll. 524–525)

Keats's description of the cave suggests the uncommon and ambiguous character of the kind of quietness and well-being that is to be experienced there by the privileged few:

---

[6] For different interpretations of the Cave of Quietude, see J. M. Murry, *Keats* (London, 1955), pp. 166–198, and N. F. Ford, *The Pre-figurative Imagination of John Keats* (Stanford, 1951), pp. 79 ff.

> Woe-hurricanes beat ever at the gate,
> Yet all is still within and desolate.
> Beset with plainful gusts, within ye hear
> No sound so low as when on curtain'd bier
> The death-watch tick is stifled.
>
> (ll. 527–531)

As to the significance of the hero's transfer from the "dark regions" to the Cave of Quietude, it is made clear later, when Endymion realizes some of the true import of his experience in the cave:

> "Alas!" said he, "were I but always borne
> Through dangerous winds, had but my footsteps worn
> A path in hell, for ever would I bless
> Horrors which nourish an uneasiness
> For my own sullen conquering: to him
> Who lives beyond earth's boundary, grief is dim,
> Sorrow is but a shadow . . ."
>
> (ll. 615–621)

It may not be superfluous to insist on the remarkable consistency of Keats's imagery, which reflects the closely knit quality of his thought. Here, as in the earlier passage, the "dark regions" are called a "hell" (l. 523); and the "wind" image is an echo of the "woe-hurricanes" (l. 527). Evidently, the "dark regions," which are the "proper home of every ill," are the poetic equivalent of the "world" of the letters, the world which is full of "troubles," of "misfortunes," of "teasing and snubbing and vexation." This is the "native" hell which all men know at some time or other, whether they experience its corruption and imperfection personally, or are "self spiritualized into a kind of sublime Misery" by their sympathy with the sufferings of others.

Furthermore, this passage expresses exactly the attitude to pain and evil which had been sketched by Keats in his letter of 22 November to Bailey. Like his author, Endymion welcomes the horrors which give him an opportunity to try the resources of his spirit. The peculiar connotations of the word "uneasiness" are confirmed by a letter of 24 April 1818. Writing to John Taylor, Keats generalizes the very mental processes if disillusionment and acceptance which he and his hero had gone through five months earlier:

Young Men for some time have an idea that such a thing as happiness is to be had and therefore are extremely impatient under any unpleasant restraining—in time however, of such stuff is the world about them, they know better and instead of striving from Uneasiness greet it as an habitual sensation, a pannier which is to weigh upon them through life (I, 270).

As to the cave itself, it is a correlative of the condition mentioned by Keats when he said that his "Nature will lie dormant for a whole Month." Under the impact of extreme misery, a defense mechanism starts operating in the soul to protect it against the destroying effect of experience. It loses its sensitiveness. Its "fine point" is "taken off"; "grief is dim, / Sorrow is but a shadow." This numbness, this apathy, is the calm sleep of the cave. It is to be equated with the "unconcernedness," the state of "abstraction" described in the letters. The soul is abstracted for some time from the common life of man; it is carried "beyond earth's boundary." This period of insensitiveness is what enables it to evade the destroying influence of extreme suffering and, therefore, to go on living in "this world" and to "save the whole" of itself (l. 544). The experience has positive value in that it allows the soul a respite which gives it the strength to "try its resources." This phrase from the letter is echoed in the poem by the words "sullen conquering," a paradoxical collocation which corresponds to the imagery used to describe the cave: "sullen" refers to the prevailing mood of the soul in the Cave of Quietude, while "conquering" explains why Endymion is ready to "bless" such miseries, to greet uneasiness. The soul comes out of this ordeal, not with a ready-made solution for its problems, but with renewed strength, with greater power to face life, and with a sharper insight into the moral nature of man and the ethical meaning of experience.

The Cave of Quietude is the key to our understanding of the end of the poem, and the last episodes illustrate Endymion's precipitous descent into selflessness, at the bottom of which he will find the plenitude he had been vainly striving to reach.

The first fruit of his "sullen conquering" of his uneasiness is his determination to give up his hope of attaining on earth the heavenly happiness represented by Cynthia. Unlike the Poet of *Alastor*, he will dedicate himself to sweet human love, represented by the Indian maiden, who is *within* his "natural sphere," although he retains the idea of meeting the goddess again "in pure elysium" (l. 658). This, however, is not yet the resolution of his problem. The delights of the life he contemplates under the aegis of Pan (l. 634) are described by Keats in a way which excludes this possibility:

> The mountaineer
> Thus strove by fancies vain and crude to clear
> His briar'd path to some tranquillity.
> (ll. 721–723)

The path image recalls lines 523 and 616–617, thus suggesting that Endymion is again wandering on the dangerous fringes of the dark regions. His expectations are "fancies vain and crude" because his hope of achieving "tranquillity" on earth through the fulfillment of natural passion is as great a delusion as was his former desire to synthetize the ideal and the actual. A new trial indeed appears to have been in store for him as the Indian girl intimates that she must bid him adieu (ll. 728–763).

Endymion can now truly be said to be "in last extreme" (l. 771). Once again, he has lost both Cynthia and the Indian maiden, and he finds himself back in the situation which was his previous to the Cave of Quietude episode. But his reaction—and this is his second step on his way to selflessness—is utterly different. He now accepts the defeat of his last hope and decides to give up not only love but also his princely power and all the "impious" and deceptive "sensations" which are the only pleasures of this world (ll. 851–854). Thus, after renouncing his "great dream" (l. 638), he now intends to renounce his "earthly realm" and to go back to Cynthia, not in the hope of winning her in any possessive way, but as a "hermit" (l. 860) in her service. And he urges the Indian maiden to do likewise. Keats's own comment on the lovers' vow of chastity makes it clear that the spiritualization of the Carian, at the present stage, is by no means complete. On the contrary, what has been achieved so far, he calls a "ghastly malady":

> Each diligently bends
> Towards common thoughts and things for very fear;
> Striving their ghastly malady to cheer,
> By thinking it a thing of yes and no . . .
>
> (ll. 895–898)

It is perhaps difficult to understand exactly what these lines mean. But if we remember that Keats had got approximately as far as line 500 by 22 November, and that he started (or intended to start) preparing his manuscript for the press on 6 January (I, 196), there is some ground for thinking that he wrote the last pages of the book in the second fortnight of December. It seems therefore legitimate to search for some similarity between these lines and what Keats was writing about "negative capability" in a letter to his brothers dated 21 December:

it struck me, what quality went to form a Man of Achievement, especially in Literature & which Shakespeare possessed so enormously—I mean *Negative Capability*, that is when man is capable of being in uncertainties, Mysteries, doubts, without any irritable reaching after fact & reason—Coleridge, for instance, would let go by a fine isolated verisimilitude caught from the Penetralium of mystery, from being incapable of remaining content with half knowledge (I, 193-194).

What I am trying to suggest, however tentatively, is that the two passages, read in conjunction, might throw some light on each other. The way to cure the "ghastly malady," that is, the frustration of the *Sehnsucht*, is *not* to think it "a thing of yes and no," a thing to be refused or acquiesced in, a thing to be decided upon by a deliberate act of the will. The faith in willpower is a form of pride which seems to be akin to that of the man who is ever "reaching after fact and reason," who is "incapable of remaining content with half knowledge." I am aware that Keats, in the letter, is speaking of literature. Nevertheless, it should be noted that negative capability is a quality of "a Man of Achievement, *especially* in Literature" (italics mine)—not, we may infer, in literature only. The phrase implies a humbleness of the mind, an acceptance of its limitations, a willingness to remain in doubt and uncertainty, a disposition to allow life to stay mysterious, beyond the grasp of either mind or will—in brief, an attitude which may apply to moral life as well as, if not better than, to poetry.

So far, Endymion has not achieved negative capability. He has been trying all the time to control his own fate, even in his renunciation of the spiritual *Sehnsucht* and afterward of his "earthly realm." This renunciation did not result from a surrender to the "Penetralium of the mystery," but from a deliberate act of the conscious will. It was something that was not lived but willed, and was, therefore, fundamentally ineffectual; hence the death-wish (ll. 927-944):

> nor much it grieves
> To die, when summer dies on the cold sward.
> Why, I have been a butterfly, a lord
> Of flowers, garlands, love-knots, silly posies,
> Groves, meadows, melodies, and arbour roses;
> My kingdom's at its death, and just it is

> That I should die with it: so in all this
> We miscall grief, bale, sorrow, heartbreak, woe,
> What is there to plain of? By Titan's foe
> I am but rightly served.
>
> (ll. 935-944)

Endymion's wish to die is not yet the final step toward spiritualization. Keats's ethical thought is here at its most complex and penetrating. The three stages of Endymion's final evolution develop on strictly parallel lines, according to a recurrent pattern. They all represent an advance on the way to detachment and acceptance, but Keats carefully emphasizes their negative aspects. First, Endymion's surrendering of Cynthia and his hopes of a tranquil life with the Indian girl were described as "fancies vain and crude." Then, his surrendering of the Indian girl and of his earthly realm, together with his decision to live like a hermit, appeared as a "ghastly malady." In his death-wish, there is likewise something blasphemous. Not only does Endymion laugh impiously at the holy beauty of nature as if it were a jest (ll. 944-949), but the main point is that he wishes to die for entirely negative reasons. The Poet in *Alastor* was seeking death in the diffident but positive hope that it might prove to be the way to fusion with the absolute. For Endymion, death is a means to evade "the slings and arrows of outrageous fortune," to escape from a world where there is no happiness, to take shelter in the oblivion of sheer nothingness. Furthermore, the Carian persists in his basic error by thinking death "a thing of yes and no," in the same way that his previous decisions had resulted, not from humble acceptance, but from a self-willed impulse to take his fate in his own hands.

The decisive stage is reached when Endymion himself realizes that his derisive attitude of irritated despair is both blasphemous and out of tune with his true self (ll. 957-962): his wish to die is "impious" (l. 961) in the same way that his clinging to an earthly realm had been impious (l. 854), and as his premature hankering after the absolute was

> Presumptuous against love, against the sky,
> Against all elements, against the tie
> Of mortals each to each, against the blooms
> Of flowers, rush of rivers, and the tombs
> Of heroes gone!
>
> (ll. 639–643)

Now, at last, Endymion has come to the end of his long pilgrimage. He has dropped all hopes of readily grasping the ideal. He has detached himself from earthly enjoyment. He has even detached himself from his wish to die. In other words, he has given up his attempt to control his own destiny. He has abandoned his earlier hubris. He accepts his own limitations. He is ready to remain in "uncertainties, mysteries, doubts." It is not too much to say that he has reached the state of negative capability. This is the climactic point in Endymion's evolution, for it is not until he answers Peona:

> "Sister, I would have command,
> *If it were heaven's will,* on our sad fate."
>
> (ll. 975–976; italics mine)

that the Indian girl reveals her true identity. And she does so because, as she soon explains, he has now been spiritualized "by some unlook'd for change" (l. 992). That he bends himself to a change he had not been consciously and willfully looking for is a mark of negative capability. That Endymion is now prepared to live in submission to "heaven's will" suggests that his evolution parallels Wordsworth's incipient recognition of God's grace—"a something given," "a leading from above"—in *Resolution and Independence.*

Like *Resolution and Independence, Endymion* is the timely utterance through which the poet overcomes his dilemma and gropes his way to growth and maturity. Endymion changes. His story is that of the growth of a mind. Book I represents his absorption in the luxurious. Books II and III, with Alpheus and Arethusa, with Glaucus, with the drowned lovers, represent the stage of active sympathy and, in a larger sense, of humanitarianism, the stage in which Endymion is "self spiritualized into a kind of sublime Misery" by keeping watch on "Man's Mortality." Book IV carries him a step further: now he has to face and conquer his own suffering, the grievous feud brought about by the equal intensity of his contrary impulses. And here, a Stoic strain merges with the Platonic and erotic tendencies. Endymion understands that he can never achieve the kind of happiness he has been hankering after, and which can be described as a sybaritic fulfillment of the opposite aspirations of his soul. He is therefore led, first to strip himself of his attachments, then to give up the attempt to mold his own destiny.[7]

It is characteristic of the romantic spiral pattern that this process of nonattachment should bring the hero back to his early ideal and allow him to gratify his early aspirations. Growth results from a combination of continuity and change, which is suggested by Keats's manipulation of light-imagery. Endymion's redemption occurs when he acknowledges the death-wish as impious because it is a sin against his own essential self:

> "I did wed
> Myself to things of light from infancy;
> And thus to be cast out, thus lorn to die,
> Is sure enough to make a mortal man
> Grow impious."
> (ll. 957–961)

And as the Indian maid reveals herself to be Cynthia in disguise,

> into her face there came
> *Light*, as reflected from a silver flame:
> Her long black hair swell'd ampler, in display

---

[7] In this respect, there is no mistaking the Christian echo in the words of the Indian maiden: "I see there is no little bird, / Tender soever, but is Jove's own care" (ll. 877–878).

>   Full *golden;* in her eyes a *brighter* day
>   Dawn'd blue and full of love.
>   (ll. 982–986; italics mine)

Endymion thus obtains the light for which he was made. Yet, it is not the same light. It is no longer the sensuous light of the butterfly world described in lines 937–939, the light of premoral enjoyment. *Endymion* enlarges upon the premonitory intuition which had given birth to *Sleep and Poetry*, and which Keats's life and thought were to verify:

>   First the realm I'll pass
>   Of Flora, and old Pan . . .
>   . . . .
>   And can I ever bid these joys farewell?
>   Yes, I must pass them for a nobler life,
>   Where I may find the agonies, the strife
>   Of human hearts.
>   (ll. 101–125)

These are the dark passages which lead from the Chamber of Maiden-Thought, and it is only by successfully passing through that "space of life between" that man can recover his spiritual health and wholeness. Only, it is no longer the health of innocence, but the health of wisdom. In the same way, some fifteen years earlier, Wordsworth, after finding that "life's business" was bound to nullify his earlier "summer mood," had recovered his gladness, thanks to the example of the leech-gatherer's firmness of mind. Thus the world of experience supersedes the world of innocence, and the sufferings and responsibilities of adult life turn the poet's youthful expectations of facile harmony into a mockery, until he finds out that his loss is even more pregnant with spiritual meaning than was his starry-eyed idealism.

On 23 January 1818, Keats, looking back on *Endymion* and forward to *Hyperion*, drew a revealing antithesis between his conception of the two poems, the written one, and the one of which he was in travail: "One great contrast between them will be—that the Hero of the written tale being mortal is led on, like Buonaparte, by circumstance; whereas the Apollo in Hyperion being a fore-seeing God will shape his actions like one" (I, 207). Endymion, indeed, reaches the final stage in the growth of his mind when he stops trying to be like a god and commends his fate unto the hands of "Jove," or "heaven." That this transformation is insufficiently realized within the framework of the narrative, nobody is likely to dispute. Nor could it be otherwise. The mainspring of Keats's inspiration has always been experience, intensely felt, deeply meditated. We can know from his letters what it was that had been "proved upon his pulse" during those autumnal months of 1817, while he was writing the last book of *Endymion*. It was first the dream of perfection, the infinite *Sehnsucht*; second, the fact that fulfillment and happiness are never given in this universe of misery and vexation; third, the notion that, in order to survive, the soul must somehow withdraw her sensitive tendrils from contact with a wounding world; fourth, the conclusion that suffering does have positive value, that it gives the spirit an opportunity to try its resources. Of the concrete way these processes worked, Keats was as yet unsure, although he sensed that they must involve some sort of detachment combined with the recognition and acceptance of the limitations of human nature. Hence it is that the last part of the poem—most, in fact, of what comes after the Cave of Quietude—seems to be the fruit of abstract ethical thought and allegorical invention, rather a symbolic embodiment of personal experience in myth. Unlike Endymion, Keats was still in the "dark passages" upon which the doors of the Chamber of Maiden Thought open. This is just why Endymion's wisdom fails to convince. The last hundred lines of the poem are an attempt to incorporate an intuition which was as yet too vague to be capable of truly symbolic treatment. Even as late as 3 May 1818, Keats could only express a dim conviction that "after all, there is certainly something real in the World" (I, 282).

It was not until a year later, in April 1819, after experiencing more of the heartbreak and the misery, that he felt able to understand completely the meaning of suffering:

The common cognomen of this world among the misguided and superstitious is "a vale of tears" from which we are to be redeemed by a certain arbitrary interposition of God and taken to Heaven— What a little circumscribe[d] straightened notion! Call the world if you Please "The vale of Soul-making" Then you will find out the use of the world . . . I will call the *world* a School instituted for the purpose of teaching little children to read—I will call the *human heart* the *horn Book* used in that School—and I will call the *Child able to read, the Soul* made from that *school* and its *hornbook*. Do you not see how necessary a World of Pains and troubles is to school an Intelligence and make it a soul? A Place where the heart must feel and suffer in a thousand diverse ways! . . . This appears to me a faint sketch of a system of Salvation which does not affront our reason and humanity (II, 101–103).

The fourth book of *Endymion* is an early attempt to figure out how an "intelligence" can become a "soul." Together with the letters of October and November 1817, it represents Keats's first gropings toward his "system of Salvation."

10 Truth Is Beauty:

KEATS'S *EPISTLE TO JOHN HAMILTON REYNOLDS* AND *ODE ON A GRECIAN URN*

THE last months of 1817 were the period when Keats became acutely aware of the gap between the youthful dream of plenitude and happiness to which a large part of his poetry had been committed, and the actual misery from which experience was ruthlessly showing him that there was no escape. From this painful awareness, two problems necessarily emerged. One, the moral problem, was about sorrow and evil, whether they have *any* function and value in the universal scheme; it was the old theological crux of the uses of evil in a world created and governed by a benevolent Providence. Keats, unlike Coleridge and Wordsworth, could not solve it by calling in orthodox Christian dogma: his was the hard way of personal experience and inner searching. (See the discussion of *Reflections Upon Having Left a Place of Retirement* and of *Resolution and Independence*, in chapters 2 and 5.) The other problem, the aesthetic one, was about art, and about its relationship with and its function (if any) in life thus apprehended. During 1818 and the spring of 1819, Keats gradually worked out the conception of life which could solve the first problem through his notion of the world as the vale of soul-making. Simultaneously, his insight into the nature and the uses of poetry developed along similar lines, checking, modulating and deepening his heart-felt belief in what he had called, in the letter to Bailey of 22 November 1817, "the truth of Imagination."

On 24 April 1818, Keats wrote to Taylor: "I have been hovering for some time between an exquisite sense of the luxurious and a love for Philosophy—were I calculated for the former I should be glad—but as I am not I shall turn all my soul to the latter."[1] And a month earlier, he had written to Bailey: "I am sometimes so very sceptical as to think Poetry itself a mere Jack a lanthern to amuse whoever may chance to be struck with its brilliance" (I, 242). These two statements should be read in conjunction: if the poetry which Keats finds trifling and useless, not worth more than "what it will fetch," was the poetry issued merely from "an exquisite sense of the luxurious," the logical alternative was either to drop poetry altogether or to turn to a kind of poetry that would have intellectual seriousness. Keats never stopped writing poetry, but expressions of his keen concern with actual life and suffering, and of his wish to help mankind, swarm in his letters of spring and summer 1818. He wrote to all his correspondents about this impassioned aspiration: to Reynolds—"I would jump down Ætna for any great Public good" (I, 267); to Taylor—"I find there is no worthy pursuit but the idea of doing some good for the world" (I, 271); to Bailey—"I am never alone . . . without placing my ultimate in the glory of dying for a great human purpose" (I, 293); to Woodhouse—"I am ambitious of doing the world some good: if I should be spared that may be the work of maturer years" (I, 387).

To the disabused mind of the twentieth-century reader, such utterances may sound childish. They are chiefly of inter-

---

[1] *The Letters of John Keats*, ed. H. E. Rollins (Cambridge, Eng., 1958), I, 271. Further quotations from the *Letters* in this chapter are from this edition and are identified by volume and page in parentheses.

est in that they confirm how little truth there is in the once orthodox portrait of Keats as the perfect aesthete. Fortunately for English poetry, Keats was neither a politician, nor a civil servant, nor a soldier, and the only way for him to solve the antinomy between life and art, and to do some good to mankind, was through art. Art itself was the way out of his dilemma. Not, of course, the kind of poetry that he sometimes thought "a mere Jack a lanthern," the poetry of summer luxury and facile escapism which had been so gratifying to his sense of sybaritic perfection. It was Keats's task to revise for himself his conception of art, to reconcile his hankering after ideal beauty, his clear-sighted perception of actual misery, and his impatient craving to help mankind.

Keats's puzzled attitude to the problem of the value of poetry in the spring of 1818 can be inferred from his letters. Although he had not relinquished his intuition about the truth of beauty and the holiness of the imagination, his confidence in poetry of the "exquisite" kind had obviously been badly shaken, as the unavoidable misery of "this world" was making itself felt more and more urgently. Keats's perplexed and self-contradictory mood is apparent in the extempore verse letter of 25 March 1818, now known as the *Epistle to John Hamilton Reynolds* (I, 259–263). However careless and rambling a piece of writing, the poem develops through three fairly distinct visions which illustrate three modes of the imaginative faculty.

The first vision (ll. 1–12) is a vision of incongruity. The poet recalls the image of "things all disjointed" that came before his eyes "as last night I lay in bed." The choice of items is revealing. The *disjecta membra* ludicrously pieced together produce mixtures of good and evil ("Two witch's eyes above a cherub's mouth"), intelligence and brutality ("Voltaire with casque and shield and Habergeon"), sublimity, wisdom, and genius on the one hand, and the burlesque—and often anachronistic—triviality of everyday life on the other ("And Alexander with his night-cap on— / Old Socrates a tying his cravat; / And Hazlitt playing with Miss Edgeworth's cat"), dramatic talent and human frailty ("And Junius Brutus pretty well so, so, / Making the best of's way towards Soho").[2] I hope I am not stretching the interpretative process too far in saying that all those pairs illustrate—in a flippant way—the incongruity of the ideal and the actual, which we know from the letters to have made a most painful impression on the young poet.

By way of transition (ll. 13–25), Keats then mentions the happy few who "escape these visitings," and whose visions are of "flowers bursting out with lusty pride" (a reference to the "exquisite" type of poetry), or of "young Aeolian harps personified" (a reference to Coleridge). In the course of this transition, he evokes a scene which will recur in the *Ode on a Grecian Urn*:

> The sacrifice goes on; the pontif knife
> Gleams in the sun, the milk-white heifer lows,
> The pipes go shrilly, the libation flows.
> (ll. 20–22)

This comes immediately after the mention of "Titian colours touch'd into real life," and the sheer beauty of the description should not make us forget that this is a scene of sacrifice, of destruction. It is no use trying to make too much of this, but

[2] To clarify this allusive passage, it is useful to reproduce W. J. Bate's comments in *John Keats* (Cambridge, Mass., 1963), pp. 307–308: "Hazlitt, who so admired the 'masculine boldness and creative vigor' of the English writers of the sixteenth and seventeenth centuries, and who constantly attacked the 'mediocrity' of the present, was playing with one of the many cats owned by the eminent 'blue-stocking,' Maria Edgeworth. The repeated attacks on the blue-stocking in Keats's letters would suggest that it had become another stock symbol of the forces that were emasculating poetry and distracting it from its pristine vigor and variety. Junius Brutus Booth, who rendered so thunderously for the present time the great passages of Shakespeare, was seen meandering tipsily toward Soho for further solace through drink."

Truth is Beauty

the fact that Keats later inserted this particular scene in one of his most ambitious poems shows that it became, for him, loaded with a significance of which he was probably unaware at the time of writing the *Epistle*.

The second vision is a vision of beauty (ll. 26–66). It deals with an enchanted castle which Keats would like to show

> in fair dreaming wise
> Unto my friend, while sick and ill he lies.
> (ll. 31–32)

The picture is drenched with magic and romantic medievalism. It is calculated to gratify Keats's "exquisite sense of the luxurious." In the transition from this vision to the last one (ll. 67–85), Keats tentatively wonders why "our dreamings all of sleep or wake" are not built of that same "material sublime" which went to the making of the enchanted castle. We shall revert to his ruminations on this point, which are all the more worthy of consideration, as this passage, too, contains a significant anticipation of the *Ode on a Grecian Urn*.

The third vision might be labeled, for symmetry's sake, the vision of cruelty:

> 'Twas a quiet Eve;
> The rocks were silent—the wide sea did weave
> An untumultuous fringe of silver foam
> Along the flat brown sand. I was at home,
> And should have been most happy—but I saw
> Too far into the sea; where every maw
> The greater on the less feeds evermore:—
> But I saw too distinct into the core
> Of an eternal fierce destruction,
> And so from Happiness I [was] far gone.
> Still am I sick of it: and though to day
> I've gathered young spring-leaves, and flowers gay
> Of Periwinkle and wild strawberry,
> Still do I that most fierce destruction see,
> The shark at savage prey—the hawk at pounce,

>The gentle Robin, like a pard or ounce,
>Ravening a worm.
>
>(ll. 89-105)

Here as in the first vision, two antagonistic elements are collocated, although the tone is no longer flippant but pathetic and instinct with high seriousness. Enjoyment of the "material sublime" (the harmony and quietness of the seascape, the luxurious beauty of the flowers) is undermined by the awareness of life—not, this time, the burlesque incongruities of everyday life, but the tragic insight into life as a process of continuous destruction. It has been claimed that this passage illustrates Keats's dissatisfaction with Wordsworth's belief in the goodness of nature.[3] Remembering the significant discrepancy between the optimistic conception of life in nature proclaimed in the Preface to *Lyrical Ballads* and the obsession with cruelty and tragedy betrayed by the poems themselves, we can only conclude that Wordsworth's view of nature was less superficial, more complex and realistic, than is commonly granted, and that Keats, in this respect, stood much nearer to the older poet than is usually admitted. For both poets, the problem was how to reconcile the opposite aspects of one same nature: its enchanting, spirit-nourishing harmony, and its heartrending cruelty.

Keats's attitude in face of this dilemma at the time of writing is forcefully expressed in the conclusion:

>Away, ye horrid moods!
>Moods of one's mind! You know I hate them well,
>You know I'd sooner be a clapping bell
>To some Kamschatkan missionary church,
>Than with these horrid moods be left in lurch—
>Do you get health—and Tom the same—I'll dance,
>And from detested moods in new Romance
>Take refuge.
>
>(ll. 105-112)

[3] H. W. Piper, *The Active Universe: Pantheism and the Concept of Imagination in the English Romantic Poets* (London, 1962), p. 92.

Truth is Beauty

The phrases "horrid moods" and "detested moods" refer primarily to the awareness of life and the world as the scene of "an eternal fierce destruction"; they may also apply to the dismayingly grotesque fantasies with which the *Epistle* begins. They are explicitly and significantly associated with the ill health of Reynolds and Tom Keats. As for romance, it is the poetry of escape, in which Keats would like to "take refuge"; it is the exquisite poetry of the enchanted-castle variety.

What disturbs Keats is, of course, that the products of the imagination are not consistently imbued with that exhilarating kind of beauty, and his puzzlement finds utterance in the transition between the second and the third visions, a cryptic passage which gives elliptical expression to a deeply-felt perplexity:

> O that our dreamings all of sleep or wake
> Would all their colours from the sunset take:
> From something of material sublime,
> Rather than shadow our own Soul's daytime
> In the dark void of Night. For in the world
> We jostle—but my flag is not unfurl'd
> On the Admiral staff—and to philosophize
> I dare not yet!—Oh never will the prize,
> High reason, and the lore of good and ill
> Be my award. Things cannot to the will
> Be settled, but they tease us out of thought.
> Or is it that Imagination brought
> Beyond its proper bound, yet still confined,—
> Lost in a sort of Purgatory blind,
> Cannot refer to any standard law
> Of either earth or heaven?—It is a flaw
> In happiness to see beyond our bourn—
> It forces us in Summer skies to mourn:
> It spoils the singing of the Nightingale.
> (ll. 67-85)

That it is a "flaw / In happiness to see beyond our bourn," is precisely what Keats had realized while he was writing

Endymion, during the last few months of 1817. And in the *Epistle* he shows himself as yet unreconciled with that truth. Art should be sheer romance; it should mean escaping from the jostling of this world into a world of "material sublime"; it should mean taking refuge—from a world where "things cannot to the will be settled"—in a world of paradisaic happiness. The daytime world of suffering and destruction teases him out of thought because he despairs of coming to terms with it, either intellectually ("high reason") or ethically ("the lore of good and ill"). Moreover, implicitly and at least for a moment, Keats seems to despair of romance as well, because the imagination, even though it is brought beyond its proper bound, yet remains confined and is unable to reach the absolute in itself, and because our perception of the world of romance increases our awareness of the shortcomings of the world in which we live. In the Preface to *Endymion*, he had described man's youth as a "space of life between," which has lost the health of boyhood and which has not yet acquired the health of maturity. The Purgatory of the *Epistle* is likewise a "space between," where the standard law of earth no longer applies and the standard law of heaven does not yet apply. Keats's perplexity results from his awareness of being in an intermediary stage, where he is as yet unable to overcome the contradictions that beset him.

Of those contradictions, those that are connected with art crystallize into the two kinds of dreams mentioned in the poem: the dreams that are made of material sublime, that are soaked in romance, that appeal to his sense of the luxurious;[4] and the dreams (like the first and the third visions) that "shadow our own Soul's daytime / In the dark void of Night," that reflect the jostling world of things which cannot to the

---

[4] W. J. Bate, *John Keats* (p. 308), finds in lines 67–69 verbal echoes of *Tintern Abbey:* "A sense *sublime* / Of something far more deeply interfused, / Whose dwelling is the light of the *setting sun*." But although the phrasing may be Wordsworthian, there is nothing in the poem to suggest that Keats had in mind the kind of visionary sublimity to which Wordsworth was referring.

will be settled. The latter are certainly not conducive to exquisite happiness, and that is why Keats is puzzled by them.

The aesthetic problem with which Keats was faced is thus seen to boil down to the question whether (and how) it is possible to account for the "disagreeables" in the products of the imagination, in dreams, in art, in poetry. A solution of a sort had been adumbrated three months earlier, when Keats discussed Benjamin West's picture, *Death on the Pale Horse*, in a letter to his brothers:

> It is a wonderful picture, when West's age is considered; But there is nothing to be intense upon; no women one feels mad to kiss; no face swelling into reality. the excellence of every Art is its intensity, capable of making all disagreeables evaporate, from their being in close relationship with Beauty & Truth—Examine King Lear & you will find this exemplified throughout; but in this picture we have unpleasantness without any momentous depth of speculation excited, in which to bury its repulsiveness (I, 192).

Since the phrase about the intensity of art is so often quoted out of context, as a final dictum, it is worthwhile to pause a little to examine what Keats really had in mind. He is comparing two products of the artistic imagination, and he finds that, while *King Lear* is intense, West's picture is not. From what he says about both, it is possible to infer that the "intensity" which gives art its excellence can take on three aspects. A close relationship with beauty is suggested by the phrase "no women one feels mad to kiss," which in turn does more than imply that Keats is, at the moment, thinking of the luxurious and the exquisite. A close relationship with human truth is connoted by "no face swelling into reality": Keats obviously means the Shakespearean gift of making characters come alive on the stage or on the printed page. A close relationship with truth (in a more philosophical sense) is referred to in the phrase "without any momentous depth of speculation excited," which suggests a possible connection between art and philosophy. As for the phrase "making all disagreeables evaporate," it should perhaps be considered a remnant of the somewhat sybaritic theory of poetry which Keats had been upholding and from which he never detached himself completely, although he felt the need to supplement it: how, indeed, could one seriously maintain that all disagreeables have evaporated from *King Lear?* The unpleasantness and the repulsiveness are buried, but they are still there; they have not evaporated; they have been transmuted because the story, as told by Shakespeare, plunges the reader (and here, Keats's critical insight is indeed at its best) into a "momentous depth of speculation." Of course, we cannot exclude the possibility that what Keats meant by that obscure phrase might precisely refer to that elusive property of art which can turn evil, sorrow, and ugliness into a source of aesthetic pleasure. However that may be, although Keats the critic could acknowledge the excellence of an art which has little connection with the exquisite and the luxurious, the truth of this proposition had not yet been "proved upon the pulse" of Keats the poet: hence the perplexed mood of the *Epistle*. Nevertheless, it seems to me that the imaginative elements were already present, however dimly, in his poetic mind: the three lines devoted to the sacrifice in the *Epistle* deal with destruction and death; yet the picture is of undeniable beauty.

It is now time to turn to the *Ode on a Grecian Urn*, which Keats wrote in May 1819, after another year of experience and meditation. It has long been a commonplace of Keats criticism that the *Ode* exalts, as Robert Bridges put it, "the supremacy of ideal art over Nature, because of its unchanging expression of perfection,"[5] or, to borrow Murry's formula, "the supremacy of the changeless and, in the strict metaphysical sense, eternal world of the imagination."[6] This is a rather simple interpretation of a poem whose complexity is probably

[5] Introduction to *The Poems of John Keats*, ed. G. Thorn Drury (London, 1896).
[6] J. M. Murry, *Keats* (London, 1955), p. 320.

destined to remain unraveled. The view I want to submit is that the main theme of the *Ode* is not the supremacy of art over life, but rather the function of art in life.

The subject matter of the poem centers round the two carved scenes on which Keats chooses to comment.[7] The main theme of the first scene is love as idealized through art. As E. R. Wasserman has shown in his elaborate analysis,[8] stanza II and the first seven lines of stanza III describe with growing intensity a state of perfect bliss (which may have mystical significance, although this is by no means obvious when the poem is considered in isolation). But it should be added that this happiness is of a kind likely to gratify Keats's sense of the luxurious rather than his love for philosophy. It prolongs the type of inspiration which had given birth to the *Ode to Psyche*. Keats's description of Eros and Psyche was focused on the particular moment when gratification has brought quietness, while desire and tenderness have not yet been destroyed by surfeit:

> They lay calm-breathing on the bedded grass;
>   Their arms embraced, and their pinions too;
>   Their lips touch'd not, but had not bade adieu,
> As if disjoined by soft-handed slumber,
> And ready still past kisses to outnumber
>   At tender eye-dawn of aurorean love.
>
> (ll. 15-20)

The artist of the Grecian urn has likewise made immortal an intensity of passion which is essentially transient.

The climax in Keats's growing identification occurs in the first seven lines of the third stanza. But the path is not as

---

[7] I cannot agree with Leo Spitzer's view that stanza I and stanzas II and III deal with two different scenes: the apostrophe "ye soft pipes, play on" refers back to the pipes of the first stanza, while the bold lover "winning near the goal" is one of the competitors in the "mad pursuit." See L. Spitzer, "The 'Ode on a Grecian Urn,' or Content vs. Metagrammar," *Comparative Literature*, VII (1955), 203-225.

[8] E. R. Wasserman, *The Finer Tone: Keats' Major Poems* (Baltimore, 1953).

smooth as a careless reading might suggest. In this respect, the ambivalence of the second part of stanza III should be noted:

> Fair youth, beneath the trees, thou canst not leave
> Thy song, nor ever can those trees be bare;
> Bold Lover, *never, never canst thou kiss,*
> Though winning near the goal—yet, do not grieve;
> She cannot fade, though *thou hast not thy bliss.*

The italicized clauses (italics mine) are negative in meaning, but even the positive statements are couched in negative terms. It sounds as if the poet were of two minds about the happiness that he is describing: while envying and projecting himself into the everlasting passion which animates the lover, he cannot help realizing that it is somehow incomplete, since it will never reach fulfillment. The alleged superiority of art over life is not so obvious, after all. The precarious poise expressed in those five lines soon gives way, however, to full-hearted acquiescence, as Keats drops all mention of the negative side of the lover's predicament and celebrates the happiness of everlasting desire: "For ever wilt thou love, and she be fair!"

The picture in stanza III is one of pure harmony. The urn, as a work of art, fixes forever what is of itself transient, and the connected secondary motifs of nature and music only strengthen the impression of flawless perfection on which the description of the lover concludes. Whether, then, the artist who carved the urn intended his characters to represent "deities or mortals," "men or gods," hardly matters: their "for ever panting" love is "all human passion far above"; if they were intended as men, art has idealized them and made them like gods in their eternal youth. Within the framework of the poem, the romantic *Sehnsucht* has been gratified, the dream of perfection has come true.

But it is typical of Keats's intellectual integrity that he makes no attempt to prolong the dream and stay in that blessed spot, where, in Chaucer's language, "grene and lusty

May shal ever endure."[9] On the contrary, the sheer intensity of the scene recalls to his mind the heartbreak of actual life. And the grammar of the last six lines of stanza III, in which the two divergent trends of thought are fused into one single sentence, shows that the climactic realization of the dream is coinstantaneous with the anticlimactic awareness of life as it actually is:

> More happy love! more happy, happy love!
> For ever warm and still to be enjoy'd,
> For ever panting, and for ever young;
> All breathing human passion far above,
> That leaves a heart high-sorrowful and cloy'd,
> A burning forehead, and a parching tongue.

This sestet thus points with almost unbearable pathos to the unbridged gap between the ideal and the actual, between art and life.

But is this gap unbridgeable? Is it due to the very nature of art? It might seem so, since the urn has created beauty only by suppressing the unavoidable condition of life: it has suppressed the dynamism which leads both to fulfillment and to decay, as well as the tensions and the contradictions which inevitably stamp all human experience with anxiety. The lover's predicament on the urn is nonhuman in two senses: it is godlike in its everlasting perfection; it is also petrified and lifeless in its immobility: the urn is with "marble" men overwrought. If there is one conclusion that might be inferred (but I hasten to add that it should not be) from Keats's treatment of the love theme in his ode, it is that beauty is not truth, that is, if we take truth to have any connection with the actual.

The third stanza, however, is only the end of the *first* episode in Keats's search for the meaning of art to life. Its last three lines are final with regard to the love theme, but in

[9] *The Parlement of Foules,* l. 130.

another respect they are transitional.[10] The poet has built up a concentrated picture of ideal love, sheltered from mutability. With the last lines of stanza III, he turns to the sufferings that necessarily accompany actual love. In the next stanza, he drops the love theme altogether to treat the theme of suffering and death, thus reaching a second stage in his poetic analysis of art. Although the second section of the poem consists only of stanza IV, the overall structure is not impaired, because that one stanza repeats the whole pattern of the first section, beginning as it does with a series of unanswerable questions and ending on a note of deep melancholy. There is of course modulation in this repetitive pattern, and it is significant that the melancholy at the end of stanza IV should be less harsh and more subdued than the melancholy at the end of stanza III.

But this parallel is accompanied by a shifting upwards of the inspirational level. In the dialectical development of the *Ode*, a new aspect of art is now envisioned. The three questions—who? whither? whence?—that control the structure of stanza IV are the fundamental questions that can be asked about man, his identity, his end, his origin, and the significance of life and death; in comparison with them, the restless questioning of stanza I seems almost futile and fussy. The distinction between the two scenes carved on the urn clarifies this difference. The first scene deals with desire and love, with beauty and happiness; it idealizes them by fixing what is inherently transitory, by subtracting it from its original context of gratification and surfeit, change and decay; but there is no inherent contradiction between the subject matter and the aesthetic treatment, since the subject matter too is exquisitely luxurious. The second picture, however, deals with the other aspect of life: its sufferings ("sacrifice"), its revolt ("lowing at

---

[10] This overlapping of the mood while the topic is changed recalls Wordsworth's peculiar handling of transitional stanzas in *Resolution and Independence* (see p. 123) and likewise enhances the impression of organic unity.

the skies"), its sadness ("desolate") and its final destruction in the mystery of death ("not a soul . . . can e'er return"). The two pictures, therefore, are complementary: one illustrates what of actual romance there is in life; the other focuses on the disagreeables. Yet, either of them is a thing of beauty.

There is, therefore, a close kinship between the paradox of nature, or life, and the paradox of art. Nature is the fountainhead of goodness and bliss. It is also the source of sorrow and evil. The reconciliation is effected in the notion that sorrow and evil have meaning and purpose within the grand scheme of universal benevolence. This comforting idea, we recall, had been anticipated in *Endymion,* and it culminated in April 1819 in the definition of life as the vale of soul-making. One month earlier, in a letter to the George Keatses, the poet had approached the same problem and reached a similar conclusion from a somewhat different angle. After mentioning that his friend Haslam was daily expecting news of the death of his father, he went on to say:

From the manner in which I feel Haslam's misfortune I perceive how far I am from any humble standard of disinterestedness—Yet this feeling ought to be carried to its highest pitch, as there is no fear of its ever injuring society—which it would do I fear pushed to an extremity—For in wild nature the Hawk would loose his Breakfast of Robins and the Robin his of Worms The Lion must starve as well as the swallow—The greater part of Men make their way with the same instinctiveness, the same unwandering eye from their purposes, the same animal eagerness as the Hawk—The Hawk wants a Mate, so does the Man—look at them both they set about it and procure on[e] in the same manner— They want both a nest and they both set about one in the same manner—they get their food in the same manner (II, 79).

In fact, Keats deals with three different aspects of the right attitude to sorrow and destruction. First, the concept of the vale of soul-making refers to the way sorrow provides the suffering individual with an occasion to try his resources. Second, "disinterestedness" refers to "a pure desire of the benefit of others" (II, 79), to sympathy with the sufferings of others. This "ought to be carried to its highest pitch, as there is no fear of its ever injuring society." Now, there is a surface contradiction between this and the next clause: "which it would be I fear pushed to an extremity"; but Keats, of course, is shifting to something else; as is made clear by the examples which follow, he is now referring to those who inflict suffering on others; and it is interesting to note that he resorts to three instances from the animal world which, in the *Epistle to Reynolds*, had been used as emblems of unrelieved fierce destruction: the hawk, the robin, the worm. De Sélincourt observed that Keats, in the 1819 letter, "shows himself far more able to grapple with the problem of nature's cruelty than in the *Epistle*."[11] The poet's third attitude consists in the realization that destruction is inseparable from perpetuation and renewal, and this brings him very close to the cyclic conception of nature which inspired Shelley's *Ode to the West Wind*.

Dealing with life, art too is concerned with opposites: with beauty and ugliness, with happiness and sorrow, with love and destruction, with good and evil, with romance and disagreeables. In art, the reconciliation is effected by the simultaneous transmutation of either into objects of genuine and permanent beauty. This is a purely aesthetic integration, which leaves intact the puzzling discrepancy between poetic apprehension and moral valuation. Keats had described the nonethical character of art on 27 October 1818, in a letter to Woodhouse:

the poetical Character . . . has no character—it enjoys light and shade; it lives in gusto, be it foul or fair, high or low, rich or poor, mean or elevated—It has as much delight in conceiving an Iago as an Imogen. What shocks the virtuous philosopher, delights the camelion Poet. It does no harm from its relish of the dark side of

---

[11] *The Poems of John Keats*, ed. E. de Sélincourt (London, 1926), p. 539.

things any more than from its taste for the bright one; because they both end in speculation (I, 386-387).

What brings together bright and dark and makes them both suitable sources of poetic inspiration is a fine display of energies which, as E. E. Bostetter rightly put it, "are to be enjoyed aesthetically, with moral detachment, regardless of whether they are erroneous or not." [12] This much is implied in a passage of the journal letter written on 19 March 1919:

Though a quarrel in the streets is a thing to be hated, the energies displayed in it are fine; the commonest Man shows a grace in his quarrel—By a superior being our reasoning[s] may take the same tone—though erroneous they may be fine—This is the very thing in which consists poetry; and if so it is not so fine a thing as philosophy—For the same reason that an eagle is not so fine a thing as a truth (II, 80-81).

On the plane of purely aesthetic integration, Keats was thus establishing a sharp cleavage between poetry on the one hand, metaphysical truth and ethical valuation on the other. But he was by no means immune from the romantic need to overcome such dichotomies and to achieve ever higher levels of integration. The *Ode on a Grecian Urn* is the outcome of this tireless endeavor. In it, the coalescence of art and nature, of truth and beauty, is carried to a successful conclusion through more than an aesthetic collocation of opposites. Its poetry consists in more than a nonphilosophical contemplation of

[12] E. E. Bostetter, "The Eagle and The Truth: Keats and the Problem of Belief," *Journal of Aesthetics and Art Criticism*, XVI (1958), 362-372. Through an unorthodox but highly interesting discussion of *The Fall of Hyperion*, Bostetter comes to the conclusion that "in theory Keats severed poetry from metaphysical and ethical responsibilities. In practice, he was unable to accept such a severance, and was constantly seeking through the poetic expression for the evidence which would give the lie to his scepticism." Although he agrees that the *Ode on a Grecian Urn* is "the resolution of his dilemma, in which the artist's vision becomes on its own terms as fine a thing as philosophy," he claims that "this triumphant vindication of the poetic vision is only momentary."

fine forms and energies. When we compare the brief vignette of the sacrifice in the *Epistle to Reynolds* with its more elaborate version in stanza IV of the *Ode*, we notice that a new note has crept in. While the former undoubtedly raises the scene to the level of aesthetic beauty, the latter raises it further—through the questions embedded in it—to the level of metaphysical significance, so that the inevitable "disagreeables" in the picture of the sacrifice and of the desolate town evaporate not only because they are transmuted into a thing of beauty, but also because they are felt to be endowed with meaning and purpose, and their portrayal prompts the mind to momentous depths of speculation. There is one thing in stanza IV which corresponds to the triumphant note of terrestrial happiness in the first section of the poem: the indirect intimation that although the ultimate truth about human destiny is unfathomable, nevertheless life has a meaning, and that this meaning—as suggested through the phrasing ("sacrifice," "altar," "priest," "pious") and through the choice of scene, is of an essentially spiritual and religious order.

The concluding lines of the *Ode* have become a matter of endless contention among critics. They have even been an obstacle to single-minded enjoyment of the poem, because the apothegm pronounced by the urn sounds to some ears like a rather empty Platonic cliché. I think, however, that this gnomic utterance is more closely and more concretely related to the poem as a whole than some critics are prepared to admit.

The function of art, as exemplified in the way the urn affects Keats's mind, is twofold. To begin with, it "teases us out of thought." Garrod has noted that the phrase is an echo from the *Epistle to Reynolds*. But the context is somewhat different. First, it is no longer "things" which tease us out of thought, but a work of art. In a way, this is a logical development from Keats's attitude in the *Epistle* with regard to the two kinds of dreams, those that take their colors "from the sunset," and those that "shadow our own Soul's daytime / In the dark void of Night." Since the latter reflect the world of actual experience, they must also tease us out of thought. But there is another and more important difference. In the *Epistle*, the poet had described his imagination as "Lost in a sort of Purgatory blind." In the *Ode*, art and imagination are associated no longer with purgatory but with "eternity." The total impression created by the letter is one of perplexity, while that created by the poem is one of wonder. In both cases, the poet is confronted with something that eludes human thinking, but the reasons for his bafflement are different. In the *Epistle*, his mind is frustrated by the apparently meaningless contradictions of life, by what Wordsworth had called, in *Tintern Abbey*,

> the heavy and the weary weight
> Of all this unintelligible world.
> (ll. 39-40)

But in the *Ode*, the contrasting elements are seen to be part of a unified whole: the urn is a "cold" pastoral which can express a love "for ever warm"; the "marble" men and maidens are "for ever panting"; although the urn is "a silent form," it is also a "historian" and a "friend to man," to whom it conveys a message of solace. The paradoxical imagery points not to chaos and confusion, but to a *coincidentia oppositorum* which is the mystery of art as it is the mystery of eternity.

The second function of art is formulated in the message itself. It is part of the ritual, when discussing the *Ode on a Grecian Urn*, to quote Keats's famous dictum of November 1817 about Adam's dream: "he awoke and found it truth." As a matter of fact, a case might be made for the argument that by 19 March 1819, Keats had recanted this youthful view, since he explicitly wrote that poetry was not truth and that it was not so fine as truth. But through the *Ode*, he worked out the synthesis of those two apparently irreconcilable propositions by establishing a much more complex relationship between poetry and truth than he could possibly have conceived in 1817. Actually, it is his old notion that "what the Imagination seizes as Beauty must be Truth" (I, 184–185) that is concisely restated in the first half of the urn's apothegm, "Beauty is Truth," which, I venture to suggest, sums up in abstract terms the meaning of the first section of the poem. Although the love scene transcends the actual conditions of human passion, it exhibits, through its sheer immutable beauty, something of the quintessential truth of love. This is a Platonic truth: the beauty of art lies in the fact that art is the perfect embodiment of an Idea which, in actual life, can only manifest itself in imperfect form owing to the limitations of human nature.

But the aphorism contains more than this favorite speculation of Keats's. The second half does not merely repeat in inverse order what the first half says. What it implies has been elucidated by the author of *The Structure of Complex Words* in a typical flash of Empsonian insight: "Keats was trying to work the disagreeables into the theory. It seemed to him, therefore, that the aphorism was *somehow* relevant to the parching tongue, the desolate streets, and the other woes of the generations not yet wasted. He, like his readers, I think, was puzzled by the remarks on the pot, and yet felt that they were very *nearly* intelligible and relevant."[13] I do not know what evidence Empson could supply for his innuendoes about Keats's defective understanding of his own poem. Much of what he says is, I am afraid, an aftermath of the once commonly held and utterly false notion that romantic poetry is chiefly concerned with moods and attitudes and that we need not expect it to convey accurate or logical thoughts. Empson's italicized words seem to me completely out of place. But he is right in linking the desolateness of stanza IV with the sorrow of stanza III and the woes of the last stanza, and in stating that "Keats was trying to work the disagreeables into the theory,"

[13] W. Empson, *The Structure of Complex Words* (London, 1951), pp. 370–371; the italics are Empson's.

that is, he was supplementing his theory of art as creation of ideal beauty with a theory of art as revelation of the beautiful in the actual.

The urn's pronouncement is thus seen as a fitting synthesis of the twofold dialectical movement of the poem: there is truth (in a Platonic sense) in the Elysian vision of the first scene; and there is beauty in the vision of suffering and death described in the second scene. Whether the apothegm is to be considered a pseudo-statement in the sense I. A. Richards gave to this word,[14] depends on the reader's own premises. It would seem that any statement dealing with the nonmeasurable world, that is, with what matters, can be construed as a pseudo-statement. Keats, no doubt, meant it as a philosophical truth, although its relevance is strictly limited. It is usual to concentrate on the urn's dictum and to overlook the last line and a half:

> that is all
> Ye know on earth, and all ye need to know.

One critic even pushed literal-mindedness so far as to point out that we do need to know other things besides! But Keats may have used "all" in the sense of "the best," "the utmost," (as in the phrase "That's all I can do"). Some such interpretation is suggested by the words "on earth," which clearly limit the range of applicability of the urn's statement. Art is not eternity, but only an analogue of it. Not until he reaches a better world will man be able to know more and to elucidate the strange interconnections of the ideal and the actual. But in this world, art is man's highest endeavor because it actualizes the ideal and it makes perceptible the presence of the ideal in the actual. A romantic commonplace, one feels tempted to say. And it is true that it sums up in five words

[14] I. A. Richards, *Science and Poetry* (New York, 1926), pp. 58–59: "A form of words which is justified entirely by its effect in releasing or organizing our impulses and attitudes."

Hazlitt's definition of the "ideal" [15] as well as Coleridge's definition of the "symbol." But by the time Keats wrote this *Ode,* he had rediscovered the symbolic function of art for himself; he had come to feel it in his blood; it had been proved upon his pulse. Through the agonizing processes of vital knowledge, he had come to a satisfactory understanding of life, he had joined the idealistic wisdom of the other romantics, and he had found, in life, a worthy and useful place for himself as a poet.

[15] W. Hazlitt, "Essays on the Fine Arts," *Complete Works,* ed. P. P. Howe (London, 1930–1934), IX, 429: "The *ideal* is the abstraction of any thing from all the circumstances that weaken its effect, or lessen our admiration of it. Or it is filling up the outline of truth or beauty existing in the mind, so as to leave nothing wanting or to desire further."

11 Conclusion:
THE PROPER BOUND

THE eighteenth century had its own various ways of appraising the dual nature of man:

> Connection exquisite of distant worlds,
> Distinguished link in being's endless chain,
> Midway from nothing to the Deity!
> A beam ethereal, sullied and absorbed,
> Though sullied and dishonored still divine,
> Dim miniature of greatness absolute!
> An heir of glory, a frail child of dust,
> . . . .
> Oh, what a miracle to man is man,
> Triumphantly distressed!

These lines from Edward Young's *Night Thoughts* sound like a rapturously optimistic retort to Pope's predominantly disabused treatment of the selfsame dual man as "The glory, jest, and riddle of the world!"

But whether in wonder or sober causticity, eighteenth-century thought was fully aware of the limitations of man. It does not seem to have entertained the notion that man could or ought to soar beyond his proper bound. The wisdom of the age can be heard in Pope's injunction to silence the metaphysical instinct: "Presume not God to scan." The main purpose of man was to make life pleasant and comfortable within the boundaries set by God. The absolute was neither to be reached, nor even to be sought. If happiness was, to Pope and many others, "Our Being's End and Aim," it was simply the happiness of moral rectitude, social adaptation, and material well-being. It was variously described as "good," "pleasure," "ease," "content." Its second-rate quality was acknowledged, yet no higher bliss was believed to be possible. As Paul Hazard has said of eighteenth-century European thinkers in general, "Leur bonheur était une certaine façon de se contenter du possible, sans prétendre à l'absolu; un bonheur de médiocrité, de juste milieu, qui excluait le gain total, de peur d'une perte totale." [1]

The starting point of romanticism is in part to be found in an increasing dissatisfaction with such a modestly sybaritic view of happiness. Happiness was also the "end and aim" of the romantics, and perhaps more conspicuously so for Keats than for any other. But it was a different happiness because it was to result from the gratification of quite different urges.

The fundamental need, which differentiates romanticism from eighteenth-century enlightenment, is what has been called by Friedrich Schlegel the "Sehnsucht nach dem Unendlichen," the "heisze Durst nach Ewigkeit," [2] and by Baudelaire "la soif insatiable de ce qui est au-delà." [3] It implies a complete reversal of previous assumptions and ideals. These had been summed up by Pope with his usual terseness in two couplets of the *Essay on Man*:

> The bliss of Man (could Pride that blessing find)
> Is not to act or think beyond mankind;
> No pow'rs of body or of soul to share,
> But what his nature and his state can bear.
>   (Epistle I, 189–192)

---

[1] P. Hazard, *La Pensée européenne au dix-huitième siècle* (Paris, 1946), I, 25.
[2] F. Schlegel, Letters of 4 October 1791, and 23 August 1793.
[3] C. Baudelaire, "Notes nouvelles sur Edgard Poe," *Oeuvres complètes* (Paris, 1935), II, 1031.

Conclusion   239

In their dissatisfaction with whatever is implied in the chain-of-being metaphor, the romantics at first rejected everything that Pope could think about the state, the powers, and the bliss of man. They did not believe that the unity of the cosmos was a hierarchized arrangement in which every class of beings has its appointed place, essentially and forever distinct from all others. There was a repetition of the historical pattern which had been exemplified two centuries earlier in the shift from Renaissance to Baroque as described by Heinrich Wölfflin: it was the passage from a concept of unity that was tectonic, mechanical, and stable to one that was atectonic, organic, and dynamic, and according to which the finite somehow participated in the infinite, the material in the spiritual, the individual in the universal. The *Sehnsucht*, therefore, did not appear to the romantics as a utopian phantasm: it was firmly grounded in and justified by an ontological intuition of cosmic oneness, which can be considered the axiological foundation of romanticism.

This intuition appears at its most explicit in the early major works of the English romantics. It is expressed in Coleridge's idea of the One Life and in Wordsworth's description of his blessed moods; in *Alastor*, it underlies the Poet's endeavor to identify himself with the absolute; in *Endymion*, it accounts for the hero's hope to achieve the fusion of the ideal and the human. But it is through the formal features and structures into which the romantic inspiration spontaneously organized itself, rather than through explicit statements, that we can best realize its intensity and its concrete modes. The metaphors of totality, of prismatic refraction, of interconnection, of fusion, the abundance of which is one of the distinguishing features of romantic poetry, all suggest the coalescence of the One and the Many. I have dealt with these elsewhere,[4] and in the present context I should prefer to concentrate on the

[4] See A. Gérard, *L'Idée romantique de la poésie en Angleterre* (Paris, 1955), pp. 41–57.

significance of structural patterns rather than of recurrent imagery.

The romantic intuition of unity necessarily entailed the need to account for the apparent dualities of day-to-day experience, and so to clarify the relations between God and the created world, between man and society, between man and nature. The oscillating rhythm of many romantic poems is a spontaneous reflection of that preoccupation, and thus, on the structural plane, a symbol of the idea which provided their inspiration. The wanderings of the poet's attention, the expansion and contraction of its focus, its swift passage from self to non-self and back to self, are all the more revealing as they are certainly unpremeditated, flowing as they do from the very heart of his inspiration, from the all-dominating need to effect the fusion of what is apparently heterogeneous. Man, therefore, is not an isolated atom of being. He is enmeshed in a complex network of interactions, in which causality and analogy are necessarily connected. The inherent structure of the Wye landscape makes it appear to be an organized microcosm, and thus causes it to kindle thoughts about the highest ethical and metaphysical issues. The thorn has become a suitable correlative of human suffering because it too has been broken and distorted by the uncontrollable forces of a malignant fate. The west wind is both a power in its own right and an adequate image of the power inherent in the human mind.

This sense of universal kinship, of oneness, participation, and totality, is a well-known feature of romanticism. What is perhaps not so commonly realized is that it raised, for the poets themselves, problems which are both of an ontological and of an ethical nature.

The ontological problem lay in the need to test the truth of the central intuition and to define—supposing it were at all possible—the nature and the modes of the unity it revealed. For the romantic poets, this was by no means an academic exercise in pure cerebration. It was a question of vital import, since it was so clearly bound to authenticate or to invalidate their most urgent and most original experience, the core of their poetic inspiration and, consequently, their own appraisal of what they were worth as poets and as men.

The dialectical and dramatic element which constitutes the hidden design of much romantic poetry was due to the clash between the romantic intuition and a number of dogmatic and experimential elements. Of course, it contradicted the dualistic tenets of the traditional, "Newtonian" cosmology: but this was exactly what the romantics were reacting against. More important, at least to Coleridge and, later, to Wordsworth, was the fact that the pantheistic trend which the intuition of oneness seemed to involve was at variance with orthodox Christian transcendentalism. The attractive idea that, in ultimate reality, God and the world were one entailed an impious confusion of the Creator and his creature: hence the damaging contradiction between the explicit message of *The Eolian Harp* and its most impassioned section. The systolic rhythm and the panoramic vision which characterize Coleridge's conversation poems testify, as eloquently as do the explicit statements, to the intensity of his sense of a fundamental kinship in which man, nature, and God are united. The misgivings kindled by the contradiction between intuition and dogma were ultimately solved through Coleridge's symbolic conception of nature. By considering nature to be not a deceitful counterfeit of infinity but a living and organized whole, bearing, in its vastness and all-inclusiveness, the stamp, and thus suggesting the idea, of the spiritual force that created it and ever animates it, he was able to account satisfactorily for his and his friend's most cherished insight without at the same time yielding to the temptation of pantheism. Neither Keats nor Shelley, brought up in a different intellectual climate and, as it were, emancipated by the early works of their elders, felt that need to accommodate their intuition of unity to the orthodox creed of Christianity.

The third challenge which the romantic *Sehnsucht* had to meet—apart, that is, from the challenge of eighteenth-century dualism and of Christian transcendentalism—was the much more formidable challenge of experiential evidence, which operated in various ways, both on the ontological and on the ethical planes.

The romantic revolution began in the eighteenth century with the revaluation of nature, and the status of nature remained one of the cruxes of mature romantic thought. Within an idealistic system, two possibilities first occur: either nature is the appropriate medium through which the infinite is revealed to man, or it is a material veil which prevents man from perceiving the absolute. The second view is that of the Poet in *Alastor;* the first is that of Coleridge and Wordsworth, and in *Alastor* it is that of Shelley in the introductory section and of the Poet previous to his enticing vision. In spite of all that has been said about pantheism, animism, and nature mysticism in romantic poetry, one thing stands out fairly clearly from a careful scrutiny of the texts: it is the extreme caution exercised by the poets in dealing with the extrasensory cognitive aspect of the experiences they describe. The meandering structure of *Tintern Abbey* is a reflection of its puzzled mood: the poet's attention oscillates between the two poles of certainty and speculation; while he feels assured that the contemplation of the forms of nature is a source of solace and moral improvement, he has no means of ascertaining whether his sense of a mystical insight into ultimate reality is valid, or whether it is a vain belief. Wordsworth knows that his ecstasies are transient, that they rest on a shaky foundation of subjectivity, that he is bound to lose them; and so, in *Tintern Abbey,* he builds his hopes of happiness and betterment, not on them, but on the sensory apprehension of nature in which they are embedded—until he realizes, in *Resolution and Independence,* that the shapes of the visible world may owe their influence on man to the grace of the benevolent God who transcends them. Similarly, Shelley shows, in *Alastor,* what happens when the poet relinquishes his hold on the world of nature and of man, and abandons himself to the mystical quest of the unmediated vision: he becomes imprisoned in his subjectivity, his self-centeredness, and although his purpose is the loftiest that can be imagined, his doubt is never dispelled, and his fate is annihilation.

There is probably no finer expression of this intellectual dilemma so characteristic of romanticism than Keats's *Ode to a Nightingale*, which, as E. R. Wasserman has observed, has its being in the "Purgatory blind" of the *Epistle to John Hamilton Reynolds*.[5] In his own way, Keats gives poetic shape to inner processes which are closely related to those of the Poet in *Alastor*. He describes himself as "too" happy in his empathy with the nightingale's happiness, in the same way that Shelley's hero has "too" exquisite a perception of absolute beauty: the same hubris is at work. The ecstasy in the first stanza is parallel to the dream-vision of Shelley's poet, and is suitably accompanied by the same night of the senses ("a drowsy numbness") which characterizes Wordsworth's mystic moods and which, in *Alastor*, takes the form of the hero's blindness to the beauty of nature and of the Arab maiden. The next stanzas recount the poet's attempt to recapture, to prolong and to intensify this ineffable bliss. But here again we find the characteristic pulsating rhythm which makes the poet's attention oscillate between blissful absorption into the ideal, and painful recognition of the real. That the poet's obsession with the world of sorrow and transitoriness takes the upper hand shows that wine, in stanza II, is only—in Wasserman's words—"a symbol of the misguided effort to engage in the sensory essence of nature without pain; a beguiling hope of penetrating to the inwardness of the sensory in such a way as to be at ease in empathy; a worldly illusion that fellowship with sensuous essence is only a distracting pleasure." It is only through imagination and poetry (of the luxurious kind) that

[5] E. R. Wasserman, *The Finer Tone: Keats' Major Poems* (Baltimore, 1953), pp. 178–223.

Keats succeeds in restoring the visionary trance ("Already with thee").[6] But this merely re-creates the condition of the first stanza, and the problem of perpetuating the visionary state remains entire: there is only one higher intensity, and that is death. The poet is now faced with the frightening mystery of death which had lured Shelley's hero to nothingness. But Keats realizes that it only *"seems"* "rich to die," and the ambiguity of death is intimated in the last two lines of the stanza:

> Still wouldst thou sing, and I have ears in vain—
> To thy high requiem become a sod.

Death would perpetuate forever the night of the senses which is part of the ecstasy; but at the same time, it would destroy the imagination, which had come alive in ecstasy: in death, the poet would become deaf not only to sensory music, but

---

[6] At this point, I find myself reluctantly compelled to disagree with Wasserman, who says that poetry "fails to function as it ideally should." This is only partly true. The lines "I cannot see what flowers are at my feet, / Nor what soft incense hangs upon the boughs" do not signify that "what should lead to the bourne of heaven is transformed into the merely mundane": they mean that the poetic ecstasy has restored the night of the senses, which leaves the imagination free to move in the realm of the ideal and "guess" at invisible beauty. This interpretation helps to clarify the second part of stanza IV. Speaking of line 35 ("Already with thee! tender is the night"), Wasserman rejects the traditional reading according to which "the poet finally succeeds in becoming united with the nightingale, and . . . then finds the night to be tender." "There would be no meaning," he claims, "in the poet's complaint that 'here there is no light' and that he cannot see the flowers at his feet, for if he is with the bird he should be able to see into essence as vividly as the bird can sing of summer, and he should be as much in the presence of the Queen-Moon as he supposes the bird is." In his view, the line means that "the night is tender with the nightingale, but it leaves the poet in blind darkness." It seems to me that the word "but" establishes an unequivocal contrast between two locations: "the night" and "here." The night is the actual night of the world, lightened by the physical moon and stars. "Here" is where the poet is, namely, with the bird, in the celestial world of the ideal, where the senses are abolished, where there is no physical light, and where the imagination can rejoice in a light that comes "from heaven."

even to the bird's high requiem; like the hero of *Alastor*, he would be no more than a sod. This realization of the vanity of the death-wish—which modulates a pattern that we have traced in *Endymion*—is enhanced by the awareness that the bird, the emblem of the ideal, was "not born for death."

What the poet has learned by now is that, although he can enjoy brief moments of ecstasy, man cannot live in the ideal world, not even by seeking death. It is of the essence of such blessed moods that they should be transient, so that the poet is brought back, in stanza III, to "the weariness, the fever, and the fret," which he had hoped to evade altogether. The bird's song, which had started "in full-throated ease" presently fades away as a "plaintive anthem"; the bird itself was not born for death, but its voice is soon "buried" deep. And as the return pattern comes full circle, when the poet is tolled back to his "sole self," he is left to face the greatest loss of all. Not only is the ecstasy painfully short-lived, but its reality, as vision, is open to doubt. Like Wordsworth wondering whether his insight into the life of things may not be a vain belief, Keats asks himself whether he has not merely been cheated by his fancy, whether his flight into heavenly light in the company of the nightingale might not be just a dream rather than a genuine vision, shadowy of truth:

> Was it a vision, or a waking dream?
> Fled is that music:—do I wake or sleep?

This ode, together with *Tintern Abbey* and *Alastor*, throws a light of its own on what might be called the ontological skepticism of the romantics, a large portion of whose poetry results from their obstinate attempt to verify their seminal insights, to assess the significance of their intuition, to draw a firm line between what of it is objective perception and what wishful thinking, to determine as accurately as possible the concrete modalities of the cosmic unity. And although they were not as much concerned with the theory of the symbol as Coleridge was, their poetic practice tends in the same direction: toward a symbolic, rather than mystical, appreception of the world. The mechanism has been described in the simplest terms by Shelley, who wrote, in *Julian and Maddalo*, that he loved all the places

> where we taste
> The pleasure of believing what we see
> Is boundless, as we wish our souls to be.
> (ll. 15-17)

The distinction between "symbolic" and "mystical" appears in the word "believing." And in *Mont Blanc*, after describing the snow-capped mountain as the seat of absolute Power, Shelley adds wistfully:

> And what were thou, and earth, and stars, and seas,
> If to the human mind's imaginings,
> Silence and solitude were vacancy?
> (ll. 142-144)

The symbolical meaning with which Mont Blanc is loaded is the result of a subjective operation of the human imagination; it is nevertheless valid and significant: the mountain is not actually the supreme Power, but it is a suitable analogue of a power that really exists. As Coleridge had said, it is in this faith that created things legitimately counterfeit infinity.

But the symbolic apprehension of nature is not limited to this metaphysical analogy between the vastness, the harmony, the power of natural objects and the spiritual absolute. The idea of the oneness of being leads to that of the kinship of beings. Hence a psychological symbolism in which the outward forms of nature are seen as correlatives of human attitudes, situations, emotions. In the same way that the expanse of the landscape gives a feeling of infinity because its very amplitude is a product of the infinite spiritual force which organizes the original chaos of inert matter, so for Wordsworth the thorn is an appropriate emblem of human misery, not merely because of its tortured shape—this would be pathetic fallacy—but because its tortured shape is the result of the action of hostile forces, as is the misery of Martha Ray: it is in this sense that the thorn, as a symbol, "abides itself as a living part in that unity, of which it is the representative."

On the ontological plane, then, the romantic *Sehnsucht nach dem Unendlichen*, backed by the romantic intuition of cosmic oneness, managed to come to terms with the dualistic outlook which is built into the Western tradition. However strongly they were attracted at first toward the idea of a unity of essence, as formulated in the doctrines of pantheism, extreme idealism, or other forms of philosophical monism, the English romantics maintained their grasp upon the actual. What they did was to reinterpret and restate the relation between spirit and matter, man and nature, God and the created world, in such a way as to substitute organic relational patterns of causation and analogy for the simple mechanistic outlook against which they were reacting. Fundamentally, symbolism is the outcome of this process.

But the cosmic intuition and the infinite *Sehnsucht* were raising problems that were even more urgent on the ethical plane because they were bound to lead not only to a conception of the nature of the universe but also to a redefinition of the good life. Here, too, romantic poetry is the response to a challenge of contradiction, for the ontological intuition of cosmic oneness was necessarily accompanied by an ecstatic bliss which sought to perpetuate itself, by a feeling that the intrinsic harmony of the universal scheme should and could result in absolute happiness, and that it was possible to raise the actual to the sphere of the ideal by pursuing single-mindedly the life of the imagination in fellowship with essence. The romantics were caught between these great expectations and the experiential evidence of human frailty, of evil and suffering. And this awareness of cruelty and destruction, in its impact on the dream of perfection, had important implications for their conception of the principles of man's ethical behavior and entailed the necessity to revise their early ideas and immature hopes. This is Wordsworth's problem in *Reso-*

lution and Independence, and it is reflected in mythical terms in *Alastor* and in *Endymion.*

The antinomy between the ideal of harmony and happiness and the darker sides of human experience can lead to a number of attitudes, among the most extreme of which is to be counted the German *Ironie,* which, as Friedrich Schlegel wrote, "enthält und erregt ein Gefühl von dem unauflöslichen Widerstreit des Unbedingten und Bedingten, der Unmöglichkeit und Notwendigkeit einer schöpferischen Mitteilung."[7] While eighteenth-century enlightenment ignored the *Durst nach Ewigkeit,* German romanticism exacerbates it by constantly reminding itself that it is both *unmöglich* and *notwendig* to gratify it: *Ironie* thus appears as a kind of masochistic contemplation of the torturing incompatibility of life and the ideal. And if anything clearly divides English romanticism from its German counterpart, it is the former's determination to overcome the poisoned delight of such unresolved paradoxes and to achieve a meaningful synthesis.

The antinomy of ideal and actual can also be evaded through a denial of the impossibility of gratifying the *Sehnsucht.* This prompts the poet to reject life altogether and to escape, through the death-wish, to a dream world of absolute perfection. As Baudelaire was to say:

> Certes, je sortirai, quant à moi, satisfait
> D'un monde où l'action n'est pas la soeur du rêve.[8]

The English romantics do not appear to have been attracted for any length of time to the extreme idealism characteristic of many of their continental colleagues. I have tried to show that *Alastor* is to be understood as a warning against, rather than a plea for, the death-wish: it is the cathartic poem in which Shelley dramatized the absolute *Sehnsucht* and worked out to

---

[7] F. Schlegel, "Kritische Fragmente" (108), published in *Lyceum* (1797); quoted in Paul Kluckhohn, *Das Ideengut der deutschen Romantik* (Tübingen, 1953), p. 19.

[8] C. Baudelaire, "Révolte," *Le Reniement de Saint Pierre,* ll. 29–30.

its ultimate absurdity the extreme idealism which was one of the temptations to which romanticism was bound to be subjected by the very nature and intensity of its spiritualistic assumptions. There is, of course, an unsolved contradiction in the attitude of the romantics to death, and it shows with what intensity they were thinking anew the perennial problems involved in the human predicament. On the one hand, for Shelley in *Alastor* and for Keats in the *Ode to a Nightingale*, death in annihilation. But on the other hand, the romantics usually held the view that death is the gate to immortality. If we take them at their face value, such statements are of course irreconcilable. But their assertive form is misleading; it conveys an impression of confidence and certainty, whereas they are the outcome of hope, anxiety, and puzzlement. It is rather significant that most of Keats's dicta on death are couched in interrogative or optative terms:

> Can death be sleep, when life is but a dream,
> And scenes of bliss pass as a phantom by?

he wrote in an early sonnet, thus setting the tone for later utterances. "I long to believe in immortality," he wrote to Fanny Brawne in June 1820 [9] and some time later, to Charles Brown: "Is there another Life? Shall I awake and find all this a dream? There must be we cannot be created for this sort of suffering" (II, 346). Neither Coleridge nor Wordsworth had tackled the problem in the same pathetic way: they were still too much immersed in the orthodox tradition of Christian dogma. But for men of a later generation, the mystery of the country from whose bourne no traveler returns was invested with fresh poignancy. Therefore, they could not yield to the temptation of the death-wish because they could not long for a death which might mean annihilation, and they could not

[9] *The Letters of John Keats*, ed. H. E. Rollins (Cambridge, Eng., 1958), II, 293. Further quotations from the *Letters* in this chapter are from this edition and are identified by volume and page in parentheses.

possibly know whether death meant anything else. They could only hope, and long to believe, and meanwhile accept the common fate of man.

What the major romantic poets of England held in common, then, was a firm determination to solve their dilemma rather than evade it. Coleridge, of course, had a ready-made solution, defined in the argument prefixed to the *Ode to the Departing Year*: "The Divine Providence . . . regulates into one vast harmony all the events of time, however calamitous some of them may appear to mortals." The very low poetic quality of the *Ode* intimates, however, that this highly orthodox and dogmatic view was a piece of dead knowledge, a mere abstraction which had not been proved upon the poet's pulse. Such facile confidence in the automatic action of providential benevolence is by no means representative. Wordsworth's case is quite different. With him, belief in divine grace is not an initial assumption blindly inherited from the orthodox tradition. It results from an organic widening of his apprehension of nature's influence, which is now provided with a proper metaphysical perspective. Nature does not only send blissful moods: she also sends trials, ordeals, sufferings, anxiety; but these too, when seen in the light of the divine grace that ordains everything, appear to be the instruments of moral improvement, and ways to surer happiness. This wider understanding of man's situation in the world is the outcome of a long and difficult inner process of moral growth, through recognition and acceptance, non-attachment and self-conquest.

It has been one of the main trends of this book to show that the major assumptions and experiences of the romantic poets organically embodied themselves in definable structural patterns. The panoramic perception of the world is a spatial correlative of the sense of infinity. The systolic rhythm of contraction and expansion is a direct outcome of the sense of kinship and interchange which presides over the poet's relation with nature. Likewise, the fundamental preoccupation of the romantics with becoming, growing, and maturing has its structural homologue in the upward spiral movement which modifies the return pattern in many romantic poems. Any definition of romantic egotism must carry two important qualifications. First, the romantics allow themselves to be self-centered because they regard themselves as suitable representatives of mankind; as Keats said, "A Man's life of any worth is a continual allegory" (II, 67). Furthermore, the self in which they seem to be absorbed is not given from the very first in a state of immutable perfection; its distinguishing feature is its flexibility, its capacity for change. In Germany, this dynamic principle of romanticism was connoted by the concept of *Werden*. But for the English romantics, there is no such thing as pure *Werden*: becoming is always purposive; it is moral growth. Whether the poet deals with the self directly—as is generally true with Coleridge and Wordsworth—or vicariously—as Keats does in *Endymion*—the self to which he returns is not the self with which he had started: it has been deepened and enriched by experience and meditation.

The combination of the return pattern with the systolic rhythm makes it possible further to define this process of growth, which seems to develop along the lines of a triadic—one might almost say Hegelian—scheme, in the sense that it is the resultant of the interaction of opposite forces. In Wordsworth's daffodil poem, the melancholy solitude ("lonely"), the grayness ("cloud"), the sedate aloofness ("floats on high") of the poet are successfully challenged by the colorful movement of the companionable daffodils ("crowd," "golden," "dancing"), so that he is drawn into their "jocund company"—an experience which, because it is an experience of communion with the otherness of nature, leaves him permanently changed and enriched ("wealth"). In some of the conversation poems, Coleridge's initial frustration is similarly relieved by his sense of humanitarian duty (*Reflections*) or through vicarious enjoyment of the symbolic landscape (*This Lime-tree Bower*). But the pattern reveals itself to be more pregnant with ethical significance when it gives poetic shape to the impact of experience upon innocence: the mystic intuition stumbles on the humdrum experience of everyday life; the multifariousness of material forms, however beautiful, prevents any immediate perception of spiritual oneness; the dream of bliss and beauty seems to be nullified by the harsh facts of evil and sorrow; rational thought shakes the foundations of faith, whether it be faith in the spirit, or in nature, or in the imagination.

Most of the poems discussed in this volume deal with this second stage, when the high expectations and the immeasurable hopes no longer reign unchallenged, but are thwarted by the uncomfortable awareness of the limitations of human nature. They are located in what Keats calls "the space of life between," where the idealistic assurance of untried innocence is shattered by a new and painful grasp of the actual, and where, consequently, perplexity is the dominant mood: the perplexity of Wordsworth in *Tintern Abbey*, of the Poet in *Alastor*, of Endymion, all of whom have to face their loss, the loss of the illusion that life can be lived in fellowship with essence, that imaginative bliss can become the daily routine, that the poet can spend his whole life "in pleasant thought, / As if life's business were a summer mood." The growth of the mind first involves the shattering of such expectations. The depth and the scope of this renunciation had been prophetically described by Keats, as early as 1816, in a passage of *Sleep and Poetry*, the first half-line of which was to be significantly echoed later in the *Ode to a Nightingale*:

> The visions are all fled—the car is fled
> Into the light of heaven, and in their stead
> A sense of real things comes doubly strong,
> And, like a muddy stream, would bear along
> My soul to nothingness: but I will strive
> Against all doubtings, and will keep alive
> The thought of that same chariot, and the strange
> Journey it went.
>
> (ll. 155–162)

It is the tragic irony of the Poet's odyssey in *Alastor* that in refusing to face the ordeal and to follow the muddy stream of real things, he embarks on another stream that will also lead him to nothingness. The common feature of the English romantics is their determination to face evil and sorrow, "the agonies, the strife of human life," while at the same time keeping alive the vision of the ideal which had first inspired them. The development of their ethical outlook is, therefore, parallel to that of their ontological insight. In *Tintern Abbey*, Wordsworth strives against the corroding effect of doubt by falling back on his assurance that nature's beauteous forms, whether or not they are a revelation of the absolute, are at least the undoubted source of all goodness and bliss. In *Resolution and Independence*, the problem is one not of knowledge but of moral behavior, and the function of restoring the poet's inner peace, of reconciling him with his new responsibilities and with the trials that are in store for him, is fulfilled not by nature but by the leech-gatherer. But in fact, the old man impersonates a new, more complex, stage in Wordsworth's idea of nature; that he is first presented in the semblance of a stone or a sea beast identifies him with nonhuman nature in the usual Wordsworthian manner; but he is also the repository of an articulate wisdom referring to purely human problems and experiences, with which nonhuman nature could not cope; moreover, his sudden appearance, then and there, is ascribed, however tentatively, to the effect of divine grace. A new element is thus introduced into Wordsworth's world view, which brings it into harmony with that of Coleridge: the idea of a transcendent godhead which, although distinct from the world it created, still acts in and through it, thus helping man to cope with an otherwise unmanageable experience.

There was nothing revolutionary in such ideas. But this growing perception of reality was vital knowledge, not inherited dogma. It was not merely conceptual but experiential, and it involved a change in the poet's ethical attitude to life.

The importance of the romantic ethos has never been sufficiently realized. For this inner evolution, as we can follow it step by step in Wordsworth's poetry and in the last book of *Endymion*, results in a second reversal of values: a reversal of some of the most widely advertised attitudes of romanticism. The desire for mystical union with the ideal makes room for a humble perception of the proper bound of human nature; the romantic *Sehnsucht* is replaced by acceptance. Paradoxically, the net result of Endymion's flight "beyond his natural sphere," "beyond the seeming confines of the space / Made for the soul to wander in," is to make him renounce his early impulse to act or think beyond mankind, to share powers of body or of soul that his nature and his state cannot bear!

The conventional image of Shelley as an ineffectual angel, as an ethereal prophet engulfed in his escapist dream of perfection and in his refusal to face the evidence of human ignorance and to come to grips with the ugly complexity of the world, is due partly to his spiritualistic vocabulary and disembodied imagery, and partly to the idealistic indictment of life which certainly does inspire much of his poetry. There is considerable truth in D. G. James's comparison of Keats and Shelley:

Shelley had nothing of the tender play of scepticism which distinguishes Keats, a scepticism which is also a humility. Scepticism of this kind neither kills nor debauches; it is completely free of any hardness of mind and heart; it deepens, steadies, enriches, and makes wise. Shelley might move from a dogmatic atheism to a dogmatic Platonism; he could not pursue his life acknowledging ignorance and submitting to uncertainty.[10]

Close reading of the poetry, however, suggests that such a statement, which reflects a commonly held conception of both poets' personalities, needs some qualification. To a large extent, Keats's intellectual quality and the source of his modern

[10] D. G. James, *The Romantic Comedy* (London, 1948), pp. 108–109.

appeal can be said to reside in his willingness to accept ignorance and submit to uncertainty; but they also reside in what we might call his "aesthetic approach," which prompted him to find the meaning of life, as far as man on earth can apprehend it, in beauty. On the other hand, skepticism was Shelley's basic attitude as well. In *Alastor* and in the second stanza of the *Hymn to Intellectual Beauty* we find him—like Keats in the *Epistle to Reynolds*—craving for answers to the questions raised by the "eternal fierce destruction" at work in the universe; and Shelley's alleged dogmatism becomes very doubtful when we recall how early he acknowledged that

> No voice from some sublimer world hath ever
> To sage or poet these responses given—

or ever will. For Shelley, as for Keats, the first lesson taught by experience was agnosticism.

Once this stage has been reached, it is of course possible to conceive a number of responses widely ranging between the two extremes of suicidal nihilism and thoughtless sybaritism. The Lake poets abolished the supremacy of experience and reason and reverted to religious idealism. Keats and Shelley attempted to make sense out of life's sorrow and evil in terms of the aesthetic approach: man's endeavors and frustrations, his revolt and his defeat are justified in the name of such intensity of beauty as may inhere in "the tempestuous loveliness of terror." [11] In the *Ode to the West Wind*, however, this is but a minor trend. The distinguishing feature of Shelley is perhaps his manly determination—which can certainly be construed as intellectual arrogance—to work out an acceptable positive philosophy on the basis of ontological ignorance. In the cosmos as man's limited senses can perceive it, the only

---

[11] The aesthetic approach is by no means foreign to modern existentialism. As Camus said, "Pour un homme sans oeillères, *il n'est pas de plus beau spectacle* que celui de l'intelligence aux prises avec une réalité qui le dépasse" (*Le Mythe de Sisyphe* [Paris, 1943], p. 78; italics mine).

enduring reality is the immanent, impersonal force of change. As an object, it is man's tragedy that he is bound to fall a victim of mutability. As a subject, it is man's greatness that he is sensitive to and aware of his fate; it is the poet's privilege that he can shape the human drama into a thing of beauty; and it is the prophet's glory that, in his recognition that evolution is a power within as well as an outside force, he can master its energy and actively curb it to alleviate the ills of mankind.

It is one of the recurring patterns of Western civilization that its wildest fits of idealism ultimately serve to deepen and enrich and revitalize a central tradition of positive acceptance of the human condition. As far as European romanticism is concerned, this has been generally acknowledged only in the case of German literature at the turn of the eighteenth and nineteenth centuries. German historians have a disconcerting habit of dividing the twin careers of Schiller and Goethe into a period of wild *Sturm und Drang* romanticism followed by a period of subdued and mature *Klassik*. What this implies is simply that both writers' youthful revolutionary idealism brought them back to a more sedate consideration of the universe and of the function of art in it. Their individualistic rebellion against constraints imposed by society led them to a renewed sense of social responsibility; their rejection of reality helped them toward a deeper understanding of it; and their emphasis on untrammeled self-expression in poetry ultimately resulted in a subtler perception of the function of formal values: in Goethe's words, they realized that "in der Idee leben heiszt das Unmögliche so behandeln, als wenn es möglich wäre." [12] The same dialectical movement controlled the swift evolution of the major romantic poets of England. Their basic intuition of spiritual oneness combined with a recognition of the inescapable duality of spirit and matter to produce a far more subtle view of both the kind of unity

---

[12] Goethe, *Sprüche in Prosa* in *Werke* (Weimar ed.), XLII, Pt. II, p. 142.

which they felt and the kind of duality which they experienced. Their youthful dream of perfection coalesced with their experience of evil and grief to provide new meaning and new vitality for the traditional, Christian-Stoic ethos of acceptance and responsibility. The net result of the dialectical struggle between the ideal premise and the experiential premise is a synthesis which brings romanticism back to the scale of values which had dominated the Western mind for centuries; indeed, it was this agonizing struggle which made them perceive, through personal experience and individual meditation, the vital rationale of those values.

Nor is this development traceable only in the intellectual field of the romantic world outlook, or in the moral field of the romantic conception of the good life. It is also manifest in the sphere of poetic practice. The romantic revolt against rules of composition that were felt to have become mechanical was actuated by an urgent need for individual sincerity and total expressiveness, both emotional and intellectual. For the romantic poet, the highest value is authenticity. He is not concerned with teaching or pleasing, because he has no palpable design upon the reader. He does not set out to impress him with his wit and skill. His main purpose is to elucidate, to clarify, and to express his inner experiences, his hopes, his insights, his puzzlement, his anxieties, with maximum accuracy—a feat which can only be performed through symbolic statement. This need to rejuvenate poetry by bringing it back to the sources of genuine experience accounts for Wordsworth's early emphasis on the "spontaneous overflow of powerful feelings." It was, as we can now recognize, a somewhat dangerous trend. For men of lesser or of no genius, the criterion of sincerity was later taken to justify the most nauseating exhibitions of cheap sentimentality, the most incoherent ramblings oozing from the sulphurous depths of the unconscious, and the most hermetic ejaculations of unbridled egotism. But all this is part of the decay of romanticism. For the romantics themselves soon came to realize that sincerity is only a prerequisite, not the sufficient condition of art as they understood it. In their theory and in their poetry, the principle of sincerity is effectively and successfully counterbalanced by two other principles which were part and parcel of the very tradition against which they thought they were reacting.

One is the principle of general truth, in which Aristotle had seen a reason for regarding poetry as "a more philosophical and a more excellent thing than history: for poetry is chiefly conversant about general truth, history about particular. In what manner, for example, any person of a certain character would speak or act, probably or necessarily—this is general; and this is the object of poetry, even while it makes use of particular names. But what Alcibiades did, or what happened to him—this is particular truth." [13] In his *Essay of Dramatic Poesy*, Dryden had accordingly described the object of a play as to give "a just and lively image of human nature"; and after him, Samuel Johnson had insisted on literature's duty to provide "just representations of general nature." Both in doctrine and in practice, the romantics upheld this principle, and its fusion with the premise of egotistic sincerity was achieved through the symbol concept in theory and through symbolic statement in poetry. This is probably one of those exceptional cases where doctrine ultimately reveals itself to have been more pregnant with consequences than actual practice. For in poetic practice, the romantic poets were innovators only in a very limited sense: writers have always made use of symbolic statement to explore areas of experience where rational logic is too coarse a tool. But it was not until Schiller and Goethe and Coleridge and Baudelaire that a valid definition of the symbol was framed, the reason being, in all probability, that a symbolic perception of the world was a necessary prerequisite for any symbolic conception of the work of art.

The symbol concept was to exercise a determining influ-

---

[13] Aristotle, *Poetics*, 1451 b. I am quoting from the 1812 edition of Thomas Twining's translation, conveniently reprinted in Everyman's Library (London, 1953), p. 20.

ence on the future of poetry, and with regard to romantic practice even the very limited number of poems that have been discussed in this book exhibits the remarkable range of its possible applications. I have dwelt at sufficient length on the metaphysical symbolism involved in the intuition of cosmic unity through the forms of nature, and on the psychological symbolism brought into play by Wordsworth in considering a thorn or a ruined cottage to be emblems of the misery of man overcome by malevolent forces. A third form of symbolism, which is more purely aesthetic, is at work in the *Ode on a Grecian Urn*, and in order to understand the workings of the symbol-making function in this particular aspect, we need only compare Keats's two treatments of the sacrificial scene: in the *Epistle to Reynolds* and in the *Ode*. Whereas all the sensory elements are the same, what stands uppermost in the *Epistle* is their plastic value, the sheer hieratic beauty of shape, color, and gesture; in the *Ode*, while the scene loses nothing of its plastic, sensuous quality—similar in kind and function to the beauty of the Wye valley in *Tintern Abbey*—it is invested with symbolic meaning because of the contrasting and complementary relationship between its desolateness and the happiness of the love scene, and because of the metaphysical questions which it raises in the mind of the poet. The sacrificial scene in the *Epistle* is an isolated incident of inherent, but apparently meaningless, beauty. In the *Ode*, the scene becomes significant of some general truth about man's mortality: the poet has become able to perceive and to make perceptible the "rays of intellect" which it had contained all the time, but to which he had been blind before.

The second principle which corrects the romantic premise of spontaneity is that of organized form. There was a time when this would have seemed a shocking statement to offer. Although the romantics had abundantly proclaimed that there is no such thing as lawless art, and although Coleridge had been the initiator of the theory of organic form in England, romantic poetry was felt to be diffuse, rambling, nebulous, and, as it were, boneless, because it seldom exhibited the strongly marked structure characteristic of neoclassical poetry. It must be admitted that although the romantic poets pondered at leisure and expatiated at considerable length on most of the problems pertaining to their art, nowhere in the vast scattered body of romantic theorizing can we find any concrete, detailed discussion of structure. Herbert Read's excellent definition of organic form will help us understand why this should be so: "When a work of art has its own inherent laws, originating with its very invention and fusing in one vital unity both structure and content, then the resulting form may be described as *organic*." [14] This implies that the creative process is primarily expressive rather than constructive. In other words, the purpose of the poet is not to fabricate an artifact according to a formal pattern preexisting in his mind; it is to provide a total and accurate rendering of the germinal idea which stirs his imagination. If this is the poet's main preoccupation, the part played by conscious artistry—at least with regard to the overall structure of the poem—is bound to be rather slight, for the work of art in its progress from beginning to end will strive to reflect as faithfully as possible the movements of the artist's mind. In the last analysis, it depends upon the quality of the poet's mind whether his poetry will turn out to be shapeless effusion or organized form. It was, I believe, some such idea that Wordsworth had in view when he stated, in his Preface of 1800, that "Poems to which any value can be attached were never produced on any variety of subjects but by a man who, being possessed of more than usual organic sensibility, had also thought long and deeply," [15] and Coleridge, when he wrote to Sotheby, in 1802, "that a great Poet must be, implicitè if not explicitè, a profound Metaphysician." [16]

[14] H. Read, "Organic and Abstract Form," *Form in Modern Poetry* (London, 1932), p. 3. This essay has often been reprinted.
[15] *Poetical Works of William Wordsworth*, ed. E. de Sélincourt and Helen Darbishire (Oxford, 1962), II, 387-388.
[16] *Collected Letters of Samuel Taylor Coleridge*, ed. E. L. Griggs (Oxford, 1956), II, 810.

Conclusion 261

In times of stress and change, the quality of a poet's mind will reveal itself in his refusal to be swayed by conventional ideas and attitudes, in his readiness to explore new areas of experience and to experiment with new forms of expression, and in his capacity to do so in an orderly way. This is how both thought and poetry renew themselves. The poets of the Renaissance rejected the fixed forms mechanically derived from the organic forms of courtly poetry by late medieval versifiers, in favor of the Pindaric ode whose freedom and flexibility made it a more suitable medium for expressing their own original living vision. This is exactly what the romantic poets did. Apparently, they were unaware of the precise nature of the new formal patterns which they were creating—or they would have discussed them. Indeed, it is most probable that those patterns were not immediately perceptible because they did not correspond to the usual criteria of formal structure, the chief of which are regularity, uniformity, and symmetry. There are two carved scenes on Keats's urn, but he devotes three stanzas to one, and one to the other; the two main parts of *Resolution and Independence* are extremely unequal in length, and they can be subdivided in two different ways with different results according as the principle of division is topical or thematic.

It was to be expected that the principle of spontaneity would make havoc of external, static unity. This does not mean that it is destructive of any kind of unity, and part of my endeavor in this volume has been to define some of the formal patterns peculiar to romantic poetry and to trace the inner dynamics from which they resulted. It is difficult to escape the conclusion that much of the profoundly satisfying quality of that poetry lies in the fact that the romantic writers successfully resisted the temptation of shapelessness in the field of aesthetic creation in the same way that they resisted the temptation of extreme idealism in the ontological field and the temptation of sybaritic egotism or querulous self-pity in the ethical field. It is one of the life-giving paradoxes of literary history that the present-day revaluation of romanticism as a stage in the wider continuity of the Western tradition—not only moral and philosophical but also aesthetic—could not have been accomplished if the twentieth-century reaction against romanticism had not renewed critical interest in the classical problem of formal structure, just as we could not have become alive to the oxymoronic quality of romantic thought and poetry if it had not been for the rediscovery of the Metaphysicals and for the stress laid by modern antiromantic critics on the significance of paradox and ambiguity.[17] The reappraisal of romanticism in our time provides a rather fascinating example of the ways in which literary history and criticism combine to sift the work of the past and so to assess what is truly valuable in the vast storehouses of our literary inheritance. When Keats wrote that "a thing of beauty is a joy for ever," he was certainly unaware of all the possible implications of the phrase. But we know that only a thing which is a joy forever can truly be called a thing of beauty. And in order to be a joy forever, it must satisfy two timeless criteria. It must provide a genuine insight into the reality of man's condition; it must express man's hopes and fears, his doubts and perplexities; it must renew our perception of the miracle and the misery of the human predicament. And through the paradox of art, it must fix this image of the transient for so long as men can breathe or eyes can see, thus mastering the power which Endymion attributed to love: the power "to make / Men's being mortal, immortal" (Bk. I, ll. 843–844). The status now awarded to romantic poetry, after it has been submitted to the exacting tests of close critical analysis, shows that it too falls within the general definition of great poetry which Shelley had proposed in his *Defence:* "A

---

[17] The cyclic irony of history aptly comes full circle when one scholar finds himself entitled to claim that, in their exaltation of poetry and criticism above all other forms of knowledge, the New Critics are, in fact, New Romantics. See R. Foster, *The New Romantics: A Reappraisal of the New Criticism* (Bloomington, 1963).

great poem is a fountain for ever overflowing with the waters of wisdom and delight; and after one person and one age has exhausted all of its divine effluence which their peculiar relations enable them to share, another and yet another succeeds, and new relations are ever developed, the source of an unforeseen and an unconceived delight." [18]

[18] *The Complete Works of Percy Bysshe Shelley*, ed. R. Ingpen and W. E. Peck (London, 1965), VII, 131.

Bibliography

Abrams, Meyer H. *The Milk of Paradise*. Cambridge (Mass.), 1934.
——. *The Mirror and the Lamp: Romantic Theory and the Critical Tradition*. New York, 1953.
——. "The Correspondent Breeze: A Romantic Metaphor." *Kenyon Review*, XIX (1957), 113–130.
——. "Belief and Disbelief." *University of Toronto Quarterly*, XXVII (1958), 117–136.
——, ed. *English Romantic Poets: Modern Essays in Criticism*. New York, 1960.
——. "Structure and Style in the Greater Romantic Lyric," in *From Sensibility to Romanticism: Essays Presented to Frederick A. Pottle*, ed. Frederick W. Hilles and Harold Bloom. New York, 1965, pp. 527–560.
Allen, Glen O. "The Fall of Endymion: A Study in Keats's Intellectual Growth." *Keats-Shelley Journal*, VI (1957), 37–57.
Allen, L. H. "Plagiarism, Sources and Influences in Shelley's *Alastor*." *Modern Language Review*, XVIII (1923), 133–151.
Aristotle, *Poetics and Rhetoric*. London, 1953.
Armour, Robert, and F. R. Howes, *Coleridge the Talker*. Ithaca, 1940.
Arnett, Carroll. "Thematic Structure in Keats's *Endymion*." *University of Texas Studies in English*, XXXVI (1957), 100–109.
Austin, Allen. "Keats's Grecian Urn and the Truth of Eternity." *College English*, XXV (1964), 434–436.
Baker, Carlos. *Shelley's Major Poetry: The Fabric of a Vision*. Princeton, 1948.

Baker, James V. *The Sacred River: Coleridge's Theory of the Imagination*. Baton Rouge, 1957.
Barron, David B. "*Endymion*: The Quest for Beauty." *American Imago*, XX (1963), 27–47.
Barzun, Jacques. *Classic, Romantic, and Modern*. New York, 1961.
Basler, Roy P. "Keats, Ode on a Grecian Urn." *Explicator*, IV (1945–1946), item 6.
Bate, Walter Jackson. *John Keats*. Cambridge (Mass.), 1963.
Bateson, F. W. *English Poetry: A Critical Introduction*. London, 1950.
———. *Wordsworth: A Re-interpretation*. London, 1954.
Baudelaire, Charles. *Oeuvres complètes*. Paris, 1935.
Beer, J. B. *Coleridge the Visionary*. London, 1959.
Benziger, James. "Tintern Abbey Revisited." *PMLA*, LXX (1950), 154–162.
———. *Images of Eternity: Studies in the Poetry of Religious Vision from Wordsworth to T. S. Eliot*. Carbondale, 1962.
Berkeley, George. *Works*, ed. A. C. Fraser. Oxford, 1871.
Berkelman, Robert. "Keats and the Urn." *South Atlantic Quarterly*, LVII (1958), 354–358.
Berland, Alwyn. "Keats's Dark Passages and the Grecian Urn." *Kansas Magazine*, 1956, 78–82.
Berry, F. *Poet's Grammar*. London, 1958.
Blackstone, Bernard. *The Consecrated Urn: An Interpretation of Keats in Terms of Growth and Form*. London, 1959.
Bloom, Harold. *Shelley's Mythmaking*. New Haven, 1959.
———. *The Visionary Company: A Reading of English Romantic Poetry*. Garden City (N.Y.), 1963.
Blunden, Edmund. "Keats's Odes: Further Notes." *Keats-Shelley Journal*, III (1954), 39–46.
Boas, Louise Shutz, and Arthur Dickson, "Coleridge's 'Ode on the Departing Year,' 149–161." *Explicator*, IX (1950–1951), item 15.
Bonjour, Adrien. "Blushful Wine and Winking Bubbles—or Keats's Nightingale Revisited." *English Studies*, XL (1959), 300–303.
Bostetter, Edward E. "The Eagle and the Truth: Keats and the

Problem of Belief." *Journal of Aesthetics and Art Criticism*, XVI (1958), 362–372.
———. *The Romantic Ventriloquists: Wordsworth, Coleridge, Keats, Shelley, Byron.* Seattle, 1963.
Boulger, James D. "Keats's Symbolism." *ELH. Journal of English Literary History*, XXVIII (1961), 244–259.
Bouslog, Charles S. "Structure and Theme in Coleridge's 'Dejection: An Ode.'" *Modern Language Quarterly*, XXIV (1963), 42–52.
Bowra, C. M. *The Romantic Imagination*. London, 1950.
Bradley, A. C. *Oxford Lectures on Poetry*. London, 1904.
Brooks, Cleanth. *The Well-Wrought Urn: Studies in the Structure of Poetry*. New York, 1947.
Brown, Calvin S. "Toward a Definition of Romanticism," in *Varieties of Literary Experience: Eighteen Essays in World Literature*, ed. Stanley Burnshaw (New York, 1962), pp. 115–135.
Brown, Leonard. "The Genesis, Growth and Meaning of *Endymion*." *Studies in Philology*, XXX (1933), 618–653.
Burgess, C. F. "Keats' 'Ode on a Grecian Urn,' 2." *Explicator* XXIII (1964), item 30.
Burke, Kenneth. *The Philosophy of Literary Form*. Baton Rouge, 1941.
———. "Symbolic Action in a Poem by Keats." *Accent*, 4 (Autumn, 1943), 30–42.
Campbell, Oscar J., and Paul Mueschke, *Wordsworth's Aesthetic Development, 1895–1802*. Ann Arbor, 1933.
Campbell, O. W. *Shelley and the Unromantics*. London, 1924.
Camus, Albert. *Le mythe de Sisyphe*. Paris, 1943.
Carlyle, Thomas. *Works*, Centenary Edition. London, 1896–1899.
Cassirer, Ernst. *An Essay on Man*. New Haven, 1944.
Cazamian, Louis. *Symbolisme et poésie*. Neuchâtel, 1947.
Chayes, Irene. "Rhetoric as Drama: An Approach to the Romantic Ode." *PMLA*, LXXIX (1964), 67–79.
Clarke, C. C. "Shelley's 'Tangled Boughs.'" *Durham University Journal*, LIV (1961), 32–36.
Clarke, Colin. *Romantic Paradox: An Essay on the Poetry of Wordsworth*. New York, 1963.

Clemen, Wolfgang. "Shelleys *Ode to the West Wind*: eine Interpretation." *Anglia*, LXIX (1950), 335–375.
Coleridge, Samuel Taylor. *Miscellanies, Aesthetic and Literary*, ed. T. Ashe. London, 1892.
———. *Biographia Literaria; or, Biographical Sketches of my Literary Life and Opinions; and Two Lay Sermons*. London, 1905.
———. *Biographia Literaria*, ed. J. Shawcross. Oxford, 1907.
———. *Biographia Epistolaris*, ed. A. Turnbull. London, 1911.
———. *Complete Poetical Works*, ed. Ernest Hartley Coleridge. Oxford, 1912.
———. *Collected Letters*, ed. Earl Leslie Griggs. Oxford, 1956.
———. *Notebooks*, ed. Kathleen Coburn. London, 1957.
———. *Shakespearean Criticism*, ed. T. M. Raysor. London, 1960.
Combellack, C. R. B. "Keats's Grecian Urn as Unravished Bride." *Keats-Shelley Journal*, XI (1962), 14–15.
Combellack, Frederick M. "Wordsworth's *Lines Composed a Few Miles Above Tintern Abbey*, 88–102." *Explicator*, XIV (1956); item 60.
Connolly, Thomas E. "Sandals More Interwoven and Complete: A Re-examination of the Keatsean Odes." *ELH. Journal of English Literary History*, XVI (1949), 299–307.
Conran, A. E. M. "The Dialectic of Experience: A Study of Wordsworth's *Resolution and Independence*." *PMLA*, LXXV (1960), 66–74.
Cornelius, David K. "Keats' *Ode on a Grecian Urn*." *Explicator*, XX (1962), item 57.
Cottle, Joseph. *Reminiscences of Samuel Taylor Coleridge and Robert Southey*. London, 1847.
Crawford, A. W. "Keats's 'Ode to a Nightingale.'" *Modern Language Notes*, XXXVII (1922), 476–481.
Danby, John F. *The Simple Wordsworth: Studies in the Poems, 1797–1807*. London, 1960.
Daniel, R. "Odes to Dejection." *Kenyon Review*, XV (1953), 129–140.
Darbishire, Helen. *The Poet Wordsworth*. Oxford, 1950.
De Man, Paul. "Structure intentionnelle de l'image romantique."

Revue Internationale de Philosophie, XIV (1960), 68–84.

———. "Symbolic Landscape in Wordsworth and Yeats," in *In Defense of Reading*, ed. Reuben A. Brower and Richard Poirier (New York, 1962), pp. 22–37.

Dickson, Arthur. "Coleridge's *Ode on the Departing Year*, 149–161." *Explicator*, VIII (1949–1950), item 15.

Dubois, A. E. "Alastor: The Spirit of Solitude." *Journal of English and Germanic Philology*, XXXV (1936), 530–545.

Durr, Robert Allen. "'This Lime-Tree Bower My Prison' and a Recurrent Action in Coleridge." *ELH. Journal of English Literary History*, XXVI (1959), 514–530.

Empson, William. "Thy Darling in an Urn." *Sewanee Review*, LV (1947), 693–697.

———. *The Structure of Complex Words*. London, 1951.

———. "The Active Universe." *Critical Quarterly*, V (1963), 267–271.

Fairchild, Hoxie, N. "Keats and the Struggle-for-Existence Tradition." *PMLA*, LXIV (1949), 98–114.

Ferry, David. *The Limits of Mortality: An Essay on Wordsworth's Major Poems*. Middletown (Conn.), 1959.

Finney, Claude L. *The Evolution of Keats's Poetry*. Cambridge (Mass.), 1936.

Flood, Ethelbert. "Keats' Nightingale Ode." *Culture* (Quebec), XXII (1961), 392–402.

Foakes, R. A. *The Romantic Assertion: A Study in the Language of Nineteenth Century Poetry*. London, 1958.

Fogle, Richard Harter. "A Note on Keats's Ode to a Nightingale." *Modern Language Quarterly*, VIII (1947), 81–84.

———. "Imaginal Design in the 'Ode to the West Wind.'" *ELH. Journal of English Literary History*, XV (1948), 219–226.

———. *The Imagery of Keats and Shelley*. Chapel Hill, 1949.

———. "Keats's 'Ode to a Nightingale.'" *PMLA*, LXVIII (1953), 211–222.

———. "Coleridge's Conversation Poems." *Tulane Studies in English*, V (1955), 103–110.

Fogle, Stephen Francis. "The Design of Coleridge's 'Dejection.'" *Studies in Philology*, XLVIII (1951), 49–55.

Ford, Newell F. "The Meaning of 'Fellowship with Essence' in *Endymion*." *PMLA*, LXV (1947), 1061-1076.
———. "*Endymion*—A Neo-Platonic Allegory." *ELH. Journal of English Literary History*, XIV (1947), 64-76.
———. "Keats's 'O for a Life of Sensations.'" *Modern Language Notes*, LXIV (1949), 229-234.
———. *The Pre-figurative Imagination of John Keats: A Study of the Beauty-Truth Identification and its Implications*. Stanford, 1951.
———. "Paradox and Irony in Shelley's Poetry." *Studies in Philology*, LVII (1960), 649-662.
Foster, R. *The New Romantics: A Reappraisal of the New Criticism*. Bloomington, 1963.
Fox, Robert C. "Keats' *Ode on a Grecian Urn*, I-IV." *Explicator*, XIV (1956), item 58.
Frye, Northrop, ed. *Romanticism Reconsidered: Selected Papers from the English Institute*. New York, 1963.
Gay, R. M. "Keats, Ode on a Grecian Urn." *Explicator*, VI (1947-1948), item 43.
Geen, Elizabeth. "The Concept of Grace in Wordsworth's Poetry." *PMLA*, LVIII (1943), 689-715.
Gibson, Evan K. "*Alastor*, A Re-interpretation." *PMLA*, LXII (1947), 1022-1045.
Gierasch, W. "Coleridge's *Ode on the Departing Year, 149-161.*" *Explicator*, VIII (1949-1950), item 34.
Godfrey, B. R. "Imagination and Truth: Some Romantic Contradictions." *English Studies*, XLIV (1963), 254-267.
Goethe, Johann Wolfgang von. *Werke*. Weimar, 1887-1920.
Göller, Karl Heinz. "Shelleys Bilderwelt." *Germanisch-Romanische Monatsschrifte*, XLIV (1963), 380-397.
Gray, Charles Harold. "Wordsworth's First Visit to Tintern Abbey." *PMLA*, XLIX (1934), 123-133.
Grob, Alan. "Process and Permanence in 'Resolution and Independence.'" *ELH. Journal of English Literary History*, XXVIII (1961), 89-100.
Guerard, Albert, Jr. "Prometheus and the Aeolian Lyre." *Yale Review*, XXXIII (1944), 482-497.
Guy, E. F. "Keats's Use of 'Luxury': A Note on Meaning." *Keats-Shelley Journal*, XIII (1964), 87-95.

Haddakin, Lilian. "Keats's 'Ode on a Grecian Urn' and Hazlitt's Lecture 'On Poetry in General.'" *Notes and Queries*, CXCVII (1952), 145–146.
Halpern, Martin. "Keats's Grecian Urn and the Singular 'Ye.'" *College English*, XXIV (1963), 284–288.
Hamilton, K. M. "Time and the *Grecian Urn*." *Dalhousie Review*, XXXIV (1954), 246–254.
Hamm, V. M. "Keats' *Ode on a Grecian Urn*, 49–50." *Explicator*, III (1944–1945), item 56.
Harper, G. M. "Coleridge's Conversation Poems." *Quarterly Review*, CCXLIV (1925), 284–298.
Harrison, Robert. "Symbolism of the Critical Myth in *Endymion*." *Texas Studies in Literature and Language*, I (1960), 538–554.
Harrison, Thomas P. "Keats and a Nightingale." *English Studies*, XLI (1960), 353–359.
Hartman, Geoffrey H. *The Unmediated Vision: An Interpretation of Wordsworth, Hopkins, Rilke and Valéry*. New Haven, 1954.
──────. *Wordsworth's Poetry 1787–1814*. New Haven, 1964.
Havens, Raymond D. "Concerning the Ode on a Grecian Urn." *Modern Philology*, XXIV (1926), 209–214.
──────. "Shelley's *Alastor*." *PMLA*, XLV (1930), 1098–1115.
──────. "Of Beauty and Reality in Keats." *ELH. Journal of English Literary History*, XVIII (1950), 206–213.
Hazard, Paul. *La Pensée européenne au dix-huitième siècle*. Paris, 1946.
Hazlitt, William. *Complete Works*, ed. P. P. Howe. London, 1930–1934.
Heidbrink, F. H. "Coleridge's *Ode to the Departing Year*." *Explicator*, II (1943–1944), item 21.
Hildebrand, William H. *A Study of Alastor*. Kent (Ohio), 1954.
Hobsbaum, Philip. "The 'Philosophy' of the Grecian Urn: A Consensus of Readings." *Keats-Shelley Memorial Bulletin*, XV (1964), 1–7.
Hoffman, H. L. *An Odyssey of the Soul: Shelley's Alastor*. New York, 1933.
Holloway, John. *The Charted Mirror: Literary and Critical Essays*. London, 1960.

Hood, Thurman L. *Literary Materials of the "Ode on a Grecian Urn."* Hartford (Conn.), 1958.
House, Humphry. *Coleridge.* London, 1953.
Hughes, A. M. D. "'Alastor, or the Spirit of Solitude.'" *Modern Language Review,* XLIII (1948), 465–470.
Hunter, Edwin R. "A Note on Keats's Idea of Beauty." *Tennessee Studies in Literature,* II (1957), 81–85.
Hutton, Virgil. "Keats' *Ode on a Grecian Urn.*" *Explicator,* XIX (1961), item 40.
James, D. G. *The Romantic Comedy.* London, 1948.
———. *Three Odes of Keats.* Cardiff, 1959.
———. "Keats and *King Lear.*" *Shakespeare Survey,* XIII (1960), 58–68.
Jones, Frederick L. "The Inconsistency of Shelley's *Alastor.*" *ELH. Journal of English Literary History,* XIII (1946), 291–298.
———. "The Vision Theme in *Alastor* and Related Works." *Studies in Philology,* XLIV (1947), 108–125.
Jones, John. *The Egotistical Sublime: A History of Wordsworth's Imagination.* London, 1954.
Kapstein, Israel J. "The Symbolism of the Wind and the Leaves in Shelley's 'Ode to the West Wind.'" *PMLA,* LI (1936), 1069–1079.
Keats, John. *The Poems of John Keats,* ed. G. Thorn Drury. With an Introduction by Robert Bridges. London, 1896.
———. *The Poems of John Keats,* ed. with an Introduction and Notes by E. de Sélincourt. London, 1905.
———. *The Poetical Works of John Keats,* ed. H. W. Garrod. Oxford, 1939.
———. *The Letters of John Keats,* ed. Maurice Buxton Forman. London, 1948.
———. *The Letters of John Keats,* ed. Hyder Edward Rollins. Cambridge (Eng.), 1958.
Keister, Don A. "Keats' *Ode to a Nightingale.*" *Explicator,* VI (1947–1948), item 31.
Kermode, Frank. *Romantic Image.* London, 1957.
Kessel, Marcel. "The Poet in Shelley's *Alastor.*" *PMLA,* LI (1936), 302–310.

Kilby, Clyde S. "Keats' *Ode to a Nightingale,* 35." *Explicator,* V (1946-1947), item 27.
Kluckhohn, Paul. *Das Ideengut der deutschen Romantik.* Tübingen, 1953.
Knight, G. Wilson. *The Starlit Dome: Studies in the Poetry of Vision.* London, 1941.
Kornbluth, Alice Fox. "Keats' *Ode on a Grecian Urn,* 1-2." *Explicator,* XVI (1958), item 56.
Kroeber, Karl. "The New Humanism of Keats's Odes." *Proceedings of the American Philosophical Society,* CVII (1963), 263-271.
Lacey, Norman. *Wordsworth's View of Nature and Its Ethical Consequences.* Cambridge (Eng.), 1948.
Leavis, F. R. *Revaluation: Tradition and Development in English Poetry.* London, 1936.
Lemaitre, Hélène. *Shelley, poète des éléments.* Paris, 1962.
Lowes, John L. *The Road to Xanadu.* Boston, 1927.
Lyon, Harvey T. *Keats's Well-Read Urn: An Introduction to Literary Method.* New York, 1958.
Lyon, Judson S. *The Excursion: A Study.* New Haven, 1950.
McLuhan, H. M. "Aesthetic Patterns in Keats's Odes." *University of Toronto Quarterly,* XII (1943), 167-179.
McNulty, John B. "Wordsworth's Tour of the Wye: 1798." *Modern Language Notes,* LX (1945), 291-295.
Marilla, E. L. *Three Odes of Keats.* Copenhagen, 1962.
Marsh, Florence C. "*Resolution and Independence,* Stanza xviii," *Modern Language Notes,* LXX (1955), 488-490.
Marshall, William H. "The Structure of Coleridge's 'Reflections on Having Left a Place of Retirement.'" *Notes and Queries,* CCIV, n.s. VI (1959), 319-321.
———. "The Structure of Coleridge's 'The Eolian Harp.'" *Modern Language Notes,* LXXVI (1961), 229-232.
Maxwell, Ian R. "Beauty Is Truth." *AUMLA (Journal of the Australasian Universities Language and Literature Association)* (May, 1959) pp. 100-109.
Meyer, George W. "*Resolution and Independence:* Wordsworth's Answer to Coleridge's *Dejection: An Ode.*" *Tulane Studies in English,* II (1950), 49-74.

Miller, Bruce E. "On the Meaning of Keats's *Endymion*." *Keats-Shelley Journal*, XIV (1965), 33–54.

Milley, H. J. W. "Some Notes on Coleridge's 'Eolian Harp.'" *Modern Philology*, XXXVI (1939), 359–375.

Moorman, Mary. *William Wordsworth: A Biography. The Early Years, 1770–1803.* Oxford, 1957.

Mortensen, Peter. "Image and Structure in Shelley's Longer Lyrics." *Studies in Romanticism*, IV (1965), 104–110.

Mueschke, Paul, and Earl Leslie Griggs. "Wordsworth as the Prototype of the Poet in Shelley's *Alastor*." *PMLA*, XLIX (1934), 229–245.

Muir, Kenneth, ed. *John Keats: A Reassessment.* Liverpool, 1958.

Muirhead, J. H. *Coleridge as Philosopher.* London, 1954.

Murry, John Middleton. *Keats.* London, 1955.

Nelson, Lowry, Jr. "The Rhetoric of Ineffability: Toward a Definition of Mystical Poetry." *Comparative Literature*, VIII (1956), 323–336.

Nethercot, A. H. "Coleridge's *Ode on the Departing Year*, 43." *Explicator*, I (1942–1943), item 64.

O'Malley, Glenn. "Shelley's 'Air-Prism': The Synesthetic Scheme of *Alastor*." *Modern Philology*, LV (1958), 178–187.

Orsini, G. N. G. "Coleridge and Schlegel Reconsidered." *Comparative Literature*, XVI (1964), 97–118.

Owen, Charles A. "Structure in *The Ancient Mariner*." *College English*, XXIII (1962), 261–267.

Owen, W. J. B. *Wordsworth's Preface to Lyrical Ballads.* Copenhagen, 1957.

Pancoast, H. S. "Shelley's *Ode to the West Wind*." *Modern Language Notes*, XXXV (1920), 97–100.

Parrish, Stephen M. "'The Thorn': Wordsworth's Dramatic Monologue." *ELH. Journal of English Literary History*, XXIV (1957), 153–163.

———. "Dramatic Technique in the *Lyrical Ballads*." *PMLA*, LXXIV (1959), 85–97.

Parsons, Coleman O. "Shelley's Prayer to the West Wind." *Keats-Shelley Journal*, XI (1962), 31–37.

Patterson, Charles I. "Passion and Permanence in Keats's *Ode on a Grecian Urn*." *ELH. Journal of English Literary History*, XXI (1954), 208–220.

Peckham, Morse. "Toward a Theory of Romanticism." *PMLA*, LXI (1951), 5–23.

———. "Towards a Theory of Romanticism. Reconsiderations." *Studies in Romanticism*, I (1961), 1–8.

Perkins, David. "Keats's Odes and Letters: Recurrent Diction and Imagery." *Keats-Shelley Journal*, II (1953), 51–60.

———. *The Quest for Permanence: The Symbolism of Wordsworth, Shelley and Keats*. Cambridge (Mass.), 1959.

Pettet, E. C. *On the Poetry of Keats*. Cambridge (Eng.), 1957.

Pettigrew, Richard C. "Keats' *Ode on a Grecian Urn*." *Explicator*, V (1946–1947), item 13.

Piper, H. W. *The Active Universe: Pantheism and the Concept of Imagination in the English Romantic Poets*. London, 1962.

Pitcher, S. M. "Keats' *Ode to a Nightingale*." *Explicator*, III (1944–1945), item 39.

Pottle, Frederick A. "Wordsworth's Lines Composed a Few Miles Above Tintern Abbey, 72–106." *Explicator*, XVI (1958), item 36.

Poulet, Georges. "Timelessness and Romanticism." *Journal of the History of Ideas*, XV (1954), 3–22.

———. *Les Métamorphoses du cercle*. Paris, 1961.

Priestley, Joseph. *Disquisitions Relating to Matter and Spirit*. 2nd ed. Birmingham, 1782.

Pulos, C. E. *The Deep Truth: A Study of Shelley's Scepticism*. Lincoln, 1954.

Raben, Joseph. "Coleridge as the Prototype of the Poet in Shelley's *Alastor*." *Review of English Studies*, n.s. XVII (1966), 278–292.

Ransom, John Crowe. "William Wordsworth: Notes Toward an Understanding of Poetry," in *Wordsworth: Centenary Studies*, ed. G. T. Dunklin (Princeton, 1951), pp. 81–113.

Rashbrook, R. F. "Ode to a Nightingale." *Notes and Queries*, CXCIV (1949), 14–16.

Read, Herbert. *Form in Modern Poetry*. London, 1932.

———. *Coleridge as Critic*. London, 1949.

———. *The True Voice of Feeling*. London, 1954.

Reiman, Donald H. "Structure, Symbol and Theme in 'Lines Written Among the Euganean Hills,'" *PMLA*, LXXVII (1962), 404–413.

Richards, I. A. *Science and Poetry*. New York, 1926.
Rivers, Charles L. "Influence of Wordsworth's 'Lines Composed a Few Lines above Tintern Abbey' upon Keats' 'Ode to a Nightingale.'" *Notes and Queries*, CXCVI (1951), 142–143.
Robson, W. W. "Wordsworth: *Resolution and Independence*," in *Interpretations*, ed. John Wain. London, 1955.
Rogers, Neville. "Shelley and the West Wind." *London Magazine*, III (June, 1956), 56–68.
―――. *Shelley at Work: A Critical Inquiry*. Oxford, 1956.
Rouge, J. "La Notion du symbole chez Goethe," in *Goethe: Etudes publiées pour le centenaire de sa mort*. Paris, 1932.
Rountree, Thomas J. *This Mighty Sum of Things: Wordsworth's Theme of Benevolent Necessity*. University (Ala.), 1965.
Rudrum, A. W. "Coleridge's 'This Lime-Tree Bower My Prison.'" *Southern Review* (Adelaide), I (1964), ii, 30–42.
Sawin, Lewis. "Wordsworth's 'Lines Composed . . . Above Tintern Abbey,' 88–93." *Notes and Queries*, n.s. III (1956), 493–494.
Sayers, Dorothy, L. *The Poetry of Search and the Poetry of Statement and Other Posthumous Essays on Literature, Religion and Language*. London, 1963.
Schero, Elliot M. "Keats' Ode on a Grecian Urn." *Chicago Review*, VIII (1954), 77–86.
Schiller, Friedrich von. *Werke*, ed. L. Bellermann. Leipzig, 1895.
Schlegel, Friedrich. *Philosophische Vorlesungen aus den Jahren 1804 bis 1806*, ed. C. J. H. Windischmann. Bonn, 1837.
―――. *Sämtliche Werke*. Leipzig, 1846.
Schlüter, Kurt. "Keats's 'Ode on a Grecian Urn' und das Dinggedicht." *Neophilologus*, XLII (1958), 128–147.
Schneider, Duane B. "The Structure of 'Kubla Khan.'" *American Notes and Queries*, I (1963), 68–70.
Schrickx, W. "Shelley's 'Ode to the West Wind': An Analysis." *Revue des Langues Vivantes*, XIX (1963), 396–404.
Schulz, Max F. "Coleridge, Milton and Lost Paradise." *Notes and Queries*, CCIV, n.s. VI (1959), 143–144.
―――. "Oneness and Multeity in Coleridge's Poems." *Tulane Studies in English*, IX (1959), 53–60.
―――. *The Poetic Voices of Coleridge: A Study of His Desire for Spontaneity and Passion for Order*. Detroit, 1963.

Scudder, Harold H. "Keats's 'Beauty Is Truth.' " *Notes and Queries*, CXCII (1947), 236–237.
Severs, Jonathan B. "Keats's 'Mansion of Many Apartments,' *Sleep and Poetry*, and *Tintern Abbey*." *Modern Language Quarterly*, XX (1959), 128–132.
Shackford, Martha H. "The *Ode on a Grecian Urn*." *Keats-Shelley Journal*, IV (1955), 7–13.
Sharrock, Roger. "Wordsworth's Revolt Against Literature." *Essays in Criticism*, III (1953), 396–412.
Shelley, Percy Bysshe. *Letters*, ed. Roger Ingpen. London, 1909.
———. *Complete Works*, ed. Roger Ingpen and W. E. Peck. London, 1926–1930 (reprinted in 1965).
Skutches, Peter. "Keats's Grecian Urn and Myth." *Iowa English Yearbook*, No. 8, pp. 45–51.
Smith, J. C. *A Study of Wordsworth*. London, 1946.
Smith, L. E. W. *Twelve Poems Considered*. London, 1963.
Spencer, Terence J. "Shelley's 'Alastor' and Romantic Drama." *Transactions of the Wisconsin Academy of Sciences, Arts and Letters*, XLVIII (1959), 233–237.
Spens, Janet. "A Study of Keats's 'Ode to a Nightingale.' " *Review of English Studies*, III (1952), 234–243.
Sperry, Stuart M., Jr. "The Allegory of *Endymion*." *Studies in Romanticism*, II (1962), 38–54.
Spitzer, Leo. "The 'Ode on a Grecian Urn,' or Content vs. Metagrammar." *Comparative Literature*, VII (1955), 203–225.
Stallknecht, Newton P. *Strange Seas of Thought. Studies in William Wordsworth's Philosophy of Man and Nature*. Durham (N.C.), 1949.
Steiner, F. G. " 'Egoism' and 'Egotism.' " *Essays in Criticism*, II (1952), 444–452.
Stillinger, Jack. "Keats's Grecian Urn and the Evidence of Transcripts." *PMLA*, LXXIII (1958), 447–448.
Strich, Fritz. *Deutsche Klassik und Romantik*. Bern, 1949.
Suther, Marshall. *The Dark Night of Samuel Taylor Coleridge*. New York, 1960.
———. *Visions of Xanadu*. New York, 1965.
Swaminathan, S. R. "The Odes of Keats." *Keats-Shelley Memorial Bulletin*, No. 12 (1961), 45–47.
Swanson, Roy Arthur. "Wordsworth's *Lines Composed a Few*

Miles Above Tintern Abbey, 72–102." *Explicator*, XIV (1956), item 31.

———. "Form and Content in Keats's 'Ode on a Grecian Urn.' " *College English*, XXIII (1962), 302–305.

Thorpe, Clarence D., Carlos Baker, and Bennett Weaver, eds. *The Major English Romantic Poets: A Symposium in Reappraisal*. Carbondale, 1957.

Trilling, Lionel. *The Liberal Imagination*. London, 1955.

Viebrock, Helmut. *Die griechische Urne und die angelsächsischen Kritiker*. Heidelberg, 1957.

———. "Keats, 'King Lear,' and Benjamin West's 'Death on the Pale Horse.' " *English Studies*, XLIII (1962), 174–180.

Wasserman, Earl R. *The Finer Tone: Keats' Major Poems*. Baltimore, 1953.

———. *The Subtler Language: Critical Readings of Neoclassic and Romantic Poems*. Baltimore, 1959.

———. "The English Romantics: The Grounds of Knowledge." *Studies in Romanticism*, IV (1964), 17–34.

———. "Shelley's Last Poetics: A Reconsideration," in *From Sensibility to Romanticism: Essays Presented to Frederick A. Pottle*, ed. Frederick W. Hilles and Harold Bloom (New York, 1965), pp. 487–511.

White, Newman Ivy. *Portrait of Shelley*. New York, 1945.

Wichert, R. A. "Shelley, *Alastor*, 645–658." *Explicator*, XII (1953–1954), item 11.

Wier, M. C. "Shelley's *Alastor* Again." *PMLA*, XLVI (1931), 947–950.

Wigod, J. D. "The Meaning of *Endymion*." *PMLA*, LXVIII (1953), 779–790.

———. "Keats's Ideal in the *Ode on a Grecian Urn*." *PMLA*, LXXII (1957), 113–121.

Wilcox, S. C. "Keats, Ode on a Grecian Urn." *Explicator*, VI (1947–1948), item 2.

———. "Keats, Ode on a Grecian Urn." *Explicator*, VII (1948–1949), item 47.

———. "The Prosodic Structure of 'Ode to the West Wind.' " *Notes and Queries*, CXCV (1950), 77–78.

———. "Imagery, Ideas and Design in Shelley's 'Ode to the West Wind.' " *Studies in Philology*, XLVII (1950), 634–649.

———. "The Unity of 'Ode on a Grecian Urn.'" *Personalist*, XXXI (1950), 149–156.
Williams, Porter, Jr. "Keats's Well Examined Urn." *Modern Language Notes*, LXX (1955), 342–345.
Wilson, Katherine M. *The Nightingale and the Hawk: A Psychological Study of Keats' Ode*. London, 1964.
Wilson, Milton Thomas. *Shelley's Later Poetry: A Study of His Prophetic Imagination*. New York, 1959.
Wimsatt, W. K., Jr. *The Verbal Icon: Studies in the Meaning of Poetry*. Lexington, 1954.
Wölfflin, Heinrich. *Principles of Art History*, trans. M. D. Hottinger. New York, 1932.
Wolpers, Theodor. "Zur Struktur der Bildlichkeit bei Keats." *Anglia*, LXXX (1962), 98–110.
Wolters, P. "Keats' Grecian Urn." *Archiv für das Studium der neueren Sprachen*, CXX (1908), 53–61.
Wood, W. R. "An Interpretation of Keats's 'Ode on a Grecian Urn.'" *English Journal*, December, 1940, 837–839.
Wordsworth, Dorothy. *Journals*, ed. E. de Sélincourt. London, 1952.
Wordsworth, William. *The Prelude, or Growth of a Poet's Mind*, ed. E. de Sélincourt and Helen Darbishire. Oxford, 1959.
———. *Poetical Works*, ed. E. de Sélincourt and Helen Darbishire. Oxford, 1962.
Wordsworth, William and Dorothy. *Early Letters*, ed. E. de Sélincourt. Oxford 1935.
———. *Letters: The Middle Years, 1806–1820*, ed. E. de Sélincourt, Oxford, 1937.
Wormhoudt, Arthur, and Richard H. Fogle. "Shelley's *Ode to the West Wind*." *Explicator*, VI (1947–1948), item 1.
Worthington, Jane. *Wordsworth's Reading of Roman Prose*. New Haven, 1946.

Index

Abrams, Meyer H., 50–51, 165n
Akenside, Mark, 22
Allen, L. H., 138n
Aristotle, 258
Armour, Robert, 31n
Arnold, Matthew, 9

Baker, Carlos, 157, 192n
Barzun, Jacques, vii
Bate, Walter Jackson, 218n, 222n
Bateson, F. W., 92, 102, 103, 120, 168, 170
Baudelaire, Charles, 62, 64, 238, 248, 258
Benziger, James, 93–94, 95, 98
Berkeley, George, 59–60, 149
Bloom, Harold, 168n
Bostetter, Edward E., 231
Bowles, William L., 43
Bradley, A. C., 120, 194n
Brandes, Georg, 15
Bridges, Robert, 224
Brown, Leonard, 194n
Burke, Kenneth, 41, 46

Campbell, O. W., 156
Campbell, Oscar J., 65, 67, 76–77, 108
Camus, Albert, 189n, 190, 255n
Carlyle, Thomas, 57–58, 61
Cassirer, Ernst, 13
Cazamian, Louis, 12

Chaucer, Geoffrey, 226
Chayes, Irene H., 170n
Clemen, Wolfgang, 171n, 186
Coleridge, Samuel Taylor, 20–63 and *passim*; *The Ancient Mariner*, 35–36, 38, 53n, 77, 130; *Biographia Literaria*, 8, 11, 12, 94; *Christabel*, 77; *Dejection: An Ode*, 20, 21, 128n, 140; *The Destiny of Nations*, 45–46, 55–56, 60–61; *The Eolian Harp*, viii, 4, 6, 7, 18, 20–53, 86, 103, 110, 116, 118, 147, 159, 160, 161, 163, 168, 241; *Fears in Solitude*, 20, 28; *Frost at Midnight*, 20, 28; *Life*, 24–25, 48–49, 50, 51; *The Nightingale*, 20; *Ode to the Departing Year*, 35, 250; *On Poesy or Art*, 16, 90, 151; *Poems on Various Subjects*, 21–23, 38; *Reflections on Having Left a Place of Retirement*, vii, 20, 29, 30–37, 44, 50, 51, 215, 251; *Religious Musings*, 34, 35, 41, 45, 56, 149; *Satyrane's Letters*, 41; *The Statesman's Manual*, 9, 13, 56, 89; *Theory of Life*, 99; *This Lime-tree Bower my Prison*, viii, 20, 21, 37–38, 52–54, 62, 251; *To a*

Gentleman, 20; *To the Reverend W. L. Bowles*, 43
Coleridge, Sara, 24, 28, 29, 34n, 36, 37, 41, 42, 44, 45, 47
Conran, A. E. M., 84, 127n, 128
Cottle, Joseph, 32–33

Danby, John F., 67, 75, 77, 79, 84n, 94, 111
Darbishire, Helen, 67, 76n, 85
Descartes, René, 39
Diderot, Denis, 15
Dryden, John, 258

Eliot, Thomas Stearns, 14, 65, 93
Empson, William, 97, 103, 234

Ferry, David, 67
Finney, Claude L., 137
Fogle, Richard Harter, 20n, 137, 171n
Ford, Newell F., 164, 201n, 203n
Forman, Maurice Buxton, 196
Foster, R., 262n

Garrod, H. W., 125, 232
Geen, Elizabeth, 133
Gibson, Evan K., 157n
Goethe, Johann Wolfgang von, 13, 62, 90, 256, 258
Griggs, Earl Leslie, 138n

Harper, G. M., 20, 28, 30, 41
Hartman, Geoffrey H., 91–93, 95, 97, 98, 106
Havens, Raymond D., 130, 157n
Hazard, Paul, 238
Hazlitt, William, 23, 94n, 218, 236
Hemingway, Ernest, 65
Hoffman, H. L., 157n
Hölderlin, Friedrich, 153, 202
House, Humphry, 28, 41, 46
Howes, F. R., 31n

Hughes, A. M. D., 159
Hunt, Leigh, 195, 196
Hutchinson, Mary, 70, 121, 126

James, D. G., 254
Johnson, Samuel, 258
Jones, Frederick L., 157n
Jones, John, 102n, 131

Kant, Immanuel, 13
Kapstein, Israel J., 185
Keats, John, 194–236 and *passim*; *Endymion*, viii, 4, 14, 136, 194–214, 222, 229, 239, 245, 248, 251, 252, 254, 258, 262; *Epistle to John Hamilton Reynolds*, viii, 7, 18, 217–224, 230, 232–233, 243, 255, 259; *The Fall of Hyperion*, 231n; *Hyperion*, 212; *Ode on a Grecian Urn*, viii, 7, 18, 218, 219, 224–236, 259, 261; *Ode to a Nightingale*, 5, 163, 164, 243–245, 249, 252; *Ode to Psyche*, 225; *Sleep and Poetry*, 212, 252
Kessel, Marcel, 138n
Kierkegaard, Sören, 63, 187, 188
Knight, G. Wilson, 170n

Lacey, Norman, 106, 115
Lamb, Charles, 37, 52
Leavis, F. R., 168, 178
Lowes, John L., 50
Lyon, Judson S., 72n

Marshall, William H., 30
McNulty, John B., 96n
Melville, Herman, 187
Meyer, George W., 128n
Milley, H. J. W., 43–44
Milton, John, 10, 22
Monro, Alexander, 51–52
Moorman, Mary, 66, 76, 96, 102, 120–121, 129n, 130, 132
Mueschke, Paul, 65, 67, 76–77, 108, 138n

Index

Muirhead, J. H., 97n, 99n
Murry, John Middleton, 203n, 224

Nitchie, Elizabeth, 117

Orsini, Gian N. G., 16n
Owen, W. J. B., 66n

Paine, Thomas, 166
Parrish, Stephen M., 66
Peacock, Thomas Love, 157
Perkins, David, 12
Pettet, E. C., 201n
Piper, H. W., 34n, 58n, 220n
Plato, 52
Pope, Alexander, 87, 237, 238, 239
Priestley, Joseph, 34n, 57–58, 59n
Pulos, C. E., 162

Raben, Joseph, 138n
Ransom, John Crowe, 125
Read, Herbert, 76, 188, 260
Richards, I. A., 235
Robson, W. W., 121, 124–125, 132, 135
Rogers, Neville, 167
Rouge, J., 62n, 90n
Rudrum, A. W., 37n

Schelling, Friedrich Wilhelm Joseph von, 13
Schiller, Friedrich, 13, 62, 256, 258
Schlegel, August Wilhelm, 13, 16
Schlegel, Friedrich, 187–188, 238, 248
Schulz, Max F., 30, 63
Sélincourt, Ernest de, 10, 66, 230
Shakespeare, William, 22
Sharrock, Roger, 67n
Shelley, Mary, 137, 138, 139
Shelley, Percy Bysshe, 136–193 and *passim*; *Adonais*, 154, 156; *Alastor, or the Spirit of Solitude*, viii, 4, 5, 7, 14, 136–162, 164, 184–185, 194, 201, 203, 206, 209, 239, 242–243, 245, 248, 249, 252, 253, 255; *The Cenci*, 166; *A Defence of Poetry*, 160–161, 165n, 189n, 190, 262–263; *Essay on Christianity*, 186; *Hymn to Intellectual Beauty*, 164, 178, 255; *Invocation to Misery*, 166; *Julian and Maddalo*, 150, 246; "Lift not the painted veil," 166; *The Mask of Anarchy*, 166; *Mont Blanc*, 163–164, 165n, 191, 192, 246; *Ode to the West Wind*, viii, 7, 17, 18, 143, 163–193, 230, 240; "Oh! there are spirits of the air," 139–141; *On Death*, 160; *On a Faded Violet*, 166; *On Life*, 149–150; *Prometheus Unbound*, 161, 163, 166; *Queen Mab*, 138, 182–184, 185; *The Revolt of Islam*, 166; *The Sensitive Plant*, 161; *Speculations on Metaphysics*, 149; *Stanzas Written in Dejection, near Naples*, 166; *To a Skylark*, 143, 190; *To Wordsworth*, 139
Smith, J. C., 96n
Southey, Robert, 72n, 139, 149
Spencer, Terence J., 152
Spitzer, Leo, 225n
Stallknecht, Newton P., 41
Steiner, F. G., 23
Stephen, J. K., 94–95
Strich, Fritz, 143n, 154n
Suther, Marshall, 41
Swinburne, Algernon Charles, 84n

Thomson, James, 127
Trilling, Lionel, 125–126
Turner, William, 178

Vallon, Annette, 76, 121, 126

Wasserman, Earl R., 165n, 184–185, 191, 225, 243–245
West, Benjamin, 223
White, Newman Ivy, 156–157
Wigod, J. D., 194n
Wilcox, S. C., 170n
Wimsatt, W. K., Jr., 90
Wölfflin, Heinrich, 17, 100, 239
Wordsworth, Dorothy, 67, 68, 70, 96, 100n, 111–113, 121
Wordsworth, William, 64–135 and *passim*; *The Complaint of a Forsaken Indian Woman*, 76; *An Evening Walk*, 76, 102; *The Excursion*, 71, 72n, 138; *The Female Vagrant*, 102; "I wandered lonely as a cloud," 36, 251; *The Idiot Boy*, 77; *Lines Written a Few Miles above Tintern Abbey*, viii, 4, 5, 7, 18, 60, 70n, 89–117, 118, 119, 120, 126, 135, 136, 147, 155, 159, 162, 163, 168, 222n, 233, 240, 242, 245, 252, 253; *The Mad Mother*, 76, 102; *Ode: Intimations of Immortality from Recollections of Early Childhood*, 121, 125–126, 148, 168; *The Old Cumberland Beggar*, 102, 131; *Peter Bell*, 68; Preface to *Lyrical Ballads*, 21, 72, 81–82, 83, 87–88, 119, 128–129, 220, 260; *The Prelude, or Growth of a Poet's Mind*, 4, 15, 36, 61, 77, 87–88, 99, 129n, 131, 148–149; *Resolution and Independence*, viii, 7, 18, 70, 102, 118–135, 166, 170, 194, 210, 215, 228n, 242, 248, 253, 261; *The Ruined Cottage*, 47n, 70–72, 77; *Stanzas Written in My Pocket-copy of Thomson's "Castle of Indolence,"* 127; *The Thorn*, viii, 7, 18, 65–88, 93, 168, 240
Worthington, Jane, 131

Young, Edward, 237

www.ingramcontent.com/pod-product-compliance
Lightning Source LLC
Chambersburg PA
CBHW021653230426

43668CB00008B/609